BEYOND THE
SHADOWLANDS

BEYOND THE
SHADOWLANDS

C.S. LEWIS
ON HEAVEN & HELL

WAYNE MARTINDALE

 CROSSWAY

WHEATON, ILLINOIS

Beyond the Shadowlands
Copyright © 2005 by Wayne Martindale
Published by Crossway
1300 Crescent Street
Wheaton, Illinois 60187

Cover design: Jon McGrath

Cover photo: Getty Images

First printing 2005

Printed in the United States of America

Extracts by C. S. Lewis copyright © C. S. Lewis Pte. Ltd. 1942, 1943, 1944, 1952. Extracts reprinted by permission: *The Last Battle; The Problem of Pain; Collected Letters of C. S. Lewis,* vols. 1 & 2; *The Weight of Glory; The Screwtape Letters; The Lion, the Witch and the Wardrobe; Out of the Silent Planet; God and the Dock; Mere Christianity; Perelandra; Miracles; The Four Loves; Of Other Worlds; Experiment in Criticism; "On Stories" and Other Essays on Literature; The Letters of C. S. Lewis to Arthur Greeves; The Great Divorce; Prince Caspian; The Magician's Nephew; Letters to Children; The Horse and His Boy; The Voyage of the "Dawn Treader," The Silver Chair; Till We Have Faces; Letters of C. S. Lewis; The Pilgrim's Regress; That Hideous Strength; The Oxford History of English Literature; "The World's Last Night" and Other Essays.*

Excerpts from *The Four Loves* copyright © 1960 by C. S. Lewis, renewed 1988, *Letters to Malcolm, Chiefly on Prayer* copyright © 1973 by C. S. Lewis, renewed 1988; *Surprised by Joy: The Shape of My Early Life* and *Reflections on the Psalms* copyright © 1956 and 1958 by C. S. Lewis, renewed 1984 and 1986 by Arthur Owen Barfield. Reprinted by permission of Harcourt, Inc.

Excerpts from *The Letters of C. S. Lewis,* by C. S. Lewis, copyright © 1966 by W. H. Lewis and the Executors of C. S. Lewis, renewed 1994 by C. S. Lewis Pte. Ltd., and *Poems* by C. S. Lewis, copyright © 1964 by the Executors of the Estate of C. S. Lewis, renewed 1992 by C. S. Lewis Pte. Ltd. Reprinted by permission of Harcourt, Inc.

Unless otherwise indicated, Scripture quotations are from the ESV® Bible (*The Holy Bible, English Standard Version*®), copyright © 2001 by Crossway. Used by permission. All rights reserved.

Scripture verses taken from the King James Version of the Bible are identified KJV.

ISBN-13: 978-1-58134-513-1
ISBN-10: 1-58134-513-5
PDF ISBN: 978-1-4335-0003-9
Mobipocket ISBN: 978-1-4335-0784-7
ePub ISBN: 978-1-4335-1709-9

Library of Congress Cataloging-in-Publication Data
Martindale, Wayne
   Beyond the shadowlands : C. S. Lewis on heaven and hell / Wayne Martindale.
      p.   cm.
   Includes bibliographical references and index.
   ISBN 1-58134-513-5 (tpb)
   1. Heaven. 2. Hell. 3. Theology, Doctrinal. 4. Lewis, C. S. (Clive Staples), 1898-1963—Religion. 5. Heaven in literature. 6. Hell in literature. 7. Lewis, C. S. (Clive Staples), 1898-1963—Criticism and interpretation. I. Title.
BT832.M27   2005
236'.24'092—dc22   2004022218

Crossway is a publishing ministry of Good News Publishers.
VP   23   22   21   20   19   18   17   16   15   14   13
16   15   14   13   12   11   10   9   8   7   6   5   4

For my grandson

JOSHUA WAYNE ELSEN

*Is there a king of earth with dominion so vast from north to south
that he hath both winter and summer together?
Is there a king of earth with a dominion so vast from east to west
that he hath both night and day together?
So much more hath God both judgment and mercy together.*[1]
A D A P T E D   F R O M   J O H N   D O N N E

"There was a real railway accident," said Aslan softly. *"Your father
and mother and all of you are—as you used to call it in the Shadowlands—dead. The term is over: the holidays have begun. The dream
is ended: this is the morning."*[2]
T H E   L A S T   B A T T L E

*"I have come home at last! This is my real country! I belong here.
This is the land I have been looking for all my life, though I never
knew it till now."*[3]
T H E   L A S T   B A T T L E ;
J E W E L   T H E   U N I C O R N   O N   A R R I V I N G   I N
A S L A N ' S   C O U N T R Y ,   H E A V E N

CONTENTS

HELL

PART I. DEMYTHOLOGIZING HELL: THE NONFICTION

PART II. REMYTHOLOGIZING HELL: THE FICTION

PURGATORY

EPILOGUE

ACKNOWLEDGMENTS

In writing a book, many debts of gratitude mount up, which may only be paid by love. Still, I must happily put down a verbal tribute as a small earnest. No one could be more blessed in family than I, and my family members are rightfully my biggest fans and best collaborators. The title, *Beyond the Shadowlands*, is the combined suggestion of my wife, Nita, and daughter, Heather Elsen. Without their encouragement to write, I would not have begun; without their careful corrections, I would not have written as well. Son-in-law David Elsen faithfully encouraged me and also read the manuscript. Heather and David have brought a great joy into our lives with grandson Joshua Wayne, whose poster pictures hung over my desk and on both sides of my study door throughout the making of this book. He inspired me more than he knows. He turned one year old as the last words were being written.

Others came to my aid in reading the manuscript before I finalized it. Lewis scholars Walter Hooper, Christopher Mitchell, and Thomas Martin gave me the counsel, confidence, and encouragement to put the book in the publisher's hands. Of course, everyone who has benefited from Lewis's writing or cares about Lewis studies owes a debt of gratitude to Walter Hooper, who through a lifetime of dedicated service has brought many of Lewis's works into easily accessible print for the first time and kept many old ones in print as well, insisting in those "early days" that publishers bring back an old book (are they ever really old?) for every new one. Then there are the wonderful new collections of letters packed with essential annotations and the magisterial *C. S. Lewis Companion & Guide*, which I pull off the shelf so often the bottom is getting frayed. Readers who track down citations in the endnotes also have Walter Hooper to thank for urging the inclusion of chapter, part, and book numbers.

Christopher Mitchell and associate Marjorie Mead and the great staff (Corey, Heidi, Mary, Shawn) at the Wade Center have opened the treasures of Lewis holdings and made me feel at home among them. Thank you to everyone who has volunteered at or contributed to the Wade Center, especially the Wade family (what a gift!). I have also been materially helped and greatly encouraged by a Clyde S. Kilby Research Grant from the Wade Center. Tom Martin has urged this project on for years, was a soul mate during his years at Wheaton, and (besides family) is the best editor I've ever had. Theologian and Pastor Jay Thomas responded with ever-insightful questions, offering a Reformed critique that deserves its own special hearing. My teaching assistants, Kathryn Welch and Ryan Hodgen, helped with permissions and indexing, and, along with Joel Sage, Wesley Hill, Marj Dolbeer, and Michael Weber, did me the honor of reading carefully and reacting most helpfully. Keith Call encouraged the project with good conversation and lots of books. All have saved me from some real howlers. The many scholars who have written or spoken on Lewis over the years have enriched my understanding and enjoyment of Lewis immeasurably; some of them are listed in the Works Cited here.

Marvin Padgett and his staff at Crossway were wonderful collaborators in this project. Marvin kindly and readily extended my due date so I could spend time with Heather and Joshua, who moved in with us while David was serving our country in Iraq. Jill Carter always had good and timely information, and Lila Bishop is the sharp-eyed editor every author dreams of getting to squeeze out the last bit of potential in a book. I'm grateful to Moody Press for permission to use the chapter on *The Great Divorce* from my *Journey to the Celestial City: Glimpses of Heaven in Great Literary Classics* (1995), part of which appears here in modified form. *Beyond the Shadowlands* had its genesis (the demythologizing Heaven part) in the Staley lectures I gave at Roberts Wesleyan in November 1994; thank you, friends, for a warm welcome, scholarly encouragement, and ongoing good work. Finally, I wouldn't have written this book without a sabbatical from Wheaton College for the spring of 2004, along with the support of my dean, Jill Baumgaertner; chairperson, Sharon Coolidge; and my other stellar colleagues in the English Department (Alan, Andrew, Anna, Christina, Christine, David, Jane, Jeff, Keith, Kent, Laura, Lee, Nicole, Roger, and emeriti colleagues Bea, Erwin, Helen, Paul, and Rolland). Wheaton College's Aldeen Fund and the English Department's Dow Fund helped greatly in the making of this book.

All of these gifts are from God, including the works of Lewis that have mentored me since college days, when George Musacchio first introduced me to Lewis's books and taught me to be a scholar. To God be the glory.

FOREWORD

By *Walter Hooper*

This splendid book has corrected a serious error in my understanding of C. S. Lewis's works. I have claimed many times that "if you dropped me down onto a desert island with copies of Lewis's works, my life would be almost as rich as it is now." I was wrong. I should have taken to heart what Lewis said about friendship: "In each of my friends there is something that only some other friend can fully bring out. By myself I am not large enough to call the whole man into activity; I want other lights than my own to show all his facets."

Before I reached the end of the first chapter of this book, I found myself saying, "I look forward to reading this *again*!" Several times I took in my breath at some comment that seemed so natural for Dr. Martindale to make, but that illuminated something about Lewis I had never noticed before. As I went on, I knew the book would become one of my indispensables. Dr. Martindale has shed new light on works I thought I knew almost by heart. If I may paraphrase the passage from *The Four Loves*, I have learned from this book that "In each of those who write about Lewis there is something only that person can fully bring out. By myself I am not *large* enough to understand all Lewis means. I need others to show me what I would clearly miss if I read him alone."

The book is important in another way as well. Shortly after Lewis died, those who knew his works were far fewer than now, and they delighted in giving and receiving new light on Lewis's books. It was a time of pleasant civility when everyone was saying to the others, "What? You like Lewis?" Those who liked Lewis liked one another. Many of us hung on the latest issue of *CSL: The Bulletin of the New York C. S. Lewis Society* and the other publications, eager to know what the others were thinking and saying about this remarkable writer. We took it for granted we needed one another.

But whatever attracted such an enormous number of fans to Lewis became, as well, a magnet for those who had different motives. Much of the early camaraderie seemed to have been lost for good. Before I had reached the end of this book, I knew it was a recovery of that friendship that ought to exist between those who love the same truth. It is the product of genuine appreciation and insight, a labor of love that well matches its subject, C. S. Lewis's brilliant illumination of Heaven and Hell.

INTRODUCTION

I begin with a confession. I have not always wanted to go to Heaven. I can see now that many myths had unconsciously crowded into my mind: Fuzzy logic conspired with pictures of stuffy mansion houses and ghosts walking on golden (therefore barren and cold) streets. Perhaps my biggest fear, until some time after my undergraduate years, was that Heaven would be boring.

I knew I *should* want to go to Heaven, but I didn't. I would have said that I want to go to Heaven when I die, but mainly, I just didn't want to go to Hell. My problem was a badly warped theology and a thoroughly starved imagination. I knew that in Heaven we would worship God forever. But the only model I had for worship was church, and frankly, I wasn't in love with church enough to want it to go on through ages of ages, world without end. My mental image was of Reverend Cant droning on forever and ever.

Somewhere in the back of my mind, quite unconsciously, Heaven was an extended, boring church service like those I had not yet learned to appreciate on earth—with this exception: You never got to go home to the roast beef dinner. What a way to anticipate my eternal destiny. But then I read C. S. Lewis's *The Great Divorce*. It awakened in me an appetite for something better than roast beef. It aroused a longing to inherit what I was created for: that which would fulfill my utmost longings and engender new longings and fulfill those, too. After reading *The Great Divorce*, for the first time in my life I felt Heaven to be both utterly real and utterly desirable. It was a magnificent gift. Small wonder, then, that *The Great Divorce* has always been one of my favorite books because when I read it, it awakened me to my spiritual anorexia. I was starving for heavenly food and didn't even know I was hungry.

Since then I've read everything Lewis has written—at least everything published—and that reading has only expanded both my understanding of Heaven and Hell and my desire for Heaven. Fewer writers bring to any subject Lewis's theological sophistication, historical grasp, imaginative range, and clarity of expression. My labor and prayer in this study is that our understanding, wonder, and desire for Christ and his kingdom may take wing and soar toward Heaven and home until the day of his appearing, when all shadows flee before the light of his glory.

The Bible tells us plainly that we are "sojourners and exiles here" and that "our citizenship is in heaven."[1] My problem often is that I don't desire this heavenly home as though I were made for it and it for me. I often feel quite at home here on earth and dread leaving it. Lewis lived in firm belief that this world is transient and that the unseen world of Heaven is permanent. Conversely, theologian Wayne Grudem suggests that if some giant computer could print out our thoughts with those taking no account of the spiritual world in black and those with spiritual priorities in red, there would be precious little colored ink.[2] I know the problem firsthand. Lewis battles such stereotypes with weapons of logic, analogy, and imaginative worlds that shatter our rigid fortifications and call us to a new home, our true country, and our legitimate King. The fiction is the chariot we ride into that new country, and I use it liberally in this section to illustrate. But before we can even see into the distant promised land clearly, we must strip away the misconceptions that blur our vision.

In thinking about why I have been afraid of going to Heaven or have desired it so little, I have identified seven myths or false ideas I have held about it at one time or another and that Lewis's thinking has helped dispel. They are seven forms of fear, really, each veiling a common human longing that has its legitimate fulfillment. In chasing these fears out of the jungle into good light, I have discovered that behind each is the one big fear: that some desire would be unfulfilled. If I went God's way, I might lose out on something. What Lewis has helped me discover is that all desires are, at rock bottom, for Heaven. All of them. "There have been times," says Lewis, "when I think we do not desire heaven but more often I find myself wondering whether, in our heart of hearts, we have ever desired anything else."[3] Even the earthly pleasures are but temporary signposts to the "solid joys" of Heaven. If we dig past the myths and fears, we will find something authentic and exhilarating to put in their place. Just as in the Bible every command is the backside of a promise, so every fear is the backside of a fulfillment.[4] Here, then, are my hopes and fears, objectified into seven myths or errors and the truth behind them. Similarly, there are six myths about Hell. I haven't held all of these, but each clarifies something important about Hell, and each drives me back to the positive heavenly quality that Hell by definition excludes. The fictional glimpses of Hell serve the same purpose, salting our thirst for the living water.

Defying Dante's precedent of putting Hell first, then Purgatory, and finally Heaven—and defying Lewis's order in *The Problem of Pain*—I have put Heaven first. I think Lewis would not object to the rationale. Heaven is our natural home in that God created Heaven for us and us for Heaven. There all human personalities and potentials are fulfilled. Hell, on the other hand, is the dustbin of humanity, all ruins and perversions of what could have been, its occupants a grotesque parody of humanity. Since Heaven is the normative state (not the same as the normal or usual destination), Hell is better understood as its perversion. And if someone is going to read only a portion, I'd rather it be the part on Heaven. Purgatory I have put last because it is least important and can wait or be dispensed with as interest dictates.

The sections with numbered myths on Heaven and Hell may be read without the sections on fiction and vice versa, though clearing the undergrowth of misconceptions may help in reading the fiction, while the fiction unfolds and dramatizes the themes introduced in the demythologizing, nonfiction sections. Though reading straight through would be ideal, skipping around among the fictional works of most interest should not create much confusion. I have arranged the discussion of Lewis's fiction by simple chronology. Though contrary to custom, I have followed Lewis's usual practice in capitalizing *Heaven* and *Hell*. In his *Pilgrim's Guide*, David Mills provides a further rationale for the practice: "Heaven and Hell are places, like, say, Oxford and Grand Rapids. Or perhaps more to the point, to Lewis's point, they are destinations."[5]

Since Lewis's books appear in multiple editions, the page numbers in the endnotes won't correspond to every reader's copy. To help the reader navigate this troubled water, in addition to the page numbers matching the edition listed in the "Works Cited," I have included chapter numbers as marker buoys, along with dates for letters, and part and book numbers, where applicable. Chapter and page numbers are separated by a colon. For example, "10:145" in the Introduction's endnote #3 refers to chapter 10, page 145, and in chapter 1's endnote 24, "IV.9:174-175" refers to book IV, chapter 9, and pages 174-175.

A comment on the word *myth* might also be of use. Lewis uses the word freely in all of its meanings, and so have I. Even on the Contents page, I use *myth* in one of the ordinary senses of false beliefs for the numbered Myths and in "Demythologizing." But I also use it to mean a story that organizes and carries special meaning in the term "Remythologizing." See chapter 2, "Making the Myths of Heaven and Hell," for a fuller discussion.

Finally, it might be useful to summarize here at the outset the essence of Lewis's thought on Heaven and Hell:

• Heaven is being in the presence of God and enjoying all good things that flow from his character and creativity.

• Heaven is utter reality; Hell is nearly nothing.

• Although Heaven is a definite place, it is more relationship than place (not unlike the experience we have in our homes).

• All our desires are, at bottom, for Heaven.

• Heaven is the fulfillment of human potential; Hell is the drying up of human potential.

• We choose Heaven or Hell, daily becoming someone more suited for Heaven or someone who wouldn't like the place even if it were offered.

• Hell is receiving our just desert; Heaven is all undeserved gift.

HEAVEN
PART I

DEMYTHOLOGIZING HEAVEN:
THE NONFICTION

1

THE MYTHS OF HEAVEN EXPOSED

Since you have been raised to new life with Christ, set your sights on the realities of heaven, where Christ sits at God's right hand in the place of honor and power. Let heaven fill your thoughts. Do not think only about things down here on earth. For you died when Christ died, and your real life is hidden with Christ in God. And when Christ, who is your real life, is revealed to the whole world, you will share in all his glory.[1]

COLOSSIANS

MYTH #1: HEAVEN WILL BE BORING

No eye has seen, nor ear heard, nor the heart of man imagined, what God has prepared for those who love him.[2]

—1 CORINTHIANS

I have confessed that for ever so long, Heaven simply held no fascination for me. Why is Heaven (aside from Hell, perhaps) the last place we would want to go? In part, our aversion stems from a fear of what we don't know and a subsequent clinging to what we do. Heaven must, in the nature of things, remain as mysterious to us in this life as adulthood is to children. Then cultural caricatures of a cloudy hereafter—a colorless, weightless, and (we presume) pleasureless existence, harp-tuned to perfect monotony—effectively turn us away. I'm afraid it creeps up on me still. My problem was a conception of Heaven as church, and church as an endless chain of bad songs and boring sermons with not even a chance of volunteering for nursery duty. How liberating to find that Lewis understood the sentiment: "The picture of Heaven as perpetual worship, a place, in the

21

hideous words of the hymn 'Where congregations ne'er break up / And Sabbaths have no end,' which has tormented many a luckless child (finding one Sabbath per week a ration only too liberal!) comes alright when one sees the real meaning: the perpetual worship *is* the perpetual vision [of God], the perfect exercise of all one's faculties on the perfect Object. Of that, one cd. [could] never have too much: of its simulacrum, 'worship' as we know it down here, one easily can."[3]

Paradoxically, my misconceptions about Heaven also came from reading the Bible, but a blinkered reading that carries over the logic of "thou shalt not" to the very architecture of Heaven. For this mind-set, Heaven is only a place of denials where we don't do this and can't do that. Or we read too literally the symbolic language and the "no mores" of Heaven. In an important address called "Transposition," Lewis acknowledges the difficulty of breaking through such misconceptions: "Any adult and philosophically respectable notion we can form of Heaven is forced to deny of that state most of the things our nature desires. . . . Hence our notion of Heaven involves perpetual negations: no food, no drink, no sex, no movement, no mirth, no events, no time, no art."[4] Against this thinking, Lewis continues, is the positive vision of God and enjoying him forever. But the positive is at a great disadvantage, since little in our earthly experience suggests it. Further, the five senses have stocked our imaginations with vivid associations from this earthly life, suggesting that home is with the old, comfortable shoes; so we plod on in contented worldliness when we might soar.

My way out of this muddle lay straight through Lewis's *The Great Divorce* and (later) *Perelandra*. These two books hooked me on Heaven. More on these stories later, but never doubt the power of fiction to tell the truth, often better than cold theological prose. Jesus knew this: He constantly taught with stories. It is impossible, I came to see, that Heaven could be boring. Heaven is that place where all that is and all that happens issues from God's creative genius. In that sense, it is like earth, except that in our present earth even nature groans, waiting for its deliverance from the curse of sin. Do you like earth? You're going to *love* Heaven! Do you enjoy earthly pleasures: the taste of cherries, the smell of morning after a rain, the feel of cool water rushing over you as you dive into a pool on a warm summer's day? Then recall Lewis's reminder that God through Christ invented all the pleasures. He is the same one who is preparing a place for us and will come again to receive us to himself.

The psalmist says, "In your presence there is fullness of joy; at your right hand are pleasures forevermore."[5] In his excellent article on Heaven, Harry Blamires gets it right:

> Whatever form your most moving earthly experiences of beauty have taken, they were foretastes of heaven. Wherever you have found loving kindness in human hands and human eyes and human words, you were confronting Christ's personality operative in God's creatures. Since the source of all that beauty and all that tenderness is God, the full opening up of his presence before his creatures can be nothing less than the aggregation and concentration and intensification of every loveliness and every goodness we have ever tasted, or even dreamed of. All the love we have ever known in our relationships with others—all that collected and distilled into the personal warmth of him from whom it all derived, and he standing before us: that is the kind of picture that the Christian imagination reaches towards when there is talk of the ultimate reward of the redeemed.[6]

Similarly, when Ransom returns from the unfallen world of Perelandra, having experienced whole new genres of pleasure, and attempts to explain these to his friend, he despairs of the task because words are too vague, imagery not concrete enough. The pleasures are too real for earthly language. As the well-known eighteenth-century hymn writer John Newton puts it:

> *Fading is the world's pleasure,*
> *All its boasted pomp and show;*
> *Solid joys and lasting treasure*
> *None but Zion's children know.*[7]

Next to the "solid joys" of Heaven, earth's are airy, misty will-o'-the-wisps. On the other hand, Hell has no pleasures and offers the world only counterfeits of Heaven's genuine article. In *The Screwtape Letters*, Lewis has senior devil Screwtape lament while cautioning junior tempter Wormwood:

> Never forget that when we are dealing with any pleasure in its healthy and normal and satisfying form, we are, in a sense, on the Enemy's ground. I know we have won many a soul through pleasure. All the same, it is His invention, not ours. He made the pleasures: all our

research so far has not enabled us to produce one. All we can do is to encourage the humans to take the pleasures which our Enemy has produced, at times, or in ways, or in degrees, which He has forbidden. Hence we always try to work away from the natural condition of any pleasure to that in which it is least natural, least redolent of its Maker, and least pleasurable. An ever increasing craving for an ever diminishing pleasure is the formula.[8]

David Fagerberg reminds us of the Devil's lie, repeated by Screwtape, that "sin affords a more robust variety of pleasure than virtue."[9] Even the movies often get right the hatred and murder that flow in the wake of sexual unfaithfulness, whether pursued for physical or egocentric pleasure. In Narnia Edmund learned this lesson the hard way with the White Witch's candy, the enchanted Turkish Delight: "anyone who had once tasted it would want more and more of it, and would even, if they were allowed, go on eating it till they had killed themselves."[10] Fagerberg finds in this idea God's reason for expelling Adam and Eve from the garden: "He wanted to save their lives." Edmund further learns that "nothing spoils the taste of good ordinary food half so much as the memory of bad magic food."[11] Sinful pleasure infects legitimate ones. Explaining how our desires become Hell-bent, Fagerberg continues, "Our appetites have been misdirected, leading us to believe that there is a contradiction between God's glory and our own happiness, that we cannot submit our lives to God and still have what we really want."[12] If we think that, we have believed a lie.

A true and legitimate pleasure is one that sweetens our lives whenever we remember it. An authentic pleasure is one we love to recall and rejoice to share. A part of both Heaven and Hell is this multiplication factor. As memories stack upon memories in Heaven, these will add luster and expansiveness to every new experience—indeed, an experience for one with a perfect memory will never get old but remain "a joy forever," to borrow from Keats. Lewis imagines such a Heaven-sent pleasure multiplied in the unfallen planet of Malacandra in Out of the Silent Planet. For his first extended time on Malacandra, the space-traveling earthling, Ransom, is mentored by a rational but quite different creature, a hross named Hyoi. Ransom learns from his new friend what must be one of the key ingredients of the increasingly layered richness of our unfolding heavenly experience: the mounding up of memories that are only and always ennobling. Hyoi explains:

A pleasure is full grown only when it is remembered. You are speaking, *Hman* [human], as if the pleasure were one thing and the memory another. It is all one thing. . . . What you call remembering is the last part of the pleasure. . . . When you and I met, the meeting was over very shortly, it was nothing. Now it is growing something as we remember it. But still we know very little about it. What it will be when I remember it as I lie down to die, what it makes in me all my days till then— that is the real meeting. The other is only the beginning of it. You say you have poets in your world. Do they not teach you this?[13]

If this is true of earthly memory, how much more of heavenly memory, which will take not only the good of earth, but the infinite accumulations of Heaven into the celestial memory bank? For this and other reasons, the hrossa are content and embrace each day without regret for the past or anxiety for the future—which itself is an element we long for in heavenly perfection. Hyoi tells Ransom, "every day in a life fills the whole life with expectation and memory and . . . these *are* that day."[14] Ransom learns a bit of what it means to live life in light of eternity. By contrast, in Hell the memory of evil chosen in this life, joined with whatever issues out of the unredeemed hereafter, will be a mounting horror. What a difference this truth would make in our earthly choices if we could keep it before us. We can see the huge implications for even our earthly lives. This explains the look of contentment and innocence in some people's faces, however old. They have no regrets dogging their consciences; their sleep is unalloyed. To be so at peace perfectly and always is very Heaven.

Christopher Mitchell reminds us of the function of pleasure: What we experience with our senses "serve in their own God-ordained way to point us to an image of the greater beauty and reality of heaven."[15] John Piper concurs that "there are merciful foretastes everywhere in this fallen world, and God is glad for us to enjoy them."[16] A common mistake is trying to grasp these pleasures with all we're worth, living as if earthly pleasures were our only reality. Lewis sets us right.

The settled happiness and security which we all desire, God withholds from us by the very nature of the world: but joy, pleasure, and merriment He has scattered broadcast. We are never safe, but we have plenty of fun, and some ecstasy. It is not hard to see why. The security we crave would teach us to rest our hearts in this world and [pose] an obstacle to our return to God: a few moments of happy love, a landscape, a symphony, a merry meeting with our friends, a bathe or a football match, have no such tendency. Our Father refreshes us on the journey with some pleasant inns, but will not encourage us to mistake them for home.[17]

Perfection—Boredom ad Infinitum

Everyone knows that Heaven and all in it will be perfect: The Bible says so—and even the biblically illiterate associate perfection with Heaven. The book of Hebrews, the book of "better things," is chock full of the word *perfect* and its many forms. For example: "You have come to Mount Zion and to the city of the living God, the heavenly Jerusalem . . . and to the spirits of the righteous made perfect."[18] We will take up the bothersome idea of being "spirits" in Myth #3, but for now, we will explore the idea of perfection. I have asked several of my classes over the years if they would choose to go to Heaven "two minutes from now" if they could, and sometimes I ask, "if I could do it, who would want me to make them perfect right now?" No small number demur. How would you answer these questions for yourself? You might try this experiment with a group of your own. Usually, most want to stay here and stay as they are. Even those who would choose perfection and Heaven often have a qualm or two about it. Why should that be so?

We are okay with perfection as a goal, but not as a steady state. That's the problem: a steady state. Perfection implies stagnation for us, a kind of fossilized goodness that goes nowhere. Where could perfection "go," anyway? It's already there. This emphasis on the journey, as opposed to the destination, comes to moderns largely from the influence of evolutionary thought: what Lewis calls "the myth of progress." All of us know that both we and the world are a mess at present; so we console ourselves that the world will be a better place in some distant future. We content ourselves to be on the way, while in earlier eras, most by far focused on the destination. Our culture conditions us to be uncomfortable with "arriving." It's no compliment to say of someone, "She thinks she has arrived."

And come to think of it, once they arrive, what do the morally pure do for kicks? If you are not getting better or working to improve, do you just sit? Adding to the problem for the biblically literate, we know that Scripture promises heavenly "rest." Perhaps we remember being forced to take those grammar school naps when what we really wanted was to play. The negative idea about rest is reinforced by the old "Rest in Peace" on tombstones, which invokes images of just lying there—insentient, dumb, and crumbling into dust.

It may help to begin by thinking of what we rest from. We rest from labors that are unfruitful, from infertile ground, unyielding clients, intractable relationships. But we won't be eternally sitting in the corner, which would be more like punishment; we'll work. But we'll work without the battle for survival and without the resistance and frustration caused by sin and its curse. It will be gardening without weeds. Work will mean the thing we love to be doing, as when an artist or hobbyist speaks of "my work." This poem by Joe Bayly helps with the relationship of rest and work.

What's a home like,
one that he prepares?

A place of peace and beauty,
of joy and glory, of celestial music,
of fresh, unchanging, purest love.

I'll say, "Hello, Lord. I'm tired."
And he'll say, "Rest,
because I have
work for you to do."[19]

I think our work will feel more like Sabbath recreation or, if you prefer, play. The only problem with *play* is the suggestion of triviality, but reigning with Jesus and helping to run the new Heaven and earth will be anything but kids' play. In fact, the reward for doing good work here on earth will be more work in Heaven: "And [the Lord] said to him, 'Well done, good servant! Because you have been faithful in a very little, you shall have authority over ten cities.'"[20] Such work will be a reward. Anyone who has been without a job knows the relief that comes from getting one, along with a sense of significance and purpose.

What form reigning in the new Heaven and earth will take is open to imagination. Perhaps the Lord will say, "You washed those dishes as unto me; now go make a star," and you'll know how. Maybe next he will call for a group project: "When you've all finished your stars, make a new constellation." In "Harleys in Heaven," John Stackhouse reviews several recent books on Heaven and observes encouragingly that "several themes stand out among the riches of these volumes. Perhaps the most crucial of these is that heaven in fact has not been portrayed as a boring place, but the location of the highest aspirations of the human heart."[21]

In John's Gospel, Jesus prays, "Father, I desire that they also, whom you have given me, may be with me where I am, to see my glory."[22] We will follow along after Jesus like apprentices. Remember that he made all that is, seen and unseen. It won't be boring in Heaven because we will always be learning. God is infinite, we are finite. We'll never get to the end of him. A pastor I know is fond of saying that the most common expression in Heaven will be, "Oh, I didn't know that!" That's the idea.

We fear that Heaven's perfection might put us in a straitjacket, that we won't be able to "be ourselves." In fact, Heaven is the only place where we can safely let our hair down. Very often, Lewis observes, when we suggest that we want to "be ourselves," we mean letting go of the demands of civility and kindness: "What often distinguishes domestic from public conversation is rudeness. What distinguishes domestic behaviour is often its selfishness, slovenliness, incivility—even brutality. And it will often happen that those who praise home life most loudly are the worst offenders. . . . The freedoms in which they indulge themselves at home have ended by making them unfit for civilized society." In our earthly lives, we must be vigilant even at home. So where can we be "comfortable and unguarded"? The answer is, "*nowhere* this side of Heaven."[23]

Here is where perfection comes to our aid. Dante understands it supremely well in his *Divine Comedy*. Surprisingly, perhaps, the favorite part of this work for many, including myself, is not *Paradiso* (Heaven) but *Purgatorio* (Purgatory), even though I don't believe in Purgatory. In explaining why, we will see how it is possible to be "comfortable and unguarded" in Heaven. Dante's Purgatory is portrayed as a mountain with seven terraces, each representing one of the seven deadly sins (pride, greed, lust, envy, gluttony, anger, and sloth or laziness). As Lewis's great friend Charles Williams explains, each is a failure to love—either the right thing at the right time or in the right proportion. In Dante's Purgatory, each person willingly undergoes the discipline to correct the sin of each terrace until the sin is turned from a perversion of love to true love. Each pilgrim on the way to Heaven emerges from Mount Purgatory fully purged of sin and loving everything perfectly. Then, truly, each can be "comfortable and unguarded."

When we are in Heaven, like these pilgrims, we can act on every impulse because every impulse will be good and right. No need to second-guess or hold back or check our feelings. There will be no need to watch our backs or guard our emotions against hurt from others because they will all be perfected in love, too. That will be true freedom, and that is the right way to think of perfection.

Lewis captures both the exhilaration and trepidation implied in being made perfect. In the core of our beings we want this perfection; yet we sense how very far we have to go and fear the cost in pain, whether seen as Purgatory or sanctification of our earthly lives:

> The command *Be ye perfect* is not idealistic gas. Nor is it a command to do the impossible. He is going to make us into creatures that can obey that command. He said (in the Bible) that we were "gods" and He is going to make good His words. If we let Him—for we can prevent Him, if we choose—He will make the feeblest and filthiest of us into a god or goddess, dazzling, radiant, immortal creature, pulsating all through with such energy and joy and wisdom and love as we cannot now imagine, a bright stainless mirror which reflects back to God perfectly (though, of course, on a smaller scale) His own boundless power and delight and goodness. The process will be long and in parts very painful; but that is what we are in for. Nothing less. He meant what He said.[24]

Here is a further implication of perfection. In discussing miracles, Lewis classifies them into two large categories: miracles of the Old Creation and the New Creation. All biblical miracles are consistent with the character of Christ and consonant with his chosen way of doing things. Jesus refused to turn stones into bread, but he multiplied a boy's loaves and fishes, which he is always doing in nature. Fish produce more fish, corn produces seeds and more corn. These are miracles of the Old Creation, focusing on what God has done or is doing. Another example is Jesus' first miracle: of turning water into wine at Cana. This, too, is just a focused instance of what he does all the time, only on a larger scale and more slowly: making vines that turn soil and water into juice, giving it proper-ties that allow for fermentation.[25] Miracles of the New Creation are hints at what our glorious future will be like. They include walking on water, which illustrates first Jesus' power over nature, but also the control of spirit over matter—including such control over our own bodies—that will characterize the New Creation, Heaven. It may be worth repeating here Lewis's reminder that we will not be magicians asserting ourselves over others or over nature on egotistical whims. Our transformed character will be among the most exciting elements of the new order, and since every impulse will be a good one, what we do with nature or each other will be in every way beneficial. What a relief that will be. Does all this sound like a bore? Of course not; it sounds, well, just perfect.

MYTH #2: WHAT! NO SEX?

You make known to me the path of life; in your presence there is fullness of joy; at your right hand are pleasures forevermore.[26]

—PSALMS

[God] made the pleasures.[27]

—SCREWTAPE

My hunch is that a house church full of persecuted Chinese Christians meeting in secret would respond to the prospect of going to Heaven very differently from churchgoing Americans. I think we comfortable Americans don't much want to go to Heaven because we are afraid of losing something. We encounter this all the time in people who don't want to come to Christ for a new life because they are afraid of missing the old one. We ourselves are afraid to turn loose of the reins of our lives in the here and now, to give everything to God, to say to him, "anything, anyplace, anytime," because we don't know what he will do with us. We are afraid we won't like it, that it will be unpleasant and difficult—maybe even, God forbid, no fun. We have the same fear about Heaven.

There are lots of "no more's" in Heaven that we happily embrace: "no more tears," "no more sorrow," "no more death." But at least one of the "no more's" we might like to have been consulted about, namely, sex. Jesus said, speaking of saved people, that "in the resurrection they neither marry nor are given in marriage, but are like angels in heaven."[28] I remember reading that and thinking, *Poor angels—poor me!* Or so I thought. As a teenager, I used to pray that Jesus would not come again until I had had my honeymoon. I didn't want to leave earth before enjoying God's great gift of sexuality. It was a mostly silly prayer, but it was nonetheless sincere, and I suspect that among those who grew up with Bible training, I was not alone.

Why do we have this fear? It is because we think, perhaps subconsciously, that Heaven will mean deprivation. What, no sex? What will people do for fun? Isn't that implied in our thinking? Of course it is. But in truth, we will be uninterested in sexuality in Heaven not because it is "atrophied" but because it is "engulfed."[29]

To explain this phenomenon, Lewis uses the apt analogy of a small boy who loves chocolates. Upon being told that "the sexual act is the highest bodily pleasure," the boy immediately asks

> whether you [eat] chocolates at the same time. On receiving the answer "No," he might regard absence of chocolates as the chief characteristic of sexuality. In vain would you tell him that the reason why lovers in their carnal raptures don't bother about chocolates is that they have something better to think of. The boy knows chocolate: he does not know the positive thing that excludes it. We are in the same position. We know the sexual life; we do not know, except in glimpses, the other thing which, in Heaven, will leave no room for it. Hence where fulness [sic] awaits us we anticipate fasting.[30]

What really awaits us is a fulfillment of our sexuality that is as unimaginable to us as sexuality itself is to a child not yet through puberty. But is that prepubescent child asexual? No. The sexuality is there, shaping crucial aspects of personality and self. It is just not yet in full bloom. I believe that death will be a kind of spiritual puberty for us and that Heaven will fulfill desires we don't even know about yet, but which are very much there *in potentia*, working even now in our personalities and our sanctification.

To help us imagine new levels of intimacy, we will look briefly to recent developments in astrophysics. Lewis often says that time and space are God's creation. To get the hang of how our earthly lives may be connected to the spiritual world, he asks us to imagine being flatlanders living in two dimensions, trying to imagine a third and how it would be related to the other two. Modern physicists are imagining in just that way. If God could invent one dimension of time, why couldn't he invent another? Astrophysicist Hugh Ross suggests the staggering implications of another dimension of time for the closeness of relationships in Heaven. First, how he came to think of it. In solving the equations for the big bang, or earth being created *ex nihilo* (from nothing), scientists came to an impasse in trying to push the mathematical possibility back toward the moment of creation until someone introduced an extra dimension. Then came more. By introducing eleven dimensions of time and space, scientists can push back to within a split second of the creation event. One speculation is that if God has time and space dimensions, he has at least eleven.[31]

Lewis believes that God is beyond time and space: They are his invention and do not contain him; rather, he contains them. But we will likely occupy both time and space in Heaven, and it is possible to think of ourselves as having more than three dimensions of space and more than one dimension of time.[32] With just one more dimension of time, we would be able to spend an infinite amount of time with every person, all the time.[33] Such intimacy we can't even have with just one person in our single dimension. The usefulness of this idea is mainly in stimulating our imaginations to think of Heaven as *more* than earth, not less: to see Heaven as adding to, not taking away. If there is no marrying in Heaven, it is because even our earthly best relationships are subsumed by Heaven's new relationships, with deeper intimacy unspoiled by sin. No sex? No problem. It is not that sex is taken away, but taken up into something even greater. Once again where we fear fasting, there is really feasting.

> Indeed, if we consider the unblushing promises of reward and the staggering nature of the rewards promised in the Gospels, it would seem that Our Lord finds our desires not too strong, but too weak. We are half-hearted creatures, fooling about with drink and sex and ambition when infinite joy is offered us, like an ignorant child who wants to go on making mud pies in a slum because he cannot imagine what is meant by the offer of a holiday at the sea. We are far too easily pleased.[34]

In *The Four Loves*, Lewis gives us another idea of how we might actually gain from the new arrangement that precludes marriage and sex with one person.

> The event of falling in love is of such a nature that we are right to reject as intolerable the idea that it should be transitory. In one high bound it has overleaped the massive wall of our selfhood; it has made appetite itself altruistic, tossed personal happiness aside as a triviality and planted the interest of another in the centre of our being. Spontaneously and without effort we have fulfilled the law (towards one person) by loving our neighbour as ourselves. It is an image, a foretaste, of what we must become to all if Love Himself rules in us without a rival. It is even (well used) a preparation for that.[35]

Unbounded and uninhibited love sounds great. But a problem, perhaps more for males, is that many of us can't easily retain the notion of deepest intimacy without sex, and we can't universalize such intimacy without implying orgies. At this point we are hamstrung by our own fallenness. Here, as in all relationships and in salvation itself, we must abandon ourselves to faith. Not a blind leap, but a leap into the arms of the one who above all is trustworthy, who is the author of love, who is love himself. It may be that our adult sexuality awaits a heavenly spring when it will blossom into something as different as a flower from a bud, just as we are sexual creatures before puberty, and yet something happens at that blossoming unimaginable to the child. Even so, that something does not eliminate but engulfs and completes the earlier latent potential. "We must believe—and therefore in some degree imagine," Lewis insists, "that every negation will be only the reverse side of a fulfilling," and that our sensory life in Heaven will differ from our earthly experience "as a flower differs from a bulb or a cathedral from an architect's drawing."[36]

MYTH #3: BUT I HATE GHOSTS!

Our citizenship is in heaven, and from it we await a Savior, the Lord Jesus Christ, who will transform our lowly body to be like his glorious body, by the power that enables him even to subject all things to himself.[37]
—PHILIPPIANS

Ever wonder how our bodies would be resurrected when their physical makeup is scattered all over creation? What about those who drown at sea and become fish food, the fish later eaten by people? Or cremated bodies with ashes strewn from a mountaintop? Of course, it is virtually the same for all of us even in this life. Our bodies replace all their cells with new ones every three and one-half years. Even the "who" of who we are physically is not that large. If all the DNA of all the five billion plus people on earth were gathered into one place, it would only be the size of two five-grain aspirin tablets.[38] But surely the thing underlying even the DNA is spirit. One definition of death, the right one, I think, is when the spirit leaves the body.

The relationship between spirit and body is one of the great unsolved puzzles of our existence. But, biblically, the superiority of spirit over matter no one can argue. God is spirit, and he created matter and energy. If the whole universe were to vanish as a dream, which it one day will, God would not be diminished and could build it all again, as he will—a new Heaven and a new earth. As a tiny but certain part of the project, he will, as promised, rebuild my body in a newer and far preferable model.

Still, in the back of my mind (and perhaps in yours), there is the haunting idea that I will be a ghost when I die—that is, something less substantial than my body. This notion we easily project onto Heaven, and the reason we easily see. In life all we can experience with our five senses is the body, and when the body dies, it returns to dust as the spirit leaves. We cannot see what leaves. Subconsciously, we associate this insubstantial spirit with images of the least substantial things we *can* see to try to grasp it with our imaginations. We imagine a vapor or a cloud ascending from the body like steam from a kettle. We imagine—we might as well come out with it—we imagine ghosts! We think of the spirit subconsciously as something *less* than the body because we can't *see* it. It's a perfectly logical—and perfectly foolish—idea. Lewis believes it a dangerous idea.

> Confusion between Spirit and soul (or "ghost") has here done much harm. Ghosts must be pictured, if we are to picture them at all, as shadowy and tenuous, for ghosts are half-men, one element abstracted from a creature that ought to have flesh. But Spirit, if pictured at all, must be pictured in the very opposite way. Neither God nor even the gods are "shadowy" in traditional imagination: even the human dead, when glorified in Christ, cease to be "ghosts" and become "saints." The difference of atmosphere which even now surrounds the words "I saw a ghost" and the words "I saw a saint"—all the pallor and insubstantiality of the one, all the gold and blue of the other—contains more wisdom than whole libraries of "religion." If we must have a mental picture to symbolize Spirit, we should represent it as something *heavier* than matter.[39]

We are comfortable with the body because it is known in the way we know other elements of the material world. But we don't perceive the spirit with eye and ear, so it belongs with "the fear of the unknown." Lewis analyzes that fear in relation to biblical accounts of the Resurrection:

> We expect them to tell of a risen life which is purely "spiritual" in the negative sense of that word: that is, we use the "spiritual" to mean not what is but what it is not. We mean a life without space, without history, without environment, with no sensuous elements in it. We also, in our heart of hearts, tend to slur over the risen *manhood* of Jesus, to conceive Him, after death, simply returning into Deity, so that the resurrection would be no more than the reversal or undoing of the Incarnation.[40]

The sense of bifurcation between spirit and body and even our embarrassment at times about our physical selves is an evidence of our fallenness and one of the very ills that Heaven will remedy. "When Nature and Spirit are fully harmonised—when Spirit rides Nature so perfectly that the two together make rather a *Centaur* than a mounted knight," our healing will be complete.[41]

What will our bodies be like? Joni Eareckson Tada in her book *Heaven: Your Real Home* suggests the difficulty of imagining it:

> Trying to understand what our bodies will be like in heaven is much like expecting an acorn to understand his destiny of roots, bark, branches, and leaves. Or asking a caterpillar to appreciate flying. Or a peach pit to fathom being fragrant. Or a coconut to grasp what it means to sway in the ocean breeze. Our eternal bodies will be so grand, so glorious, that we can only catch a fleeting glimpse of the splendor to come.[42]

We find the best clue available in Jesus' resurrected body. On the one hand, Jesus appears suddenly in a room with locked doors and ultimately floats into Heaven. On the other, Jesus takes pains to calm this fear for his followers: He eats fish, breaks bread, converses in audible language that uses "normal" bodily functions. He was recognized by his disciples as the Jesus who had been with them over miles of dusty road. He was so substantial that he had to admonish Mary Magdalene to let go. Thomas was invited to touch his wounds. The resurrection body of Jesus, like the new body he promises to bestow on us, has amazing capabilities. It is not an issue of giving up the things about our present bodies we know and love and that God in Christ created good. It is more like getting a new model with expanded capabilities that we will assuredly like.

In Jesus' resurrection "a wholly new mode of being has arisen in the universe. The body, which lives in that new mode is like, and yet unlike, the body his friends knew before the execution. It is differently related to space and probably to time, but by no means cut off from all relation to them."[43] Yet Jesus could go from place to place without passing physically (in our normal sense) through space—he appeared and disappeared at will. He entered rooms through walls and closed doors. With three more dimensions of space, he could do it: one substance passing through another substance without dislodging either.[44] This helps, but it is a matter of following the logic of physics equations, not intuiting it in an imaginative leap. Lewis's reflections on space and time suggest that he would have been intrigued by such creative speculations, not as an article of faith, but as suggestions that help us feel or imagine that it might be done. Such a thing is not essential to belief, but it certainly plays a good supporting role.

The imagination (not belief) is at an almost insurmountable disadvantage when it comes to spirit. To which of the five senses may we successfully appeal for aid? The advantage is all with the flesh. But like a judo fighter, Lewis uses the weight of this enemy against itself. The classic example is *The Great Divorce*, where Lewis gives ordinary solid earthly bodies to the "Solid People" from Heaven and portrays the folks arriving from Hell as ghosts whose feet cannot even bend the grass of Heaven. After walking in the Solid People's moccasins through several pages, our imagination does the work of throwing the ghost-fear to the mat. We see that Heaven is the real place, Hell the ghost town. Similarly, when Weston yields himself to demonic possession in *Perelandra*, a process that began long ago, "only a ghost was left—an everlasting unrest, a crumbling, a ruin, an odour of decay." The negative imagery of ghosts goes in the Hell column where it belongs.[45]

In imagining Heaven, the job of the imagination is not to predict the details even of our new bodies, but to mull over enough possibilities that we are cured both of thinking too small and of thinking we know the unknowable.[46] We can know that Heaven is the place where we grow into our true selves. In "Man or Rabbit?" using rabbit as a metaphor for our merely natural selves, Lewis describes the process of transformation as painful but worth it, even with the handfuls of fur and bleeding necessary to the change, but "we shall find underneath it all a thing we have never yet imagined: a real Man, an ageless god, a son of God, strong, radiant, wise, beautiful and drenched in joy."[47]

One significance of Jesus' ascension into Heaven is that a body has to go someplace. He goes "to prepare a place for us," the Bible says. Lewis reminds us that "it is not the picture of an escape from any and every kind of Nature into some unconditioned and utterly transcendent life. It is the picture of a new human nature, and a new Nature in general, being brought into existence. . . . That is the picture—not of unmaking but of remaking. The old field of space, time, matter, and the senses is to be weeded, dug, and sown for a new crop. We may be tired of that old field: God is not."[48] Lewis reminds us that every other major religion in the world sees the body as an irrelevance in the hereafter and that it is Christianity that has always affirmed the body. God declared his physical creation good and entered it in the person of Jesus that it might be completed and perfected through him.[49]

MYTH #4: I WON'T BE ME

I am sure of this, that he who began a good work in you will bring it to completion at the day of Jesus Christ.[50]

—PHILIPPIANS

And what else are we afraid of? We are afraid of giving up the self. It is true, of course, that we must die to self. It is Jesus himself who calls us to unconditional surrender. He insists on making us perfect. In the final analysis, he won't settle for anything else. But dying to self does not mean the death of selfhood. We become more ourselves in Christ. In fact, when we insist on making ourselves the center, the result is pathology. Self-consciousness is part of the Fall, as when Adam and Eve felt shame over their nakedness only after they had disobeyed God and chosen their own way. Isn't the "journey back to the habitual self" the very thing the poet Keats complained of? Isn't the romantic love of nature chiefly driven by a desire to forget the self and become absorbed into something greater and grander?

For our own health, we must learn to give ourselves away, but we do it in a way that we get back a healthier self, a fuller, richer, more differentiated self so that we have more and better to give away; then give that away, too. In so doing, we will not only enjoy earth more, but we will be preparing ourselves for the symbiosis of Heaven. It is the very pattern of behavior we find in the Godhead. As Lewis says in *The Problem of Pain*:

> In self-giving, if anywhere, we touch a rhythm not only of all creation but of all being. For the Eternal Word also gives Himself in sacrifice; and that not only on Calvary. For when He was crucified He "did that in the wild weather of His outlying provinces which He had done at home in glory and gladness." He surrenders begotten Deity back to begetting Deity in obedience. . . . From the highest to the lowest, self exists to be abdicated and, by that abdication, becomes the more truly self, to be thereupon yet the more abdicated, and so forever. . . . This is not a heavenly law which we can escape by remaining earthly, nor an earthly law which we can escape by being saved. What is outside the system of self-giving is not earth, nor nature, nor ordinary life, but simply and solely Hell. Yet even Hell derives from this law such reality as it has. That fierce

imprisonment in the self is but the obverse of the self-giving which is absolute reality.[51]

Heaven is a place where the self is realized, or else why did God make us different from each other? Our diversity enables us all to worship him in a unique way and teach others what we are uniquely gifted to see in him. Lewis says:

> God . . . makes each soul unique. If He had no use for all these differences, I do not see why He should have created more souls than one. Be sure that the ins and outs of your individuality are no mystery to Him; and one day they will no longer be a mystery to you. . . . Your soul has a curious shape because it is a hollow made to fit a particular swelling in the infinite contours of the divine substance, or a key to unlock one of the doors in the house with many mansions. For it is not humanity in the abstract that is to be saved, but you. . . . Blessed and fortunate creature, your eyes shall behold Him and not another's. All that you are, sins apart, is destined, if you will let God have His good way, to utter satisfaction. . . . Your place in heaven will seem to be made for you and you alone, because you were made for it.[52]

> Each of the redeemed shall forever know and praise some one aspect of the divine beauty better than any other creature can. Why else were individuals created, but that God, loving all infinitely, should love each differently?[53]

By contrast, Hell involves a loss of personal distinctiveness. Sin is ultimately the choosing of self over God. Damnation and Hell are receiving that choice of self over God forever. Hell is the drying up of human potential; Heaven is the fulfillment of human potential. Hell is the final inability to choose anything but the self: nothing other, neither God nor other creatures, nor the Heaven that is the created destiny of human beings. The fear of losing our selfhood is justified, but it belongs with our fear of Hell, not Heaven. We will see this played out amply in examining the philosophy of Hell.

In *Perelandra* Ransom has seen Weston yield to demon possession and has experienced his unrelenting assault even on his sanity, as when Weston plies him with unsleeping banalities, incessantly calling Ransom's name until Ransom asks, "What?" and is answered only with, "Nothing." In being anti-God, Weston has been consumed by the satanic self, which opposes all selfhood but his own. Ransom concludes: "There was, no doubt, a confusion of persons in damnation: what Pantheists falsely hoped of Heaven, bad men really received in Hell. They were melted down into their master, as a lead soldier slips down and loses his shape in the ladle held over the gas ring."[54] By implication, Hell is not an arbitrary punishment. Hell, in Lewis's view, is to have as one's sentence not something imposed upon him according to some arbitrary rule, but what a person has chosen for himself. That is, "to live wholly in the self and to make the best of what he finds there. And what he finds there is Hell."[55]

Nor is Heaven an arbitrary reward. It is the completion of what God has begun in us as his creatures. It is the thing for which we were ultimately made. Heaven is the place where we achieve ultimate, fully differentiated selfhood. Think of how different this concept is from the man-made heavens of pantheism or Buddhism in which we merge into some great cosmic, amoeba-like One. That's a hellish view of Heaven. Thoughts of self-annihilation *ought* to cause us fear. But it has no place in our thoughts about the Heaven in which we will "know as we are known" and say of an old friend, "Ah—he is himself at last."[56] In his *C. S. Lewis Encyclopedia* entry on Heaven, Colin Duriez sums it up this way: "Heaven is founded upon the paradox that the more we abandon ourselves to Christ, the more fully ourselves we become. Thus, while redemption by Christ improves people in this present life, the consummation of human maturity is unimaginable. In heaven both the individuality and society of persons will be fulfilled, both diversity and harmony. Heaven is varied, hell monotonous. Heaven is brimful of meaning; hell is the absence of meaning. Heaven is reality itself, hell a ghost or shadow."[57]

MYTH #5: JUST A HARP AND CROWN TRIP

Blessed be the God and Father of our Lord Jesus Christ! According to his great mercy, he has caused us to be born again to a living hope through the resurrection of Jesus Christ from the dead, to an inheritance that is imperishable, undefiled, and unfading, kept in heaven for you, who by God's power are being guarded through faith for a salvation ready to be revealed in the last time.[58]

—1 PETER

Are you afraid that you'll have to take in Heaven those harp lessons your mother never made you take on earth? Or that some heavenly Emily Post will make you wear your crown whenever you go out? Will you actually be allowed to walk on golden streets with your shoes on? Ironically, a big source of the unappealing stereotypes we have of Heaven come from symbolic biblical descriptions. In our post-romantic fondness for the natural world, a path through a wood with a stream running by might be more appealing than streets of gold, especially if we have been conditioned to beware of materialism. The problem is not in the biblical imagery, though; it is in our inability to read symbolic language symbolically.

All attempts to express the inexpressible have the same inherent difficulty. If streets of gold are suggested, it is only to imply that the care in its design is lavish beyond imagination. Who uses gold as a paving material? If crowns are suggested, it is only to imply that we will be given tasks of exhilarating importance and fascination. Lewis quips:

> There is no need to be worried by facetious people who try to make the Christian hope of "Heaven" ridiculous by saying they do not want "to spend eternity playing harps." The answer to such people is that if they cannot understand books written for grown-ups, they should not talk about them. All the scriptural imagery (harps, crowns, gold, etc.) is, of course, a merely symbolical attempt to express the inexpressible. . . . People who take these symbols literally might as well think that when Christ told us to be like doves, He meant that we were to lay eggs.[59]

We are not always as "grown up" in our handling of biblical symbolism as we should be or want to be. Our imaginations are often too literal.

Lewis laments that the man on the street thinks of God having a Son in the same way a Greek god might, this son descending to earth from Heaven "like a parachutist," going to some underworld place, then ascending back to Heaven to take his place on an ornate throne next to his father. "The whole thing seems to imply a local and material Heaven—a palace in the stratosphere."[60] The church has always had to battle against this kind of literalism and has condemned anthropomorphism from its earliest days. Our job is to "distinguish the core of belief from the attendant imagining."[61] He is also clear that non-metaphorical language is impossible even for scientists.

Let's acknowledge at once that even the most imaginative of artists have their backs against the wall when it comes to depicting Heaven. On the literary side, we find that Dante, in *The Divine Comedy*, could give us fascinating portraits of Hell and Purgatory, which are often taught, but his rarely assigned treatment of Heaven resorts to highly complex symbolism and abstraction, concluding with a vision of God as spinning wheels within wheels that result more in vertigo than love and longing for God and our heavenly home. Similarly, John Milton imagined his way into literary "immortality" with *Paradise Lost*, with unforgettably tragic speeches from the Devil and scenes in Hell, but his *Paradise Regained* is a comparative flop. Lewis, in his *Preface to "Paradise Lost,"* faults Milton as downright misleading in making Hell and its occupants so intriguing.

Lewis sympathizes with the difficulty and suggests why even the best falter at describing Heaven, when they score a success with Hell. Evil, he explains, is easy to imagine. All you have to do is let your mind go. Unchecked, it will wander naturally into that weedy terrain. This is what it means to be fallen or have a sin nature and to be in need of redemption. Similarly, we have done evil. On the other hand, to imagine unalloyed holiness is to attempt a projection of our minds into a place they have never been. It is no different for artists. We will ever, in this life, be at a disadvantage when trying to portray goodness. *The Screwtape Letters* is Lewis's own huge success in imagining his way into the diabolical mind. Lewis thought, ideally, that these letters should be answered by a balancing set of letters from an unfallen archangel's point of view, but he withered under the task of projecting himself into a holy mind and despaired at finding an answerable style.[62]

The Bible writers, even those given a glimpse into Heaven, had the same disadvantage of relating something outside human experience. So overpowering is unveiled holiness, goodness, and glory that mortals must be shielded from it or die. Moses wished to see God's face, but had to be sheltered by a rock and covered by God's own hand, seeing only his back. Other biblical visionaries have a similar reaction at seeing Heaven, proclaiming with Isaiah their unworthiness and falling down, like John, as though dead. "So," concludes Kenneth Kantzer, "the Bible accommodates itself to our insensitivity. Heaven is portrayed as essentially unlike earth— no sorrow, no sighing, no tears, no pain, no sin. Most of what we know about heaven from the Bible is the listing of things we do not like on earth."[63]

We know from biblical witnesses allowed to see Heaven 1) that it is a real place, and 2) that it is a stretch describing it in human language. Paul was caught up into the third heaven but not permitted to tell what he saw. Peter, James, and John got a taste of it on the Mount of Transfiguration. Stephen gave witness to Heaven opening up and seeing God as he was leaving this life as the first Christian martyr. In the Old Testament, Moses glimpsed God and came off the mountain with a glowing countenance himself. Elisha's eyes were opened to see an army of angels in flaming chariots arrayed around him. The two fullest visions are also the most perplexing. The first is Ezekiel's in the Old Testament. The opening describes a storm with constant flashes of light and "four living creatures" in the midst of the storm, shining like polished bronze. They were like humans and not like humans with four faces, four wings with hands beneath, and feet like a calf's. It sounds a little like something I saw in The Lord of the Rings that put me on the edge of my seat. That was Ezekiel's reaction, too: "I fell on my face," and "I sat there overwhelmed among them seven days."[64]

John's vision in Revelation 21 and 22 is similar in its otherworldliness, featuring rainbow thrones, gates of pearl, streets of gold, a 1,400-mile cube, and walls of jasper 200 feet thick. Joni Eareckson Tada says, tongue in cheek, it sounds like Minnesota's Mall of America. It seems the ultimate in city planning, but as post-romantics, we have largely lost our taste for city scenes, preferring the pastoral countryside. I'm tempted to say, "Couldn't I just go dirt-biking for a couple hundred years?"

I don't think we have to worry about missing nature because we will have it still. In Genesis nature is cursed. In Revelation the curse is removed. What would be the point of removing a curse from something that was to be simply destroyed? No, there will be a new heaven and a new earth. Here heaven and earth mean nature—the whole creation made to order by God for his human creation. Nature will become what it was always meant to be, just as our redeemed and glorified selves will be what they were always meant to be. Lewis says of nature, "She will be cured, but cured in character: not tamed (Heaven forbid) nor sterilised. We shall still be able to recognize our old enemy, friend, play-fellow and foster-mother, so perfected as to be not less but more, herself. And that will be a merry meeting."[65] "God never undoes anything but evil, never does good to undo it again. The union between God and Nature in the Person of Christ admits no divorce. He will not go out of Nature again and she must be glorified in all ways which this miraculous union demands."[66]

Clarence Dye says about Lewis's handling of this issue that he "did not so much invent new images of heaven, as interpret to the modern mind the images already given in the New Testament."[67] Lewis's rejoinder on reading symbolic language catches me up short: "Heaven is, by definition, outside our experience, but all intelligible descriptions must be of things within our experience. The scriptural picture of heaven is therefore just as symbolical as the picture which our desire, unaided, invents for itself; heaven is not really full of jewellery [sic] any more than it is really the beauty of Nature, or a fine piece of music."[68] Lewis finds the appeal of such imagery small himself, but he encourages us to pursue the biblical imagery as authoritative and ultimately the most valuable.

For example, the cubic design of the New Jerusalem (1,400 miles long, high, and wide) is meant to remind us of the Old Testament Holy of Holies, which was twenty cubits in all three dimensions. It was the place of God's presence. In the New Jerusalem, the whole city is a temple because God is everywhere present in it. Streets of gold suggest that what many have died for on earth is so paltry in Heaven that we tread it beneath our feet. Gates of pearl, single pearls large enough to make a gate for a wall 200 feet thick, are meant to boggle our minds. It sets Anne Graham Lotz to musing on what size oyster and how much suffering [69] The New Testament mentions many kinds of crowns—crowns of life, rejoicing, glory, righteousness, incorruptibility. Joni Tada puts the fun and freshness back in by calling them "God's party favors." Any way we take it, we are in for a stretch, as the Bible warns: "No eye has seen, nor ear heard, nor the heart of man imagined, what God has prepared for those who love him."[70] But in the end would we want a Heaven suitably described in ordinary legal language? We can trust the God who made the glories of this temporary earth to multiply the wonders of our permanent home and multiply our capacity to enjoy it and him forever.

MYTH #6: HEAVEN IS ESCAPIST THINKING

So we do not lose heart. Though our outer nature is wasting away, our inner nature is being renewed day by day. For this slight momentary affliction is preparing for us an eternal weight of glory beyond all comparison, as we look not to the things that are seen but to the things that are unseen. For the things that are seen are transient, but the things that are unseen are eternal.[71]

—2 CORINTHIANS

Isn't Heaven just "pie in the sky," a bribe to make us good, a crutch for people who can't otherwise cope with the harsh reality of cold facts, an escapist's dream? In answering a related question about whether a good life can be lived without Christianity, Lewis shifts the ground to a more foundational question: Is Christianity true? If false, we will not want to promote it whether it helps or not; rather, we should squash it as a pernicious lie. But if true, we should embrace it even if the consequence makes life uncomfortable. Belief always determines action; so it stands to reason that our view on the question will make a difference.

A Christian believes that while God created the universe and all in it, the universe's days are numbered, but the human creation will live forever. Further, human happiness, both here and through eternity, depends on "being united with God," so that anything else is secondary. The materialist, on the other hand, believes that humanity emerged by blind chance and that the seventy or so years of life on earth must be made as happy as possible by social planning and good political policy. In its idealist forms, materialism generates utopias: versions of Heaven on earth. Lewis argues in the essay "Man or Rabbit?" that Christianity will make us good, but it will change the definition of good. The first thing we discover is that we can't be moral on our own, "not for twenty-four hours."[72] We are flawed at the core so that the very standard we use for judging others will condemn us as well. We don't need more moral teachers but a new heart, a new set of inner motivations. The second thing we learn is that "mere *morality* is not the end of life. . . . The people who keep on asking if they can't lead a decent life without Christ, don't know what life is about."[73] Rather, our purpose, in the words of the catechism, is to "know God and enjoy him forever." To be united to God is, at last, to be in Heaven. To love him is to take on his character, which is the very ground of morality. Until we are rid of sin, that is until nothing impedes our love for God and others, we will need a crutch. Better for the wounded to hobble home than wait for the enemy to overrun them.

In presenting the challenge of Christ's truth claims, Lewis poses his famous trilemma in *Mere Christianity*. You can't take Jesus simply as a great moral teacher and leave it at that. He claimed to forgive sins, to be the power behind creation, in fact to be God. Someone making those claims has left us only three options: He is liar, lunatic, or Lord. If he is a liar, he is evil beyond description. If self-deceived, he is on the level of a man who thinks he's a "poached egg."[74] If speaking truth, as one of Flannery O'Connor's characters says, "It's nothing left for you to do but throw away everything and follow him."[75] In other words, he is worthy of worship, so worthy that becoming his sons and daughters should be the only ultimate goal of our lives. "For from him and through him and to him are all things," as the apostle says.[76]

Regarding Heaven as a bribe, we have seen already Lewis putting morality in its place and insisting on truth and belief as an end and not a means. This is a good place to remember that Jesus said, 'I am the way, and the truth, and the life."[77] If Heaven is real, it might still be possible to try to take it as a bribe for good behavior. Lewis solidly takes the biblical view that no one can be good enough to earn Heaven: "all have sinned and fall short of the glory of God" and "the wages of sin is death.'[78] It is impossible to take Heaven as a bribe because it comes exclusively as God's gift or not at all. Lewis explains in "The Weight of Glory" that marrying a person for money or fighting as a hired gun are mercenary, but marrying for love and winning a victory to protect the homeland are the activities in consummation. They are their own rewards. Do we have to worry that taunts about "pie in the sky" are true or that we are merely mercenary and self-serving in desiring Heaven? Though we can be self-serving (and Lewis warns against this danger), we have the assurance that all desires have their proper satisfactions and that both the yearnings and fillings are of God. The question is whether we want God as a means or an end.

> We are afraid that heaven is a bribe, and that if we make it our goal we shall no longer be disinterested. It is not so. Heaven offers nothing that a mercenary soul can desire. It is safe to tell the pure in heart that they shall see God, for only the pure in heart want to.[79]

Since Heaven is union with the divine nature (God), and Hell is separation from it, Lewis thought it a corruption of doctrine to think much of our eternal destiny "apart from the presence or absence of God."[80] Lewis sees the doctrine of Heaven and Hell as "corollaries to a faith already centred upon God." Further, apart from Heaven as "union with God" and Hell as "separation from Him, the belief in either is a mischievous superstition; for then we have, on the one hand, a merely 'compensatory' belief (a 'sequel' to life's sad story, in which everything will 'come all right') and, on the other, a nightmare which drives men into asylums or makes them persecutors."[81] Lewis believed in God for "a whole year" before he had "any belief in the future life," a year of "very great value."[82] In my own case, no less legitimate, I came fleeing the thing I feared. Lewis came more nobly, if more rarely, from the dogged pursuit of truth and the constraints of logic. Heaven, unity with God in Christ (not mansions for their own sake), was simply the answer to his heart's desire and satisfied his mind and soul.

As Lewis puts it in "The Weight of Glory": "Those who have attained everlasting life in the vision of God doubtless know very well that it is no mere bribe, but the very consummation of their earthly discipleship; but we who have not yet attained it cannot know this in the same way, and cannot even begin to know it at all except by continuing to obey and finding the first reward of our obedience in our increasing power to desire the ultimate reward."[83] The triune God is "the ultimate Fact" and "fountain of all other facthood." All places, even Heaven itself, exist "in Him," so that being united with "the Divine Life in the eternal Sonship of Christ, is strictly speaking, the only thing worth a moment's consideration."[84] If Heaven is the ultimate and permanent reality and this the shadowlands, then worldliness is escapism.

MYTH #7: HEAVENLY MINDED, BUT NO EARTHLY GOOD

Seek first the kingdom of God and his righteousness, and all these things will be added to you.[85]

—JESUS

We've all heard it: "Too heavenly minded to be of any earthly good." It is patently false. In a sense, this statement could only be made by a nonbeliever because *if* it were true, which would a wise person choose: to be earthly minded and think our three score and ten worth our utmost energy or to be heavenly minded and build for time out of mind in paradise? This cliché gives Heaven a bad rap amongst earthlings. For example, in his recent book on religion and culture in America, Alan Wolfe is "offended" by the central Christian teaching that we are "resident aliens": that is, we are sojourners on earth with our true home in Heaven. Wolfe, a self-described secularist, wants Americans to be "full citizens."[86] It is true that Christianity has a historical strand of separatism. Instead of following Jesus' teaching to be "in the world but not of it," many Christians, in trying not to be "of the world," have had nothing to do with it. When this has happened, it has not had the desired effect of making us pure; rather, it has made us legalistically self-righteous and evangelistically impotent.

The tension between living in the "City of Man" while journeying toward the "City of God" is as old as Abraham and is a major theme throughout the Bible and in writers as historically and theologically spread out as Augustine, Luther, and Richard Niebuhr.[87] As these writers affirm, nothing could be further from the truth than the notion that a person focused on Heaven has his head in the clouds and does nothing of practical value. If you are thinking of the heavenly streets of gold, so this line of thinking goes, you are likely to hit the potholes in the streets of Chicago. But history shows that the people most interested in the streets of gold are most likely to do something about the ones made of concrete and asphalt. Lewis points out, though he was not the first or last to do so, that it is precisely those who have the strongest belief in Heaven who have done the most earthly good. And this is quite apart from the fact that the best possible use of earthly time is to prepare for heavenly eternity. In *Mere Christianity*, Lewis says,

> Hope . . . means . . . a continual looking forward to the eternal. . . . It does not mean that we are to leave the present world as it is. If you read history you will find that the Christians who did most for the present world were just those who thought most of the next. . . . It is since Christians have largely ceased to think of the other world that they have become so ineffective in this. Aim at Heaven and you will get earth "thrown in": aim at earth and you will get neither.[88]

What contributions to earthly good have the heavenly minded made? In an essay entitled "Some Thoughts," Lewis tells us that Christianity is responsible for:

> [preserving] such secular civilization as survived the fall of the Roman Empire; . . . to it Europe owes the salvation, in those perilous ages, of civilized agriculture, architecture, laws, and literacy itself. . . . This religion has always been healing the sick and caring for the poor; . . . it has, more than any other, blessed marriage; . . . arts and philosophy tend to flourish in its neighbourhood.[89]

There are many reasons for this benevolence by Christians, but chief among them is the belief that God is the creator of all, and creation deserves respect because it is his. The human part of that creation, as something in his own image and something destined to live forever, demands our special regard. "Because we know the natural level also is God's creation we cannot cease to fight against the death which mars it, as against all those other blemishes upon it, against pain and poverty, barbarism and ignorance. Because we love something else more than this world we love even this world better than those who know no other."[90] Lewis rightly and often proclaims the truth that loving God first and most enables us to love everything and everyone more, an idea we will see more of later.

George Weigel elaborates the reason for Christian charitable achievement: "History is not simply the by-product of the contest for power in the world—although power certainly plays an important role in it. And neither is history the exhaust fumes produced by the means of production. Rather, history is driven, over the long haul, by culture—by what men and women honor, cherish, and worship; by what societies deem to be true and good, and by the expressions they give to those convictions in language, literature, and the arts; by what individuals and societies are willing to stake their lives on."[91] This "Christian way of thinking," Weigel suggests, can be traced back to Augustine's *The City of God*. In fact, this thinking is biblical. Jesus, after all, commanded that we "render to Caesar the things that are Caesar's": Among other things, pay taxes.[92]

Citing Henri de Lubac, Weigel gives the corollary: "It is not true, as is sometimes said, that man cannot organize the world without God. What is true is that, without God, he can only organize it against man." And, Weigel states, "that is what the tyrannies of the twentieth century had proven—that ultra mundane humanism is inevitably inhuman humanism."[93] This will immediately put readers of Lewis in mind of his *Abolition of Man* and *That Hideous Strength*, where he argues and illustrates the destructive consequences of stepping outside God-given morality in human affairs. The result, for twentieth-century Europe, was what Solzhenitsyn calls a "'rage of self-mutilation': multiple totalitarian regimes, the Great Depression, two world wars, and a Cold War in which Europe cannibalized itself."[94]

In a statement with parallels in Lewis, historian Christopher Dawson concludes that "the modern dilemma is essentially a spiritual one, and every one of its main aspects, moral, political, and scientific, brings us back to the need of a spiritual solution."[95] Lewis concurs: "Christianity really does two things about conditions here and now in this world: (1) It tries to make them as good as possible, i.e., to reform them; but also (2) It fortifies you against them in so far as they remain bad."[96] Any society that wants to thrive in art, culture, science, and humanitarian services, and any government that knows history and wants to serve its people will make a welcome home for the "heavenly minded."

HEAVEN
PART II

REMYTHOLOGIZING HEAVEN:
THE FICTION

2

MAKING THE MYTHS OF
HEAVEN AND HELL

The Mythical Mode "can give us experiences we have never had and thus, instead of 'commenting on life,' can add to it."[1]

C. S. LEWIS

Harry Blamires, a former pupil of Lewis and a considerable scholar, apologist, and author of fiction, remembers that Lewis's friend "Owen Barfield once recommended to scholars the need for 'unthinking.'"[2] We need the same gift when attempting to think of Heaven. All of our present categories will lead us astray. We are limited by a very small amount of time and can sustain very few close relationships. We do not live our lives for very long at a time with our eternal destiny in view, though we are commanded to try and rewarded when we do. In helping us get outside the box, Blamires points out that when we look up *caterpillar* in the dictionary or encyclopedia, we find it described in terms of the butterfly: what it *will* be. He suggests imagining how an angel looking up our own species might find us described, since our own "metamorphosis" will be far more radical than the caterpillar's: "I cannot help wondering what an angel would find if he looked up *Man* and *Woman* in the *Encyclopaedia Caelestis*":[3]

> The name given to the larvae of the saved in their prepupal stage as terrestrial beings. They are two-legged, two-armed, two-eyed, and two-eared (and the most degenerate specimens are said to be two-faced). They are wingless. They have only a rudimentary sensitivity to reality. They tend to measure everything wholly on the basis of their immature understanding as creatures imprisoned in the space-time continuum.[4]

But how do we "unthink" entrenched images and ideas, as Barfield suggests? The best way is to leave this world behind and go to a new one where we can start all over again without all the old assumptions and hang-ups. Where do we do that? In imaginative literature of the sort Lewis excelled at creating. And how do we, along with Blamires, think into our future? Again, through imaginative literature. The unique gift of good fiction is to appeal simultaneously to our intellects, imaginations, and emotions. It can deliver such an integrated experience that our mental landscapes are permanently altered.

This is one reason why Jesus always taught with stories. Indeed, much of the Bible is in narrative form. The advantage is in defying all the abstract categories that can foster legalistic applications. Almost any parable would serve to illustrate. As Colin Duriez so aptly puts it: "C. S. Lewis believed that heaven is probably unimaginable, even though we have the biblical images to take us as far as they can. Parable, allegory, and fiction are the closest that we can come to speaking of heaven. This is why he explored heaven so much through fantasy."[5] To put it another way, Lewis's whole enterprise in helping his readers grasp biblical truth was a process of demythologizing the false and remythologizing the true.

Lewis loved myth from his earliest childhood, especially Norse. Myths of dying gods who sacrificed themselves for others powerfully captured his imagination. The action and emotion rang morally true, but he thought them "lies breathed through silver" until his friends Tolkien and Dyson explained on an extended walk around the Magdalen College grounds in the wee hours that the old myths were "a real though unfocused gleam of divine truth falling on human imagination." As David Downing summarizes it:

They argued that one of the great and universal myths, that of the dying God who sacrifices himself for the people, shows an innate awareness of the need for redemption not by one's own works, but as a gift from some higher realm. For them, the incarnation was the pivotal point at which myth became history. The life, death and resurrection of Christ not only fulfilled Old Testament types but also embodied—literally— central motifs found in all the world's mythologies. . . . No more were his beloved Greek myths, Nordic sagas and Irish legends mere escapist tripe unworthy of a thinking person. They became reservoirs of trans-rational truths; they provided insights, admittedly partial and distorted, about realities beyond the reach of logical inquiry. In Christianity, the true myth to which all the others were pointing, Lewis found a world-view that he could defend as both *good* and *real*. It was a faith grounded in history and one that satisfied even his formidable intellect.

For Lewis, Christianity would thence become the fountainhead of all myths and tales of enchantment, the key to all mythologies, the myth that unfolded itself in history.[6]

Of course, using the term *myth* in the precincts of Christianity is understandably going to raise red flags and get the hackles up on some who have defended Christianity against the charges that it is "only a myth." Before venturing further, the first thing to remind ourselves of is Lewis's commitment to defending the truth of Christianity. No one was more convinced of it than he, and few have paid such a price without suffering physical torture and martyrdom. Against his nature as a bookish stay-at-home man, he traveled and spoke to diverse audiences. This resulted in a massive correspondence that obliged him to labor one to two hours each morning at a task he prayed to be delivered from but never was. Perhaps harder, he bore for nearly thirty years the scorn of many in the Oxford scholarly community, including his own college, who felt that he had violated the unwritten code of staying in your own academic field and not popularizing for the unlearned. Add to this the rampant disbelief of atheists and agnostics and the unavoidable jealousy in that very closed community.

The second thing, and more to the point, is getting down some definitions. Lewis uses the term *myth* in its two most common forms, plus a third specialized sense, much as he used the term *joy* in its ordinary sense of "happiness" and in the special sense of "longing and desire," which confusingly means the lack of something versus its possession. Similarly, *myth* usually means either ancient stories formerly believed but now seen as fictions or something false, which only the ignorant or foolish would believe. This makes for tough sledding when the two are linked by a true believer like Lewis into an apparent oxymoron like "Christian myth." In the third sense, as in "Christian myth," Lewis means a story that embodies values, that gives us at once an imaginative experience and relates truths of the most important kind. In this meaning, it shares something with the first definition in that the myths embodied the beliefs and values of a culture. The importance for Lewis is clear from the opening account of his literary taste and conversion. The importance for those who may not share those tastes may not be obvious at first, but the effort of understanding it pays off because it explains why we love his fiction and why it has been so hugely successful.

In "Myth Became Fact," Lewis observes a basic human problem that myth solves. Ordinarily, we cannot *have* an experience and *think* about the experience at the same time without fundamentally altering it. We can't kiss a beloved and think about kissing without ruining the moment. We can't laugh at a joke and discuss the principles of effective humor at the same time. In one case we are *in* an experience, and in the other *outside* it examining it. The unique contribution of mythic writing is in allowing us to have an experience while getting insight into elemental truth. Here is how Lewis puts it in his essay "Myth Became Fact": "What flows into you from the myth is not truth but reality (truth is always *about* something, but reality is the *about which* truth is), and, therefore, every myth becomes the father of innumerable truths on the abstract level."[7] We see this in the application of Jesus' parables to innumerable life situations, which is why "he said nothing to them without a parable."[8] Fortunately, we can receive this benefit without understanding how myth works, but wanting to know how things work is part of being human, as well as a means of doing the thing ourselves. The mythic element in Lewis's fiction is the very thing that has captivated millions with "wonder and delight." His work, like few others, arouses our elemental longing for heavenly satisfactions and vibrates many other cords of authentic human experience.

Lewis cautions that we should not confuse mythic writing with artistic writing. Myth, in Lewis's special sense, works because it is a certain kind of story and can be effective in literary writing, painting, or even dull prose. His fullest definition occurs in *Experiment in Criticism* in the chapter "On Myth," where he lists six characteristics. Myths: are "extra-literary"; don't depend on the usual storytelling techniques of suspense and surprise, and may in fact have a sense of the inevitable; don't foster identification with the characters, though we feel "a profound relevance to our own life"; deal with the supernatural; are solemn; and raise a sense of awe attaching to characters or worlds unlike us (like angels, ghosts, or gods).[9]

Myth also involves what Lewis terms a "world picture" or understanding of value, meaning, and significance. Obviously, these can be mistaken beliefs. Lewis's writing renders two signal services. First, the nonfiction demythologizes false beliefs, in two ordinary senses of the term "myth": exposing error and knocking the props from under modern myths like progressive evolution.[10] In general, he remythologizes in his fiction, all of it meeting the above six criteria. Unlike any other writer I know, Lewis's nonfiction is often mythic and remythologizing, too, as anyone who has read "The Weight of Glory" must know. Clearly, anything meeting these standards will take us to the realm of ultimate issues where questions of Heaven and Hell are never far away. And since Lewis's work is both high quality literature and thoroughly Christian, he prepares the mind, will, and emotion to receive ultimate truth.

Marjorie Hope Nicholson, a contemporary of Lewis's and notable scholar, makes the case for Lewis as mythmaker, commenting on one of his earliest works of fiction in her study *Voyages to the Moon* (1948):

> *Out of the Silent Planet* is to me the most beautiful of all cosmic voyages and in some ways the most moving. . . . As C. S. Lewis, the Christian apologist, has added something to the long tradition, so C. S. Lewis, the scholar-poet, has achieved an effect in *Out of the Silent Planet* different from anything in the past. Earlier writers have created new worlds from legend, from mythology, from fairy tale. Mr. Lewis has created myth itself, myth woven of desire and aspirations deep-seated in some, at least, of the human race. . . . As I journey into worlds at once familiar and strange, I experience. as did Ransom, "a sensation not of following an adventure but of enacting a myth."[11]

Lewis believes that in Christ's incarnation, the three elements of myth, truth, and fact come together. In *Perelandra*, the second book of the space trilogy, the hero, Ransom, must fight the Un-man, Weston. On the outcome of this fight rests the destiny of a world. The narrative voice recognizes the mythic quality of the story as Ransom, under God's direction, does what Christ did in a more profound act for our own world:

> Long since on Mars, and more strongly since he came to Perelandra, Ransom had been perceiving that the triple distinction of truth from myth and of both from fact was purely terrestrial—was part and parcel of that unhappy division between soul and body which resulted from the Fall. Even on earth the sacraments existed as a permanent reminder that the division was neither wholesome nor final. The Incarnation had been the beginning of its disappearance. In Perelandra it would have no meaning at all. Whatever happened here would be of such a nature that earth-men would call it mythological. All this he had thought before. Now he knew it. The Presence in the darkness,

never before so formidable, was putting these truths into his hands, like terrible jewels.[12]

What Lewis is up to can scarcely be put better than in these words concluding "On Stories":

> In life and art both, as it seems to me, we are always trying to catch in our net of successive moments something that is not successive. Whether in real life there is any doctor who can teach us how to do it, so that at last either the meshes will become fine enough to hold the bird, or we be so changed that we can throw our nets away and follow the bird to its own country is not a question for this essay. But I think it is sometimes done—or very nearly done—in stories. I believe the effort to be well worth making.[13]

In remythologizing Heaven, Lewis develops six major themes through a breathtaking array of characters and situations: 1) Christ is the center of all things; 2) Heaven is utterly real and our earthly life its shadow; 3) Heaven flows from the character of God, which means it is fully integrated and love reigns supreme, accompanied by goodness, justice, mercy, and creativity; 4) here humanity finds the fulfillment of its created potential—it is our true and natural home; 5) all of our longings are at their core for Heaven; and 6) we choose Heaven by choosing the preeminence of Christ. These themes are biblical, and reading them in Lewis's fiction takes me back to that great original not only with deeper understanding but with new depth of passion.

3

RECLAIMING THE HEAVENS FOR HEAVEN:
Out of the Silent Planet

When I look at your heavens, the work of your fingers, the moon and the stars, which you have set in place, what is man that you are mindful of him?[1]

PSALMS

Lewis's Ransom trilogy (*Out of the Silent Planet*, *Perelandra*, and *That Hideous Strength*) is perhaps the first work to combine science fiction and theological heft.[2] Lewis didn't begin with a Christian message and then decide on science fiction as a good way to smuggle it in. As David Downing tells us, and Lewis himself recounts in his autobiography and many letters, something of the reverse is true.[3] Lewis was a lifelong fan of fantasy literature of all kinds, but especially the mythic past. When, on a late night turn around Addison's Walk in Oxford, his friends Tolkien and Dyson helped Lewis make the connection of Christian truth with ancient mythology, the keystone for his conversion slipped into place.

In the Ransom series, Lewis simply reverses the process. Lewis's fiction shimmers throughout with mythic overtones because it was so integral to his imagination. As much of the literary critical work on Lewis shows, his fiction is a veritable remythologizing of ancient and medieval stories and outlooks recast in modern settings with supreme relevance. Similarly, as readers of his fiction all know, Lewis didn't merely tack on a Christian theme; rather, his thought was so fully integrated and his Christian commitment so deep that he would have been artificial and superficial had he attempted to leave it out. The Christian element, as much as the mythic, suffuses this and other works as the very mark of the author's integrity. He is true to his own principle that "the only moral . . . of any value . . . inevitably arises from the whole cast of the author's mind."[4]

Clyde Kilby aptly summarizes the direction the theological themes take in the trilogy: "Perhaps we could properly say that the aim of *Out of the Silent Planet* and *Perelandra* is to indicate what might have been and of *That Hideous Strength* to indicate what might yet be."[5] That is, the first two show what a world might have been unwounded by sin, and the third shows the hellish nightmare of sin run amuck. We could say with equal validity that the first two also foreshadow what Heaven will be like as a sinless, harmonious place and the third what Hell will be like as a place permanently marred by the ravages of sin.

Though the first of the trilogy, *Out of the Silent Planet*, does not deal with Heaven and Hell directly, it puts into imaginative perspective several key connected themes:

• harmony with an unfallen creation (between created beings and their environment);

• harmony with other created beings from animals to humans, angels, and God;

• the loss that comes by sin;

• death as necessary to the new and better thing God wants to do;

• humanity and this present creation (universe) as provisional in the context of God's bigger plan;

• God's care for individuals and details (even the grossly sinful people, like Weston, who is shown mercy by the Oyarsa, who sees hope in him despite his "bentness" or sinfulness);

• humility about what we don't know (for example, by our physical limitations to what we can see; Lewis provides a view beyond time and space to give us an inkling of what may be, including dimensions of Heaven hard to imagine);

• the heavens as gloriously full instead of empty.

As we would expect, many of the same themes will recur in the other two books, especially *Perelandra*. In discussing *Perelandra*, I will focus on the first three themes and for *Out of the Silent Planet* the last five.

SPACE AS HEAVEN

Lewis saw God as "the glad Creator," to borrow the words of his beloved Spenser. Everywhere, if we have eyes to see it, the world blazes with the glory of God. If we look down, we may even "see the universe in a grain of sand," says Blake; if we look up, "the heavens declare the glory of God," as the psalmist announces. But it was not always so for Lewis, looking into the vast reaches of space. In his years as an atheist, the emptiness of space was, in fact, one of the reasons for his unbelief, as he lays it out in the beginning of *The Problem of Pain*. Space seemed to him then a vast, empty waste without life, and even our own planet, perhaps the only one supporting life, was void of life for millions of years and may be so again when the sun runs out of fuel and life on earth has vanished. The Oyarsa of Malacandra (angelic ruler of Mars) puts his finger on the problem, knowing how the limitations of time and space and our relatively minute position in space handicap our imaginations. As he explains to Ransom: "My people have a law never to speak much of sizes or numbers to you others, not even to *sorns* [the most philosophic of rational creatures on Malacandra]. You do not understand, and it makes you do reverence to nothings and pass by what is really great."[6]

But this and all dark views of creation were illumined by the light of Christ at Lewis's conversion. Everything took on a new significance, redolent of eternity. The sky itself became to him a mythic element in God's creation: "If God chooses to be mythopoeic—and is not the sky itself a myth—shall we refuse to be *mythopathic*?"[7] In *Miracles* Lewis offers a view of creation as intentionally analogical and subject to mythologizing: "It is not an accident that simple-minded people, however spiritual, should blend the ideas of God and Heaven and the blue sky."[8] We do, in fact, get life-giving light and heat from it that makes the earth fruitful. Besides that, the sky is the thing we see that most suggests infinity. "And when God made space and worlds that move in space, and clothed our world with air, and gave us such eyes and such imaginations as those we have, He knew what the sky would mean to us. And since nothing in His work is accidental, if He knew, He intended. We cannot be certain that this was not indeed one of the chief purposes for which Nature was created."[9]

With his conversion, Lewis began to look into space with new eyes, and his transformation of empty space into a womb of teeming, vibrant life is one of his great gifts in helping us to imagine Heaven and one of the unique contributions of *Out of the Silent Planet*. Lewis didn't have to look far for a model of the heavens swarming with life. Throughout his work, he makes fulsome use of the medieval worldview, which includes the "doctrine of Plenitude." As George Musacchio explains: "It means that, because of God's very nature, the universe is full of all the multivarious kinds of life possible. An omnipotent and benevolent God would of course create a plenitude, a fullness, of life and energy and goodness through His creation, not wasting all that space out there beyond our ken."[10] Without believing the medieval worldview as an article of faith, Lewis transforms it into an imaginative insight into God's splendor in elements of creation known to us but scarcely imagined and little understood.

Before he ever gets to Malacandra (Mars), the space-traveling Ransom, though kidnapped by evil scientists, sees the error of his old view of space:

> A nightmare, long engendered in the modern mind by the mythology that follows in the wake of science, was falling off him. He had read of "Space": at the back of his thinking for years had lurked the dismal fancy of the black, cold vacuity, the utter deadness, which was supposed to separate the worlds. He had not known how much it affected him till now—now that the very name "Space" seemed a blasphemous libel for this empyrean ocean of radiance in which they swam. He could not call it "dead"; he felt life pouring into him from it every moment. How indeed should it be otherwise, since out of this ocean the worlds and all their life had come? He had thought it barren: he saw now that it was the womb of worlds, whose blazing and innumerable offspring looked down nightly even upon the earth with so many eyes—and here, with how many more! No: Space was the wrong name. Older thinkers had been wiser when they named it simply the heavens—heavens which declared the glory—the
>
> > "happy climes that ly
> > Where day never shuts his eye
> > Up in the broad fields of the sky."
>
> He quoted Milton's words to himself lovingly, at this time and often.[11]

On leaving "the heavens" for the gravitational pull of Malacandra, Ransom is loath to leave the newfound glories behind, and "sensations of intolerable height and of falling—utterly absent in the heavens—recurred constantly. . . . Suddenly the lights of the Universe seemed to be turned down. As if some demon had rubbed the heaven's face with a dirty sponge, the splendour in which they had lived so long blenched [sic] to a pallid, cheerless and pitiable grey."[12]

They were falling out of the heaven, into a world. Nothing in all his adventures bit so deeply into Ransom's mind as this. He wondered how he could ever have thought of planets, even of the Earth, as islands of life and reality floating in a deadly void. Now, with a certainty which never after deserted him, he saw the planets—the "earths" he called them in his thought—as mere holes or gaps in the living heaven—excluded and rejected wastes of heavy matter and murky air, formed not by addition to, but subtraction from, the surrounding brightness.[13]

Conversely, when he is journeying to Meldilorn much later in the story and is nearly free of the Malacandrian atmosphere, nearer the heavens, "he felt the old lift of the heart, the soaring solemnity, the sense, at once sober and ecstatic, of life and power offered in unasked and unmeasured abundance. If there had been air enough in his lungs he would have laughed aloud."[14] In the heavens, as in Heaven, even the most ordinary of experiences are sublime and all the senses keener.

If the atmosphere around Malacandra disappoints Ransom by comparison to space, the surface of the new planet gains by comparison to earth. His first and lasting impression sums it up: "Before anything else he learned that Malacandra was beautiful."[15] This "exquisitely beautiful" landscape features an ocean that is "'really' blue," not just a reflection or effect of "certain lights," with shores of "pinkish-white vegetation," a horizon purple in the distance, and beyond "upright shapes of whitish green," and farther yet a "rose-colored cloud-like mass." In short, he likes it. The environment of Malacandra is not only beautiful, but life-sustaining and spirit-refreshing. Even the ground cover is nourishing.

Lewis's contemporary Evelyn Underhill Moore, herself a writer of spiritual books, praises *Out of the Silent Planet* for its "delightful combination of beauty, humour, & deep seriousness" and what Lewis thought his best contribution, "the substitution of heaven for space."[16] We use the same word, *heaven*, to describe both the sky and the place of eternal abode for the saved. His revisioning gives us a kind of *a fortiori* presentation: If something is true of the lesser, how much more in the case of the greater. The heavens we see will "melt with a fervent heat" at Jesus' second coming, but the redeemed will spend eternity in the permanent Heaven.

Beyond the homonyms "heaven" and "Heaven," there are two other important links to Heaven in this book. The first is Maleldil, the word used interchangeably for God and Jesus, and the second is the ruling spirits or angels, called eldila (plural for eldil), who people the heavens and move at Maleldil's command. The eldila perform many of the biblical tasks of angels and have in common that grandeur about them that the art and literature of the past several centuries has blunted. The eldila strike terror or at least awe in the wise. Only the foolish and spiritually ignorant, like the evil Weston, dare to bandy words and attempt to manipulate them, of course to no avail. The eldila move at speeds faster than light and have insubstantial bodies. One of the philosophic creatures of Malacandra, a sorn, explains to Ransom that bodies are motion. If they move at one speed, you smell them, at another you see them, and faster yet, you don't perceive them at all. The highest order of all, God, moves so fast that he is everywhere at once and may be said to rest and "have no body at all."[17]

When the eldila speak, their voices sound "inorganic," and they assume forms such as dim lights when they wish humans to, in some sense, see them. These powerful beings are sometimes given the position of ruling a world. Such a ruler, even when human, is called the "Oyarsa." In perfect humility, the Oyarsa of Perelandra, an eldil, prepares the planet for rule by the humanlike creatures Maleldil puts there and gladly helps the humans learn how to run it. The eldila may well be doing what God's angels do for us. We are certainly looked after by some of them, and Scripture promises that we, too, will reign with Christ—help run things. Through the eldila, the door of Heaven is cracked a little further open.

Despite their goodness, even the creatures of Malacandra with physical bodies terrify Ransom at first, not only with the natural fear of the unknown, but intensified by the monstrous sense of "the other." As with his prejudice about space, Ransom has been conditioned by contemporary fictional representations of creatures in other worlds. In H. G. Wells's science fiction and that of his contemporaries, the inhabitants of space are grotesque, monstrous, and malevolent, invoking fear in human visitants. "The tellers of tales in our world make us think that if there is any life beyond our own air it is evil," says Ransom to the Oyarsa of Malacandra.[18] Similarly conditioned, Weston and Devine saw only projections of their own prejudice in past encounters with the Malacandrians, and Ransom overhears their horrific reports of sorns as demon gods requiring human sacrifice (him!). Ransom expects the worst. But in the event, the three rational species of Malacandra—sorns, hrossa, and pfifiltriggi—all prove to be unfallen, skilled, intelligent, hospitable, and even delightful upon further acquaintance.

For example, soon after meeting the large, black, furry, seal-like hrossa with "glossy coat, liquid eye, sweet breath and without teeth," Ransom learns that looking at them as rational animals with "the charm of speech and reason," rather than animalistic humans, it seems "as though Paradise had never been lost and earliest dreams were true."[19] They live in harmony with each other and their environment, as well as with the spiritual world of the eldila and Maleldil.

On his journey to Mars and later to Venus, Ransom finds beauty, harmony, hospitality, and vitality. Even bolder words are needed: He finds splendor and glory. This view of creation is part of what Christ redeemed in Lewis himself. When Ransom returns to earth from Malacandra, he presents to his sole confidante a rationale for publishing his story and a good part of Lewis's reason for writing these books: "If we could even effect in one per cent of our readers a change-over from the conception of Space to the conception of Heaven, we should have made a beginning."[20]

NO HEAVEN ON EARTH

Besides suggesting many of the values and characteristics of Heaven, Lewis's book shows the futility and perversity of trying to create a heaven on earth. Lewis was alarmed to find students, scientists, and serious writers propagating the idea that the hope and meaning of the universe was wrapped up in human colonization of space coupled with the evolutionary myth that we will get better and better until we become divine and immortal, at least as a species. H. G. Wells popularized this notion in his science fiction. Lewis's character, the scientist Weston, holds exactly this view.

> The danger of "Westonism" I meant to be real. What set me about writing the book was the discovery that a pupil of mine took all that dream of interplanetary colonization quite seriously, and the realization that thousands of people in one way and another depend on some hope of perpetuating and improving the species for the whole meaning of the universe—that a "scientific" hope of defeating death is a real rival to Christianity.[21]

In *Out of the Silent Planet*, Weston is impervious to beauty and intelligence in other forms than his monomaniacal philosophy of progress, and he's certainly blind to goodness. He is not yet fully in the bent Oyarsa's (Satan's) control, as happens in *Perelandra*. The Oyarsa of Malacandra tells Weston that he is only "bent," unlike his sidekick Devine, who is "broken" and has become merely greed personified. "He is now only a talking animal," says the Oyarsa.[22] The one good quality left to Weston that gives the Oyarsa hope for him is loyalty to his species, though he has perverted it, as happens to all things not subordinate to God. What would space as settled by Weston and Devine look like? Nothing but cosmic killing fields, peopled by the deluded and self-centered.

In virtually all of the science fiction written before Lewis, space was something to be gotten over or through, and space creatures were grotesque and evil, with earthlings as good guys. This, too, Lewis deliberately countered in his science fiction. The other planets are all ruled by good Oyaresu (plural of Oyarsa) under the direct guidance of God. Only earth, the silent planet, has been cut off from their society by our "bent Oyarsa," Satan, who has rebelled against God. The Oyarsa of Malacandra is eager to learn what God has done to counter this evil and ultimately save those of earth. The Oyarsa's wish alludes to 1 Peter 1:12, which says these are "things into which angels long to look." Ransom explains the incarnation, life, death, and resurrection of Jesus, a plan that fills even the Oyarsa with admiring wonder.

On his own planet, the Oyarsa is fully aware that evil has entered in Weston, who kills some of the good creatures of Malacandra and would eliminate them if he could to make way for earthlings. Thus, Lewis counters the false view of making Heaven on earth (or from it), seeing rightly that sinful beings would propagate sin, not progress, except in the most blatantly technological of terms. This, of course, is a very necessary clearing of the jungle to make way for the garden, the new Eden, the true Heaven.

DEATH AS THE GATEWAY TO HEAVEN

If we do not come to Heaven in *Out of the Silent Planet*, we come at least to the threshold in the Malacandrians' view of death, which these unfallen creatures welcome. They die, not because of sin, but because Maleldil (God) is in the process of remaking all of his creatures and even the universe itself. Using "drink" as a metaphor for life experiences, Hyoi explains to Ransom that on one occasion he was alone with Maleldil by Balki pool in which the *hnéraki* lived that could alone bring an early death to hrossa. "That was the best of drinks save one." Ransom asks, "Which one?" and Hyoi replies, "Death itself in the day I drink it and go to Maleldil."[23] Here is an embodiment of the apostle Paul's passion for his eternal destiny: "To live is Christ, and to die is gain."[24]

This view is affirmed again by the sorn, Augray, carrying Ransom to Meldilorn: "A world is not made to last for ever, much less a race; that is not Maleldil's way."[25] As Ransom explains Weston's diabolical belief in perpetuating human life by exterminating living creatures beyond earth planet by planet and so on forever, the Oyarsa of Malacandra exclaims at his ignorance, "Does he think Maleldil [God] wants a race to live for ever?"[26] In Lewis's view, God never does the same thing twice. He always multiplies the goodness when he makes a new creation, moving not to an improved model of the old, but to a whole new order of being that incorporates and subsumes the old. As he explains in *Mere Christianity*: "People often ask when the next step in evolution—the step to something beyond man—will happen. But on the Christian view, it has happened already. In Christ a new kind of man appeared: and the new kind of life which began in Him is to be put into us."[27]

This idea is repeated toward the end, as the hrossa sing a dirge over the dead bodies of the three killed hrossa, whose bodies they have brought to Oyarsa to unmake: "Let it go hence, dissolve and be no body. . . . Let it go down; the *hnau* [rational, soul] rises from it. This is the second life, the other beginning. Open, oh coloured world, without weight, without shore. You are second and better; this was first and feeble."[28] The Oyarsa responds: "Let us scatter the movements which were their bodies. So will Maleldil scatter all worlds when the first and feeble is worn."[29]

The Oyarsa critiques the people of earth who are "wise enough to see the death of their kind approaching but not wise enough to endure it." By contrast, "the weakest of my people does not fear death. It is the Bent One [Satan], the lord of your world, who wastes your lives and befouls them with flying from what you know will overtake you in the end. If you were subjects of Maleldil you would have peace."[30]

4

PARADISE REGAINED:
Perelandra

And to Adam [God] said, . . . "cursed is the ground because of you."
GENESIS

No longer will there be anything accursed.[1]
REVELATION

If the special contribution of *Out of the Silent Planet* is remythologizing outer space and its spiritual inhabitants, the special contribution of *Perelandra* is remythologizing earth: in casting a new vision of an unfallen world teeming with life and goodness. Every good book in some way permanently changes the landscape of our minds. More than any other book, *Perelandra* best evokes in me the longing for heavenly pleasures. In this volume, the character Ransom must travel from earth to Perelandra (Venus) for reasons unknown to him until he meets the evil scientist Weston, who is bent on making the new world conform to his warped and sinful vision. Apropos of his name, Ransom's task is to save this planet from a fall like earth's.

As in the Narnia books and *Out of the Silent Planet*, the first step involves detaching us from the broken world we have come to think of as normal. The narrator, a Lewis-like character named "Lewis," must run the gauntlet of spiritual and psychic assaults to get to his friend Ransom's house in answer to a summons, like Ransom, for an unknown mission. In approaching this semi-deserted house, Lewis fights his natural caution against getting "drawn in." It was night and the wartime blackout was on. He feels an uncanny depression that comes from, he learns later, spiritual assault from the demonic world that attempts to block him. Upon entering the house, he stumbles onto a "coffin," symbolizing both our universal need to die to ourselves and Ransom's doing so as the Christ-figure assigned a special role in saving Perelandra. To cap it off, Lewis becomes aware of "a very faint rod or pillar of light" and had no doubt that he was "seeing an eldil."[2]

We will have learned from *Out of the Silent Planet* that an eldil is an angel. Lewis changes the names of all spiritual beings, including God, whom he calls "Maleldil," "mal" meaning "chief" in Hebrew. Maleldil is not an eldil himself, but their "chief" as creator and commander. Why the new names and all the relearning that goes with it? Lewis believed our conceptions of both God and angels are seriously flawed from centuries of unbiblical cultural influences, but the new names and the travel to a new place both cause us to approach the story without stereotypes.

One special case of unsettling our "normal" perspective belongs to the category Lewis calls the "numinous," discussed at the beginning of *The Problem of Pain* and keenly exemplified here. Numinous experience comes from anticipating or being in the presence of a being unlike ourselves in kind. We get the hang of it if we imagine a ghost awaiting us in the next room. Lewis sees it as another evidence for the existence of the spiritual world. His characters' encounter with it at the book's opening knocks us out of our materialistic lethargy and prepares us for the world of Perelandra, which teems with spiritual life.

To be sure, appearances of angels in the Bible were accompanied by human terror, which Lewis gets right in his space trilogy. In the first book, *Out of the Silent Planet*, the Oyarsa (ruling angel) of Malacandra addresses Ransom's fear head-on when they first meet at Meldilorn: "'What are you so afraid of, Ransom of Thulcandra [earth]?' it said. 'Of you, Oyarsa, because you are unlike me and I cannot see you.'"[3] The evocation is even more powerful at the opening of *Perelandra* as the narrator, Lewis, bumbles around in a dark house on a foggy night, tripping over a "coffin," his imagination fired by Ransom's wild stories and his anxiety that he might have to face a spirit being called an eldil alone. Even meeting Ransom again was a thing to be feared because "a man who has been in another world does not come back unchanged," and Ransom had been to Mars.[4]

Lewis knows, and reminds himself, that Ransom is "sane and wholesome and honest."[5] He therefore knows that the eldil he might meet in Ransom's house is also good, on Ransom's word. That very fact—that the eldil is unalloyed goodness—is itself another cause of fear. If it is evil,

Lewis reasons, there is still a chance of appeal to goodness. But if it is good and other (a different order of being, hence "dreadful"), then there is no hope of escape. Lewis puts it this way: "Here at last was a bit of that world from beyond the world, which I had always supposed that I loved and desired, breaking through and appearing to my senses: and I didn't like it, I wanted it to go away."[6] The special edge to this fear is the knowledge that he, Lewis, is not unalloyed goodness. He feels that inevitable sense of being exposed with no place to hide, which is just what Orual feels as she stands before the gods in judgment at the end of *Till We Have Faces.* As the Oyarsa of Malacandra rebukes Ransom for taking "many vain troubles to avoid standing" before him, Ransom must admit: "Bent creatures are full of fears."[7] In facing the spiritual world imaginatively in the space trilogy, we not only bring this fear into the open, but we come to experience a world filled with goodness and desire to be part of it. Fear is replaced by "perfect love" and awe.

Upon arriving in the new world, Ransom revels in a landscape of unspeakable beauty and hospitality to him as a human. He floats on the oceans, finding the water refreshing to drink; enjoys the help of the animals, who delight in aiding him; is dazzled by its colors, including a sky that suggests the aurora borealis; and discovers a new genus of pleasure in the taste of its fruits and the refreshing baths of the bubble trees that burst over him with a kind of super Gatorade invigoration. Perelandra's human-like couple, the Adam and Eve of this new world, are in harmony with nature, both flora and fauna, and are in easy, regular communion with God. In no other reading experience have I felt so keenly, so imaginatively, the price in our world exacted by sin. And more than any other book, it suggests to my imagination how marvelous the re-creation of our own world will be when God restores the harmony shattered by disobedience. No wonder *Perelandra* was Lewis's personal favorite among the books he had written. To the twin elements of heavenly pleasure—the absence of sin and its consequences, and the positive enjoyments of pleasures only foreshadowed on earth—we turn our attention.

As with all experience suggesting Heaven in Lewis's work, the presence of God claims central importance. This he communicates on Perelandra in three ways: a perfectly integrated environment; creatures in direct unimpeded, communion with God; and a palpable sense of freedom and fulfillment in God's presence. Ransom at last meets a human, like our race in appearance, but green. He dubs her the Green Lady and eventually learns that her name is Tinidril. As with Milton's conception of Eve being tempted by Satan when working separately from Adam, Tinidril's husband, Tor, the only other human on the planet, is away when the tempter comes. Unlike Milton's version, in which Eve follows Satan's suggestion of working apart from Adam so that she seems to commit the sin of pride before eating the forbidden fruit, Tor is elsewhere at Maleldil's behest. That the Green Lady, unfallen, hears Maleldil's voice directly communicated to her mind has a peculiar effect on Ransom. When she leaves and he is alone, he nevertheless senses "Someone's Presence," from which he was distracted by her company. But now he must attend to it and finds it at first "almost intolerable."

> There seemed no *room*. But later on, he discovered that it was intolerable only at certain moments—at just those moments in fact (symbolized by his impulse to smoke and to put his hands in his pockets) when a man asserts his independence and feels that now at last he's on his own. When you felt like that, then the very air seemed too crowded to breathe; a complete fullness seemed to be excluding you from a place which, nevertheless, you were unable to leave. But when you gave in to the thing, gave yourself up to it, there was no burden to be borne. It became not a load but a medium, a sort of splendour as of eatable, drinkable, breathable gold, which fed and carried you and not only poured into you but out from you as well. Taken the wrong way, it suffocated; taken the right way, it made terrestrial life seem, by comparison, a vacuum.[8]

Ransom is learning to abandon himself to God in exchange for a fullness, exhilaration, and freedom he would never otherwise know. It must be learned and practiced; our sinful habit of claiming ourselves, our time, and our possessions as our own must be unlearned. As Lewis states in "Christianity and Culture": "There is no neutral ground in the universe: every square inch, every split second, is claimed by God and counterclaimed by Satan."[9] Heaven is where God's claim reigns without contest. Our true natural state, the one we were created for, is the easy submission and delight in God that comes effortlessly to the Green Lady.

Of course, the challenge in self-surrender intensifies as Ransom comes slowly to the realization that Weston's temptations are wearing down Tinidril's resistance and that the only option available is the physical destruction of Weston in hand-to-hand combat—and Ransom is a sedentary philologist. Weston has also abandoned himself in a Faustian exchange of his soul for supernatural powers. His body and personality are possessed by the Devil (or a devil) such that he needs no sleep and has a diabolical facility in twisting truth and misrepresenting events from earth's history. He ignores goodness "to the point of annihilation."[10] The idea of fighting him to physical death naturally repulses Ransom, but it cannot be shaken.

Ransom here enacts Paul's command in Romans 12:1 (my italics): "I appeal to you therefore, brothers, by the mercies of God, to present your *bodies* as a living sacrifice, holy and acceptable to God, which is your spiritual worship." I often wondered why "bodies" and not something like mind, will, or soul. The Bible (and Lewis) embraces the physical as integral to God's good creation so that what we do in the body expresses what has been embraced in the mind, will, and soul. Our actions are the result of character and belief and the end result of a chain of decisions. The ultimate example is Jesus, whom Ransom imitates as the Christ-figure of Perelandra. Jesus redeemed us, bearing our sins on the cross in the flesh. In Heaven, we will forever be in bodies. Jesus took on a body in the Incarnation, never to lay it down. Ransom's physical fight is very much a spiritual act of worship.

Ransom's abandonment to God is reminiscent of Lewis's conversion to Christianity. The long struggle ended, the event itself was devoid of emotion. "I was driven to Whipsnade one sunny morning," Lewis recounts at the conclusion of his spiritual autobiography. "When we set out I did not believe that Jesus Christ is the Son of God, and when we reached the zoo I did." He recalls that it felt like awaking from a long sleep. "Freedom, or necessity?" Along with will and emotion, they seem not to matter. He surrendered.[11] Similarly, when Ransom must decide to fight the Un-man (Weston's demon-possessed body) to determine the destiny of a world, after the long struggle,

> without any apparent movement of the will, as objective and unemotional as the reading on a dial, there had arisen before him, with perfect certitude, the knowledge "about this time tomorrow you will have done the impossible. . . ." You might say, if you liked, that the power of choice had been simply set aside and an inflexible destiny substituted for it. On the other hand, you might say that he had [been] delivered from the rhetoric of his passions and had emerged into unassailable freedom. Ransom could not, for the life of him, see any difference between these two statements. Predestination and freedom were apparently identical.[12]

The fusion of what was formerly distinction and contradiction is a large part of the peace found in the presence of Christ. To put it another way, Heaven will resolve all our paradoxes. But, as Lewis says elsewhere, it is not so much that in Heaven we get answers to our questions as that the questions will seem unimportant when we are in the presence of Truth himself.[13]

The absence of questions that plague our minds; the restored harmony of spirit, mind, and body; the harmony of all creation, creatures with each other and all with their environment; and harmony with God—all these Lewis pictures in *Perelandra*. The book portrays Eden restored and the curse lifted. In Genesis the curse was levied; in Revelation it is removed. In Heaven we get back, through Christ, what was lost by sin—and then some. God is not only restoring, but ever creating, adding to.

> Never did He make two things the same; never did He utter one word twice. After earths, not better earths but beasts; after beasts, not better beasts, but spirits. After a falling, not a recovery but a new creation. Out of the new creation, not a third but the mode of change itself is changed for ever. Blessed is He![14]

The final segment shows Tor and Tinidril embarking on a new stage in their growth. As such, they image the heavenly reality that we will not be static, but always growing as we move more and more into the infinitude that is God. In their next stage, the Perelandrian pair reign over the planet, the very kind of thing we are promised in Heaven. The angelic Oyarsa now turns over responsibility to the humans she has served and will continue to serve in teaching them until fully independent.[15] The Oyarsa had built the land and mountains and spun the very air of the atmosphere, guiding the whole through the galaxy. But "to-day," says Perelandra, "all this is taken from me. Blessed be he." With no sense of loss, but with joy and a sense of fulfillment in created purpose, Perelandra announces to Ransom that this day "the world is born" and that Tor and Tinidril will "step up that step at which your parents [Adam and Eve] fell, and sit in the throne of what they were meant to be."[16]

In Perelandra's giving of this gift, in Ransom's gift of thwarted evil to a world he must now leave, each reflect the heavenly truth that "all is gift."[17] Such "gift-love," embodied in the Trinity itself, characterizes all who dwell in the heavenly presence. This reality the spirits celebrate in a rhapsodic benediction, announcing that everything and everyone is at the center because wherever God is, there is the center, and he is everywhere. And though he needs nothing, everything has "immeasurable use" to him to show forth his "love and splendour." This harmony of belonging to God Lewis calls, after classical models, The Great Dance. In the concluding pages of *Perelandra,* the dance has begun, and we are invited to join.

THE FULFILLMENT OF HUMAN POTENTIAL:
The Great Divorce

Heaven enters wherever Christ enters, even in this life.[1]
C. S. LEWIS

In discussing this book, we'll have to spend a little time in Lewis's imaginary Hell, but we'll leave that mildewed place for the fresh outdoor world of Heaven before long to look at some of the positive truths that make it so desirable. First, a disclaimer: Lewis's own. He says in the Preface that he is not attempting to describe either Hell or Heaven as he thinks it literally appears as landscape. His real concerns are to show that Heaven is more real than any present physical reality and is the fulfillment of God's desires for us, and that Hell is by comparison "so nearly nothing." He is also concerned to show that we choose our own eternal destiny by turning ourselves—with the Devil's help or Christ's—into a soul fit for Hell or a soul fit for Heaven.

DESIRE

Throughout his works, Lewis's most persistent theme is our desire for Heaven. Lacking a word to adequately describe this inmost hunger, he borrows one from Wordsworth and Coleridge: The word is *Joy*. It is a problematical term in that its usual meaning is happiness, satisfaction, and fulfillment, whereas Lewis's special use is nearly the opposite: It is the absence of satisfaction and fulfillment. He defines *Joy* as a "stab of desire" for something never satisfied on earth. When all of our natural desires have been fulfilled, "we remain conscious of a desire which no natural happiness will satisfy."[2] For this reason, it is a major pointer to Heaven and was key in Lewis's own conversion.[3]

Lewis believes that every desire is at its root a desire for Heaven. Solomon knew it, observing that God has put eternity in our hearts.[4] Augustine put it this way: "our heart is restless, until it repose in thee." We are all pilgrims in search of the Celestial City: some lost and looking for joy in all the wrong places, some saved with eyes fixed on the heavenly prize, some sidetracked on dead-end streets and byways—but all longing for Heaven, whether we know it or not. Nearly all of Lewis's works have the aim of arousing this desire for Heaven or showing us how to live in proper anticipation of our true home.

Heaven is more sharply defined and more keenly desired when contrasted with Hell. So Lewis's story, like Dante's, opens in Hell. And as Dante has his mentor, Virgil, for a guide, so Lewis's narrator has his mentor, George MacDonald, as guide. Lewis had his desires for Heaven aroused at the age of sixteen when he read George MacDonald's *Phantastes*; so halfway through *The Great Divorce*, on the outskirts of Heaven, the narrator (whose biographical details fit Lewis exactly) meets George MacDonald, who becomes his teacher.

In the narrator's story, all who are in Hell can take a bus to Heaven if they wish, though few even wish it. Does Lewis believe that souls in Hell actually have a "second chance"? Absolutely not. He says in the Preface that he chose *The Great Divorce* as the title to deliberately contradict William Blake's notion expressed in his title *The Marriage of Heaven and Hell*, a satiric minefield, claiming that "the road of excess leads to the palace of wisdom" and that opposites must marry before progress is possible.[5] But, Lewis insists, reality presents us with an "'either-or.' If we insist on keeping Hell (or even earth) we shall not see Heaven: if we accept Heaven we shall not be able to retain even the smallest and most intimate souvenirs of Hell."[6] Lewis deliberately casts the whole story as a dream vision (as we learn at the end) to emphasize the fictional nature of the story—and anything can happen in dreams.

Why, then, does Lewis allow the "hellians" to journey to Heaven and stay if they want?[7] Simply to stress 1) that we choose our eternal destinies, and 2) that by our life choices we turn ourselves into beings suited for one or the other. By presenting his characters at the entrance to Heaven, Lewis can show at once both the process that damns and the result. We hear the hellians' reasons for rejecting Heaven, and as they leave for the "grey town"

(Hell), we instantly see the consequence. Tellingly, those from Hell usually fail to even see the beauties of Heaven, and most hasten back to Hell. The very first Ghost from the grey town to be mentioned (besides the narrator) doesn't last even a minute in Heaven. "'I don't like it! I don't like it,' screamed a voice, 'It gives me the pip!'"[8] With that she ran to the bus and never returned.

When the narrator asks his teacher if everyone has a chance to get on the bus, MacDonald replies with these soaring words:

> Everyone who wishes it does. Never fear. There are only two kinds of people in the end: those who say to God, "Thy will be done," and those to whom God says, in the end, "*Thy* will be done." All that are in Hell, choose it. Without that self-choice there could be no Hell. No soul that seriously and constantly desires joy will ever miss it. Those who seek find. To those who knock it is opened.[9]

The theme of choice and our responsibility to choose not only permeates *The Great Divorce* but is found throughout Lewis's works. Here's another example from *The Problem of Pain*:

> In the long run the answer to all those who object to the doctrine of hell is itself a question: "What are you asking God to do?" To wipe out their past sins and, at all costs, to give them a fresh start, smoothing every difficulty and offering every miraculous help? But He has done so, on Calvary. To forgive them? They will not be forgiven. To leave them alone? Alas, I am afraid that is what He does.[10]

ASCENT INTO HEAVEN

Lewis has another good reason for allowing the trip from Hell to Heaven: to provide multiple contrasts as a way of highlighting both hellish and heavenly qualities, contrasts between physical things like landscapes and bodies, and contrasts in the character of the people. Upon arriving at Heaven, the first thing the narrator notices is its expansiveness. Though Hell seemed vast from within, by contrast to Heaven, it is claustrophobic. Heaven "made the Solar System itself an indoor affair."[11] We later learn that the hellians, though it seemed to them a long journey up the side of a cliff, emerged in Heaven from a miniscule crack in the soil between two blades of grass. If a butterfly of Heaven were to swallow all of Hell, the teacher MacDonald tells the narrator, it would make no more difference than swallowing a single atom.[12] How real is Heaven, how much more substantial? Hell could not contain the minutest part of it.

After the landscape, the next thing the narrator notices is the bodies of the hellians. They appear as ghosts, as dirty stains on the air. Because people in Hell are really what remains of their human selves with their potential shriveled by sin, when they are expanded to the size of a normal person in Heaven, they are so thin and unsubstantial that they look like ghosts. This is a very effective technique for showing that Heaven is ultimate reality and Hell so nearly nothing.

But the most telling contrast comes in the character of the people. The diabolical and warped are met by the holy and whole. Those from Heaven are fulfilled, content, overflowing with love and the reflected glory of Christ that makes them luminous. The Ghosts have all come to Heaven for some bogus and selfish reason. The Solid People, as those from Heaven are called, have all made great sacrifices to come long distances from Deep Heaven to the outskirts in hopes of winning some of the Ghosts to Heaven.

The longest journey, however, is made by Christ himself. We know from some key, though subtle, clues that the bus driver who brings the Ghosts to Heaven is representative of Christ. First, the narrator's teacher, MacDonald, says that only the greatest can become small enough to fit into Hell. Second, the driver is described as being "full of light." Third, he is rejected by those he came to save: "God! I'd like to give him one in the ear-'ole," snarls one of the Ghosts. The narrator responds: "I could see nothing in the countenance of the Driver to justify all this, unless it were that he had a look of authority and seemed intent on carrying out his job."[13] This episode is a literal enactment of the Apostles' Creed: "He descended into Hell."

What follows upon their arrival in Heaven is a series of loosely organized encounters between the Ghosts and an appropriate heavenly counterpart. Like its cousin, *The Screwtape Letters,* the design is episodic: There isn't much plot. Although we come to identify with the narrator and his final fate, the interest is not mainly in the resolution of a central conflict or the development of a single character. Rather, our interest is in what sort of persons will take the stage next, what has kept them from Heaven, and what their response will be to the invitation to enter all joy. In the process, we get a short course on human nature and the psychology of sin.

Also like *The Screwtape Letters,* in *The Great Divorce* Lewis blends elements of earth with his vision of Hell. In the latter book, he blends elements of earth with Heaven, too. This not only makes Hell and Heaven more understandable because of the familiar earthly elements, but it makes us grasp the truth that "there is no neutral ground in the universe."[14] It points up the further truth that we bring into our earthly experience intimations of either Heaven or Hell by our choices. We are becoming every moment souls suited for one or the other.

You will have met people who are so full of the Spirit of Christ that any destiny other than Heaven is unthinkable. These people also have many of the joys that will characterize Heaven, even in the midst of earthly pain. You will also have met people who hate goodness: who prefer evil companions and evil acts, though these make them wretched and miserable. When they do encounter good persons, they condemn them, perverting their sense of reason by rationalizing evil, even finding ways to blame the good or God or religion for their problems and those of the world. They already hate goodness because it implicitly condemns the evil they have chosen. They wouldn't like Heaven if they could have it. They are, in a sense, already in Hell, preferring darkness to light. This we see in each Ghost that returns to Hell.

On the book's design, Evan Gibson notes that the Ghosts and the people from Heaven who meet them are presented in three divisions: five in the first half, five in the last half, and a group in the middle getting short treatment, all having in common a foolish desire to criticize Heaven. Some come all the way from Hell just to spit at Heaven in spite.[15] The first five Ghosts are all inwardly focused. Their besetting sins are "their inflated inner-image, their intellectual dishonesty, their materialism, their cynicism, their false shame."[16] The five in the second half are also selfish, but their sin involves the desire to control others. Except for the first one, an artist, all in this last group exhibit some kind of perverted family relationship.

As with *The Screwtape Letters*, we learn by negative example how not to behave and by inference how we should behave. The book is a series of lessons in Kingdom values, like the parables of Jesus. From the Theological Ghost, we learn that we can slip from a desire to know God and a love of God to a desire to know about God and a love of mere academic, theological pursuit. The Theological Ghost would rather return to Hell where he can dispute about Christ than enter Heaven and know him. Similarly, the Painter Ghost has slipped successively from loving light and truth to loving the medium, to loving his own opinions of truth, to loving his reputation. He learns from a heavenly counterpart that no one is much interested in his work, now that he has been dead for a while. He instantly abandons Heaven in a vain attempt to restore his now discredited reputation and resurrect his school of painting. Journals, lectures, manifestos, publicity—these fill his mind as he abandons Truth and ultimately his true self for pretensions.

We also meet a mother who is possessive of her son and a wife whose earthly life was devoted to remaking her husband in her own image. Both would rather see their family members in Hell for the chance of controlling them than find true love in Heaven, love that cares about the real good of another. In the process of grasping, like all the hellians, they pervert their own personalities and become the sin they choose. Though on the brink of Heaven, all the Ghosts from Hell could say with Milton's Satan:

The mind is its own place, and in itself
Can make a Heaven of Hell, a Hell of Heaven.[17]

Which way I fly is Hell; myself am Hell.[18]

The Great Divorce shows us a parallel truth, one preeminently displayed in Dante's vision: that neither the punishment of Hell nor the reward of Heaven is arbitrary. Lewis's heavenly guide MacDonald explains this in the case of the Grumbling Ghost:

"The whole difficulty of understanding Hell is that the thing to be understood is so nearly Nothing. But ye'll have had experiences . . . it begins with a grumbling mood, and yourself still distinct from it: perhaps criticising it. And yourself, in a dark hour, may will that mood, embrace it. Ye can repent and come out of it again. But there may come a day when you can do that no longer. Then there will be no *you* left to criticise the mood, nor even to enjoy it, but just the grumble itself going on forever like a machine."[19]

One of the central truths the book teaches is that Heaven is the fulfillment of human potential, Hell the drying up of human potential. "To enter heaven is to become more human than you ever succeeded in being on earth; to enter Hell is to be banished from humanity. What is cast (or casts itself) into Hell is not a man: it is 'remains.'"[20] Hell strips away distinctions, and unrelieved sin is shown to be boring. On the other hand, in Heaven we blossom into fully differentiated personalities.

Having seen the long parade of Ghosts who come to the outskirts of Heaven only to return to Hell for the same reason they went there in the first place, the narrator naturally inquires of his guide whether any actually accept the invitation to enter Heaven. There are allusions by MacDonald to many who make it in, but we only see one actually making the passage. This is the case of a man whose besetting sin is lust, symbolized by a red lizard who sits on his shoulder, reminding him that his very identity is wrapped up in his lust and that life would be insipid without the flame of desire. An angel meets the Lustful Ghost and implores him for permission to kill the lizard. Through many struggles and though fearful that it may mean his death, he gives permission. Wondrously, the lizard is transformed into a white stallion, which the now Solid Man rides joyously into Heaven.

The point is not that people once in Hell can go to Heaven or that sin can progress to goodness: Lewis explicitly denies both, as we have seen. The point is 1) that we must die to self to live, and 2) that all desires, however masked, are ultimately for Heaven. When we give our desires to God, the Author of all the pleasures, he fulfills the desires. The very thing that when grasped would drag us to Hell and pervert our personalities, when given to God is not only fulfilled but becomes a means of grace. God created all things good. Sin is not self-existent; it is a perversion of good.

A word on the Solid People: None in the book who come from Heaven are "great" in an earthly sense. The only one besides Lewis with a popular earthly reputation is his guide, MacDonald. The others are all ordinary people with sins running the gamut from pride in one's own talent to apostasy to murder. The main difference is that the Solid People all recognized their need of God and repented; they turned from their sin and received the gift of a new heart (new motives) and eternal life. None suffers the illusion that he or she deserves Heaven. It is a completely undeserved gift. The Solid People urge each of the Ghosts to receive the gift and "enter into joy." Pride keeps the Ghosts out. All try to justify their sins. One of the impressions we are left with is how easy Heaven is to gain, and how easy it is to lose.

The last paired Ghost and Solid Person are treated at the greatest length and deserve special attention. Here, using the technique of analogy (using the earthly to describe the heavenly), we have Lewis's fullest description of a Solid Person. Throughout the book, Lewis has used the technique of distancing. Scripture says, "no eye has seen, nor ear heard, nor the heart of man imagined, what God has prepared for those who love him."[21] Since Heaven is beyond our experience or even our imagining, Lewis avoids error and enhances our anticipation of it by never giving us a glimpse of "Deep Heaven" or even "Deep Hell." Throughout the narrative, we are always in the in-between time before night falls in Hell or the day dawns in Heaven. Geographically, we are also never allowed into Hell or Heaven proper; we are always on the outskirts. Yet what we see of the fringes is both unspeakably horrific and unspeakably enchanting by comparison to earth. Even here on the outskirts, we see enough to make our blood run fast.

In the last pairing, a Self-pitying Ghost named Frank appears as a Dwarf leading by a chain a projection of himself called a Tragedian. He is met by Sarah Smith of Golders Green, who was his wife on earth. Frank's interest in making the pilgrimage from Hell is not in gaining Heaven; it is in gaining pity for his condition, thereby holding the joy of Heaven hostage. In this scene, Lewis answers the age-old question of how there could be joy in Heaven when even one soul suffers the torments of everlasting Hell. Pity cannot hold love hostage. MacDonald, the narrator's guide, explains to him that Heaven will not make a dunghill of "the world's garden for the sake of some who cannot abide the smell of roses."[22] In the end, the Dwarf Frank chooses his self-pity over Heaven and shrinks until nothing is left but the projection of his sin, the Tragedian, which vanishes back to the constriction that is Hell.[23]

Sarah is not brokenhearted; it is not possible in the presence of him who is true love and joy. She is joined by angels who sing a psalm of her overcoming joy and protection by God. She appears by earthly standards to be a goddess. Indeed, she is a "Great One" in Heaven, though on earth she was the lady next door. She is reaping the rewards of nameless acts of love that characterized every contact with every person and all creation. This love extended even to the animals. Now, in Heaven, these very animals make up a part of her sizable entourage, which also included gigantic emerald angels scattering flowers, followed by numerous boys and girls and musicians. Of the indescribably beautiful music, the narrator can only say that no one who "read that score would ever grow sick or old."[24] "Dancing light" shone from the entourage. All was in honor of Sarah Smith, who was so ordinary on earth. And to this the Self-pitying Ghost and all from Hell were invited. We wonder at the depth of pride and per-version that would embolden so many, both in the book and in our own experience, to thumb their noses at the sublime largesse of God.

The Great Divorce ends with dizzying reflections on time and eternity, predestination and free will. Lewis deftly shows that all attempts to solve this ancient paradox fail if they are posed from within time. God, being outside of time, sees all in an ever-present now; so from his point of view, all is known and done, even what is yet in the future for us. But from our point of view within time, choices are still before us. Even now, in what may be my twentieth reading of *The Great Divorce*, the concluding pages move me to tears for people without the hope of Heaven and my own des-tiny were it not for "Bleeding Charity." Throughout the book, it has been perpetual evening twilight in the grey town of Hell and perpetual pre-sun-rise dawn in the hinterlands of Heaven where the meetings take place.

Now, at the end, as the pilgrim narrator looks into the face of his teacher, George MacDonald, and with the east at his back, the promised sunrise breaks. It will mean eternal day for Heaven and a darkening to eternal night for Hell. The sunlight falls in solid blocks upon the narra-tor's insubstantial body, and he is stricken with terror, for he has come to these precincts of Heaven as a ghost from Hell: "'The morning! The morn-ing!' I cried, 'I am caught by the morning and I am a ghost.'"[25] In the moment when he is seized by the terror of damnation, the narrator awak-ens from his dream, clutching at a tablecloth and pulling down on his head, not blocks of light, but books. With sweet relief, we realize that he and we are still pilgrims, and Heaven is still before us. There is yet time to choose and to guide the choice of others.

6

LAND OF WONDER
AND DELIGHT:
THE CHRONICLES
OF NARNIA

Delight yourself in the LORD, and he will give you the desires of your heart.[1]

PSALMS

Narnia is mostly about this world. Even the parts that feature Aslan (who parallels Christ) evoke the actions of Jesus in our world, from the grand pre-incarnate acts of creating the world in *The Magician's Nephew* to its dissolution in *The Last Battle*. Most of Aslan's actions recall Christ's earthly ministry: bringing salvation by his sacrifice on the Stone Table, canceling the penalty of death required of each sinner by the Law when he dies in Edmund's (our) place; reenacting Jesus' first miracle of turning the water to wine at Cana in *Prince Caspian* through the agency of Bacchus; and echoing the long oppression of Israel awaiting its Messiah, with many doubting the promise, but a remnant believing and praying.[2] There are also earthly issues like usurping kings, rightful heirs, wars, valor, and growing up.

But always in Narnia, it is life lived in the shadow of eternity, with Heaven and the "Heaven sent one" in view. Questions of belief and unbelief point to this bigger reality. In *Prince Caspian,* for example, the question of belief takes two main forms. In the first, before Aslan returns, hundreds of years since his last appearing, Trufflehunter the badger remembers the stories of Old Narnia and believes them: "We don't change.

We hold on," he says of the badgers.[3] But the Dwarfs, typically out for their own interests, have little use for the past or future. When Trumpkin, one of the better Dwarfs, asks derisively, "Who believes in Aslan nowadays?" Caspian answers without hesitation, "I do."[4]

When Caspian repeats the question later to the Black Dwarf Nikabrik, "Do *you* believe in Aslan," he asks the question central to human destiny.[5] Nikabrik's strictly pragmatic answer, "I'll believe in anyone or anything . . . that'll batter these cursed Telmarines . . . Aslan *or* the White Witch," betrays an attitude toward ultimate issues that leads to perdition. The question of belief arises in every book. In the first written, *The Lion, the Witch and the Wardrobe*, it comes early to the Pevensie children as Lucy, the youngest, is the first of them to encounter Aslan. They are slow to acknowledge her fantastic discovery of another world and take a long time getting to Aslan, slowed by Edmund's skepticism that turns to cynicism and unbelief, even when he knows in his heart that Aslan has a rightful claim on it. Like all of us, in one way or another, Edmund must come to the end of himself before turning to Aslan for salvation.

Once more in *Prince Caspian*, Lucy is the first to meet Aslan. The children are racing against time to get to Aslan's How and Prince Caspian before the army of his usurping uncle, Miraz, but they are uncertain of the way. Lucy sees Aslan's face and senses his summons in the direction opposite their present resolve. All reject her vision and follow Peter's mistaken instincts. After much delay, futile work, and weariness, they give in to Lucy's renewed sightings of Aslan, who takes them in the opposite direction, which turns out to be the shortest. This is a common theme in The Chronicles of Narnia, from *The Lion, the Witch and the Wardrobe* on: The quickest way, and the only way in the end, to solve a problem is to find Aslan and rely on his plan. Do-it-yourself schemes always go bust, in Narnia as in real life.

Since Jesus is central to all of human history and is the central figure in the Bible and Christian fiction taken as a whole, we should expect the Narnia stories to unfold around Aslan, the Christ-figure in Narnia. Lewis explains to a young correspondent that Aslan is not Jesus, but the result of asking himself if Jesus were a lion and occupied a world of talking beasts and living rational trees, what might he do in given situations.[6] Of course, the parallels are strikingly close to the biblical account. So much is unknown about what Heaven will be like, but what is certain is here: our relation to Aslan, who mirrors Christ in many ways.

• He is the Lord: "King of the wood" and "son of the great Emperor-Beyond-the-Sea."[7]

• He is (in *The Magician's Nephew*) the creator of Narnia and of all worlds; the sustainer and protector of this world.

• He is judge (of the Telmarines in *Prince Caspian* and of all in *The Last Battle*, destroying the Old Narnia) and maker of a New Narnia (Heaven).

• When Aslan is present, all goes right and is put to rights.

• The prospect of separation from him is lamented by those who love him.

• When he is absent, he is longed for.

• He is the savior as with Edmund in *The Lion, the Witch and the Wardrobe* and Eustace in the powerful undragoning episode of *The Voyage of the "Dawn Treader."*

• He brings joy and feasting (as in Revelation). Feasting is a common motif in Narnia when Aslan has finished some great work. It draws on both the chivalric elements that thread through the stories and parallels in Jesus' ministry, who was always feeding the poor. On more than one occasion, Jesus fed multitudes miraculously, and he promises the grandest feast of all when he gathers us in Heaven for the wedding feast of the Lamb. Feasting is associated both with life, as a necessity, and with joyful celebration in peace and plenty.

• He is the resurrection, rising first himself, then raising others as when he awakens tree spirits in *Prince Caspian* and stone characters in *The Lion, the Witch and the Wardrobe.*

A Note on the Order

Readers debate the proper sequence for reading the seven Chronicles of Narnia. Lewis published them much as he wrote them, in this order: 1) *The Lion, the Witch and the Wardrobe*, 2) *Prince Caspian*, 3) *The Voyage of the "Dawn Treader,"* 4) *The Silver Chair*, 5) *The Horse and His Boy*, 6) *The Magician's Nephew*, and 7) *The Last Battle*. Macmillan paperbacks, for years the most available, used this ordering.

In a letter to a young correspondent, Lewis suggested that the best reading order would be chronological by Narnian history, starting with the creation of Narnia. This order goes: 1) *The Magician's Nephew*, 2) *The Lion, the Witch and the Wardrobe*, 3) *The Horse and His Boy*, 4) *Prince Caspian*, 5) *The Voyage of the "Dawn Treader,"* 6) *The Silver Chair*, and 7) *The Last Battle*. HarperCollins now has the copyright and has been publishing the

Chronicles in Narnian historical order for the past several years. Scholars have entered the fray over the best order. I have noticed that people tend to prefer whatever order they first read them in, and I see little loss one way or the other, as our minds can slot the events as easily as we do flashbacks. The thing I like about the original order is getting the excellent theological background of the basic gospel first in *The Lion, the Witch and the Wardrobe*. (Can you tell which order I read them in?) But I have decided to follow the current norm (Narnian history) in discussing the books here, as being most convenient for most readers.

THE MAGICIAN'S NEPHEW: REGAINING PARADISE AND SEEING THE FACE OF GOD

As with the pristine worlds of Malacandra and Perelandra, we are stabbed by the beauty of sinless perfection in the newly created Narnia of *The Magician's Nephew*, realizing what has been lost through sin, waiting in the certain hope that it will be created anew as our permanent inheritance. Through the work of magical green and yellow rings, Polly and Digory, Jadis, Uncle Andrew, a London cabby, and his horse Strawberry all find themselves in Narnia as it is being sung into existence by Aslan. Aslan's voice works on the good-hearted as seeing his face does in other books. The voice sounds wonderfully familiar and full of promise, bringing a sense of well-being. It even sounds so to Strawberry, who whinnies in response as if "it found itself back in the old field where it had played as a foal, and saw someone whom it remembered and loved coming across the field to bring it a lump of sugar."[8] Tellingly, Jadis hated Aslan's creative music and "would have smashed that whole world, or all worlds, to pieces, if it would only stop the singing."[9]

Aslan sings Narnia into existence, just as God through Christ spoke the universe into being. The Narnian world shimmers with elements of the medieval worldview, even shaping the order and choices about tone and content, as Michael Ward has recently discovered.[10] Having Aslan sing the worlds into being echoes the belief in the music of the spheres, the medieval idea that the heavenly bodies made music as they turned through their orbits. Lewis has just taken Digory and Polly through the ruined and dying world of Charn, destroyed, in a grotesque parody of Aslan's creative word, by Jadis's "deplorable word." On the principle "if I can't have it, no one can," she kills every living thing on the planet, converting even herself to stone until Digory revives her and provokes the final fall of Charn by pursuing a kind of forbidden knowledge. This contrast heightens our delight and wonder at the new world Aslan calls into being "before our eyes." Lewis gives us Eden before the Fall, a piece of our own history and an important part of our longing for an unspoiled world that Heaven will satisfy.

In moving between the worlds of Charn, Narnia, and earth, Digory and Polly pass through an interim place called "Wood between the Worlds." The very words are enough to set our hearts to longing. In these woods are several pools with "a world at the bottom of every pool." Digory and Polly have a foretaste of Heaven here, probably by virtue of being out of their own world and its curse from sin. In this wood, "if anyone had asked him, 'Where do you come from?' he [Digory] would have said, 'I've always been here.' That was what it felt like—as if one had always been in that place and never been bored although nothing had ever happened." In other words, the wood embodies everything we idealize in the notion of "home": a place where we belong, though it is not our final home.[11]

In the new world of Narnia, one of the objects that evokes Heaven (and Eden) is the tree for the healing of the nations that grows in Narnia. This Narnian tree alludes to its original, the tree in the apostle John's vision of the new Heaven and earth in Revelation 22:2: "also, on either side of the river, the tree of life with its twelve kinds of fruit, yielding its fruit each month. The leaves of the tree were for the healing of the nations." At Aslan's bidding, Digory goes on a quest with Polly to bring back a piece of fruit from the Narnian tree. While in the secret garden where the fruit is growing, Jadis tempts Digory to eat the fruit, rather than take it to Aslan. When Digory won't eat it, she tempts him even more sorely with the idea of taking the fruit to heal his terminally ill mother. But Digory obeys Aslan and is rewarded lavishly. Aslan tells him, "no hand but yours shall sow the seed of the Tree that is to be the protection of Narnia."[12]

The very smell of the tree brings "joy and life and health" to the Narnians, but "death and horror and despair" to the White Witch.[13] This episode shows how a single thing can elicit opposite responses, depending on the respondent's heart (like seeing Aslan's face and as illustrated in 2 Corinthians 2:15-16): "For we are the aroma of Christ to God among those who are being saved and among those who are perishing, to one a fragrance from death to death, to the other a fragrance from life to life."

Aslan gives Digory fruit from the tree to heal his mother when he returns to earth. The boy buries the core in the backyard, which grows into a tree that is felled by a storm years later. Its wood is used to build the magic wardrobe through which the Pevensies enter Narnia in the next book. The episode of the tree illustrates the principle of the ripple effect of single acts of obedience or disobedience. Digory's earlier sin in Charn, which brought Jadis into Narnia, had huge ripples in the other direction. Here is a key theme in Lewis's writing on Heaven and Hell: Choice is destiny. Obedience brings life and Heaven; disobedience brings death and Hell. As with others in the Chronicles, Digory gets Aslan's "well done" when he obeys in the face of great temptation. This will be one of the great rewards of Heaven, to see God taking pleasure in us.

The Beatific Vision: Aslan's Face, the Face of God[14]

Narnia seems most like Heaven in the presence of Aslan. He is its creator and sustainer. When he is absent, he is longed for; when he is present, problems are resolved and all is put "to rights."[15] "He's the King. He's the Lord of the whole wood," Mr. Beaver informs the Pevensie children.[16] He's the subject of Narnian prophecy, and when he shows up, the end is near, as Mr. Beaver surmises. He is good but "not safe": those who seek goodness long for him. On hearing Mr. Beaver describe Aslan, Peter says, "I'm longing to see him . . . even if I do feel frightened when it comes to the point."[17]

The hope of Heaven is embodied in Aslan. As St. Augustine said, the Lord is "The One Whom we love in everything."[18] The children in Narnia often have transforming experiences with the great Lion that fill them with joy, wonder, vitality, excitement, and a deep-seated sense of well-being and security. It is like taking in all that is implied of goodness in Maslow's hierarchy of need in one gulp of magical air. Just before Digory and Polly come tumbling back into the "noise, heat, and hot smells of London," they have a final encounter with Aslan that gives them a life-sustaining hope of Heaven. It comes as the Beatific Vision always comes in Narnia: by contemplating the face of Aslan. The promise of Scripture for the believer is to see the face of Jesus. Lewis explains the concept well in *Perelandra*:

> As there is one Face above all worlds merely to see which is irrevocable joy, so at the bottom of all worlds that face is waiting whose sight alone is the misery from which none who beholds it can recover. And though there seemed to be, and indeed were, a thousand roads by which a man could walk through the world, there was not a single one which did not lead sooner or later either to the Beatific or the Miserific Vision.[19]

There is no more potent theme in the Chronicles than this. It emerges in every book and always fires our hearts with longing. Readers who know nothing of Jesus and the promise of Heaven feel it. The mother of a nine-year-old American reader named Laurence wrote to Lewis on her son's behalf because the boy, who did know Jesus, feared his liking Aslan even more might be displeasing to Jesus. Lewis reassured her that "Laurence can't *really* love Aslan more than Jesus, even if he feels that's what he is doing. For the things he loves Aslan for doing or saying are simply the things Jesus really did and said. So that when Laurence thinks he is loving Aslan, he is really loving Jesus: and perhaps loving Him more than he ever did before."[20]

A splendid example of the Beatific Vision comes toward the end of the first book, *The Magician's Nephew*.

> Both children were looking up into the Lion's face as he spoke these words. And all at once (they never knew exactly how it happened) the face seemed to be a sea of tossing gold in which they were floating, and such a sweetness and power rolled about them and over them and entered them that they felt they had never really been happy or wise or good, or even alive and awake, before. And the memory of that moment stayed with them always, so that as long as they both lived, if ever they were sad or afraid or angry, the thought of all that golden goodness, and the feeling that it was still there, quite close, just round some corner or just behind some door, would come back and make them sure, deep down inside, that all was well.[21]

And later, back in his mother's sickroom on earth, before she has come around, Digory starts to lose hope amidst the mundane things of ordinary life. He "hardly dared to hope; but when he remembered the face of Aslan he did hope."[22] We will be revisiting this theme often in the Chronicles, right to the very end of Narnian history in *The Last Battle*.

THE LION, THE WITCH AND THE WARDROBE: PURCHASING HEAVEN—ASLAN AND "THE WAY"

In The Chronicles of Narnia, as with Jesus in the Bible, Aslan creates Narnia, saves all inhabitants who believe in him and go to his side, conquers death, destroys Old Narnia, and creates the New. As with Jesus, no one but his Father is over him; no one else is more powerful. His character defines what is good, and he is the desire of every heart—even those hearts that have so perverted that desire in sin that they can no longer choose him. Jesus said, "I am the way, and the truth, and the life. No one comes to the Father except through me."[23] In The Chronicles of Narnia, no one comes to Narnia from our world or goes on to the new eternal Narnia unless Aslan calls the person. And while in Narnia, Aslan is the way out of every fix and his presence the deepest longing of everyone who meets him and accepts him as the rightful Lord of the wood.

As Mr. and Mrs. Beaver tell the children about Aslan, by their response to the very mention of his name, the children reveal the condition of their hearts well before they meet him.

> And now a very curious thing happened. None of the children knew who Aslan was any more than you do; but the moment the Beaver had spoken these words everyone felt quite different. Perhaps it has sometimes happened to you in a dream that someone says something which you don't understand but in the dream it feels as if it had some enormous meaning—either a terrifying one which turns the whole dream into a nightmare or else a lovely meaning too lovely to put into words, which makes the dream so beautiful that you remember it all your life and are always wishing you could get into that dream again. It was like that now. At the name of Aslan each one of the children felt something jump in his inside.[24]

Edmund responds with "mysterious horror" because he has already fallen for the White Witch's temptation to pride in reigning over his siblings and has an insatiable appetite for Turkish Delight. Peter feels "brave," Susan smells something "delicious" and hears "delightful" music, while Lucy feels a sense of new beginnings—as at the start of summer or a holiday. This is one of Lewis's ways of illustrating the truth that "Heaven is an acquired taste" and that we are every day turning ourselves into someone who will love Heaven or hate it.[25] And, of course, it is impossible to love Heaven without loving Heaven's creator, in part because the key definition of Heaven is being in Christ's presence, unimpeded by the effects of sin. We are reminded that at Jesus' return "every knee should bow, in heaven and on earth and under the earth, and every tongue confess that Jesus Christ is Lord."[26] Some knees will gladly bow, having learned joyous submission to the Lord who fulfills us in himself; some will bow grudgingly, having chosen self as preeminent, but all will serve his glory, nonetheless.

We may not yet *feel* excitement at Jesus' name, even if we know that being in his presence is the "fullness of joy."[27] With Aslan, here in the book published first, Lewis gives us a character who is the Jesus of Narnia. Along with the children, our excitement for him builds all the way to our meeting him. He is the one who will break the White Witch's spell of making it "always winter but never Christmas." Winter signifies death, and Christmas the birth of Jesus who will triumph over death in his own resurrection and the promise of ours. The Beavers' description of Aslan gives us a sense of his unfathomable nature: good but not safe. Our excitement mounts through the mention of his name; our anticipation grows with the advent of spring, which means that Aslan is in the land and the power of the Witch is starting to wane. Finally, we meet him, learning that something can be "good and terrible at the same time." When the children "tried to look at Aslan's face they just caught a glimpse of the golden mane and the great, royal, solemn, overwhelming eyes; and then they found they couldn't look at him and went all trembly."[28]

In a move that reenacts the central conflict of human history, Edmund willingly deceives himself and his siblings, selling out all of Narnia to the White Witch for a chance at showing up his big brother and indulging his appetite. With this choice, he gambles life and soul. Edmund has put himself under a power so strong that, as the Beavers advise, it's no use their trying to beat the White Witch themselves. The only hope for Edmund— indeed, for all Narnia—is to go to Aslan. He has the power and wisdom to defeat evil—no one else. Edmund here stands for all humanity, collectively and individually: "All have sinned and fall short of the glory of God"; "the wages of sin is death."[29] The Witch has the right to a kill for every traitor; so Aslan saves Edmund the only way possible, by giving his life in Edmund's place. The execution takes place on the Stone Table, an apt and easy symbol for the law of God, which was written by the finger of God on tablets of stone given to Moses and hence to us all. This is the same law, the New Testament says, that is "written on our hearts." The law puts us under penalty of death, for all have broken it. But Christ, the perfect sacrifice, has taken the penalty of death in our place.

Aslan's death is meant to resonate with Christ's. There is a meal, a last supper, the night before. Aslan tells the girls that he would be "glad of company" in his final hours, just as Jesus asked his disciples to accompany him for prayer in Gethsemane. The girls attend him at his death, just as it was mostly women disciples who attended Jesus at his crucifixion, and the girls are the first to see him after his resurrection, just as Mary Magdalene was first to see Jesus after he rose. The deeper magic that the White Witch didn't know is that "when a willing victim who had committed no treachery was killed in a traitor's stead, the Table would crack and Death itself would start working backwards."[30] First, Aslan rises from the dead; then he frees everyone else the White Witch has turned to stone (symbolically kept under the power of the law) by breathing life into them. This act shimmers with the suggestion of creation, salvation, and the coming of the Holy Spirit, but mostly it suggests resurrection. Whereas the Witch and Satan bring death, Aslan and Christ bring life, first originating it, then conquering death with life everlasting.

The disciples who met Jesus after his resurrection were permanently changed from fearful cowards to courageous martyrs who knew truly that "to live is Christ, and to die is gain."[31] Similarly, the Narnians who meet the resurrected Aslan charge boldly into battle. They realize that evil and death have been defeated. Paul longed to be with Christ, but he willingly underwent a life of suffering for the gospel that will scarce find a parallel, from spiteful and envious adversaries to flogging, stoning, and martyrdom. He died daily to himself that he might live for Christ. Why such courage? I am confident that Paul's willingness to give his all was owing primarily to two things: One, he had been given a look into Heaven, and two, he had been with Christ—personally taught by Jesus. Paul knew where he was going and who awaited him there. Anyone who knows Jesus and Heaven in this way has been set at liberty in this life. Such a one is free to serve God and others without stint, even to the point of laying down life itself. There is nothing on earth so good that it couldn't be traded in a heartbeat for Heaven. Not goods, not family, not life itself.

Lewis prepares us in the Chronicles for this kind of commitment by awakening and cultivating our innate longing for Heaven and training our affections to love and desire the presence of Christ in the person of Aslan. Nowhere are the Chronicles more joyous, more nourishing to the soul than in these two places. First, Aslan's conquest of death, rising from the Stone Table. Lucy and Susan witnessed Aslan's humiliation as the forces of evil jeered, spat, hurled abuse and blasphemy, beat and tied him, and ultimately killed him. After honoring his memory by loosing the muzzle, the girls hear a loud crack and see the Stone Table split up the middle, just as the temple curtain barring the people's access to God's presence was torn in two. Susan utters the ironic words, "Is it more magic?" referring to the magic in the Witch's command. When Aslan answers with, "Yes. . . . It is more magic," he gives the true meaning to the word: that a magic beyond the knowledge and power of the Witch has been at work.[32]

Then Susan and Lucy turn to see the best sight ever: Aslan "shining in the sunrise, larger than they had seen him before, shaking his mane."[33] After Aslan explains the deeper magic, the girls play with him, running and chasing and rolling "together in a happy laughing heap of fur and arms and legs." It was "like playing with a thunderstorm" and a kitten at the same time.[34] Then the children "climbed onto his warm, golden back," holding his mane in a ride that "was perhaps the most wonderful thing that happened to them in Narnia."[35] Nothing is more solemn and yet uninhibited fun than time with Aslan. That is the way we should feel about Jesus, and Heaven is the place where the fun happens. Conditioned by most of our culture to reject Heaven as "pie in the sky" and Jesus as a myth—or worse, the whole thing as a crashing bore—by sojourning in Narnia, our imaginations have been baptized and restored to their rightful function. Now instead of leading us away from Jesus and Heaven, they are better equipped to lead us to them. Though Narnia is not Heaven, much of it intentionally suggests Heaven. As will certainly be the case for us in Heaven, the children lived in Narnia "in great joy and if ever they remembered their life in this world it was only as one remembers a dream."[36]

THE HORSE AND HIS BOY: "GOD OPPOSES THE PROUD BUT GIVES GRACE TO THE HUMBLE."[37]

On the way to warn Archenland and Narnia of a coming invasion, the talking warhorse Bree experiences a failure of nerve when a lion attacks his companion, Aravis. He runs on instead of turning back to defend her. The lion turns out to be Aslan, who is at once forcing them to speed ahead and bringing justice to Aravis, scratching her back with his claws, one scar for every lash a servant had to take as a consequence of Aravis's uncaring deception in her escape. In the aftermath, Bree is crestfallen over his cowardice. The wise Hermit of the Southern March counsels Bree that he has "lost nothing but [his] self-conceit."[38] In his dejection and sense of injured pride, Bree considers going back to the evil land of the Calormen rather than face the Narnians humbled. The Hermit continues his counsel: "You're not quite the great horse you had come to think, from being among poor dumb horses. Of course you were braver and cleverer than *them*. You could hardly help being that. It doesn't follow that you'll be anyone very special in Narnia. But as long as you know you're nobody very special, you'll be a very decent sort of Horse."[39]

The theme of pride, so central in both Lewis's fiction and nonfiction, here gets another powerful treatment. Bree has been the leader of these adventures, and as the wisest and strongest, we have identified with him. Now we feel keenly his necessary humiliation. He was raised among dumb beasts, but in Narnia, where rational animals are the norm, he will be quite ordinary. The competition to be the center of everything Lewis dubs in *Mere Christianity* "the complete anti-God state of mind" because God simply *is* the center as a matter of fact, and everything goes wrong when he isn't recognized as such.[40]

Similarly, we are hurtful to others when we try to make ourselves the center. We only relate properly to God and others when God is at the center. No one is special in Heaven because everyone is special—that is, no one will have the sense that "I'm better than you." That attitude belongs to Hell, which is why Bree must be broken of it now. As Lewis says in *Christian Reflections*, "pride does not only go before a fall but is a fall—a transfer of attention from God the Creator to ourselves, mere creatures."[41] The solution is not to go to Calormen and eat dirt, to engage in a poor-me trip, but to conclude that "everyone is as special as me."[42]

Bree has no corner on the poor-me attitude. At several points, Shasta ("his boy" and companion on the escape from Calormen to Narnia) laments that he is "unlucky" or "unfortunate." At his lowest, separated from his friends, tired and hungry, having narrowly escaped Rabadash and the Calormen army, and unsure of his way in the dark of night and shrouded in fog, Shasta feels sorry for himself and has reached the point of tears, declaring, "'I *do* think . . . that I must be the most unfortunate boy that ever lived in the whole world. Everything goes right for everyone except me.'"[43] At this very point, Aslan makes his undisguised appearance, but even then it seems like another bit of rum luck: a new and unknown presence beside him in the dark. After his initial exchange with the new presence, but before he learns who Aslan really is, Shasta repeats, "'Oh, I am the unluckiest person in the whole world.'"[44]

The irony for readers who know other books in the series is delicious, for the parts of the Chronicles we like most, the ones that fill us with longing for the Christ of whom Aslan is but a type, are the passages where Aslan comes unexpectedly and yet inevitably on the scene. Characters often fear meeting Aslan, while we know that all will be set aright, that the lover of souls is orchestrating events for good, that we will see his glory and share his glory, and that comfort is at hand. As Shasta feels the warm, sweet breath of the lion and receives assurance that this "is not the breath of a ghost," Aslan commands the "unluckiest person in the world" to "tell me your sorrows."[45] Is not Shasta at this moment, in our imaginations, the luckiest person in the world? Who would not trade places with him if it were granted? And, of course, the point is that we *will* be granted the same privilege. What follows Shasta's lament is Aslan's unveiling of the providence behind every experience in which all the "bad" turns out to be for Shasta's good and the good of all Narnia. Aslan has not only been sparing Shasta's life and building his relationships and character, but he has been leading Shasta to the point of receiving his new name and new status as Prince Cor, heir to a kingdom. The biblical texts behind this episode are many and include:

I will never leave you nor forsake you.[46]

You are no longer a slave, but a son, and if a son, then an heir through God.[47]

The Spirit himself bears witness with our spirit that we are children of God, and if children, then heirs—heirs of God and fellow heirs with Christ, provided we suffer with him in order that we may also be glorified with him.[48]

All that is Christ's will be ours, but, as Lewis helps us see, the deepest longing of our heart is to be with him. The children often long for Narnia, but would rather be anywhere with Aslan than any other place without him. He wipes away our tears, turns sorrow into joy, and surrounds us with his glory. In a parallel event, the Hermit corrects Aravis on her comment that she is lucky that the lion (not yet known to be Aslan) hadn't scratched her back with permanent injury. The Hermit says, "'I have now lived a hundred and nine winters in this world and I have never yet met any such thing as luck.'"[49] Later they learn that Aslan is not only behind this attack for Aravis's good, but is behind all the stories. Aslan tells everyone their own story: interprets their lives, giving each the true meaning.

The Beatific Vision: Shasta Meets Aslan

The genius of these stories is simply but powerfully tapping into the often unrecognized desire beneath all desires—to be with God. Lewis moves us from the abstraction "God's glory" to an imaginatively lived experience of it. He uses two primary techniques to engage our emotions. One is the immediate appeal of the regal Aslan, who has been doing selfless good all along, now physically present. Here is the king of beasts, bigger than a horse, with sweet breath, an indescribable perfume in the air, a resonant voice, comforting kisses from the moist lion's tongue to a child's forehead, the velveted paw (claws safely withdrawn)—so much power controlled by so much love. The recognition scene, when Shasta is first permitted to see Aslan as he is, enchants us. Shasta loses his fear that he had heard a ghost's voice or that some beast of prey would eat him. He encounters a shining mist so bright he blinks, next a golden light "he thought was the sun," and then, taller than his horse, a Lion. "It was from the Lion that the light came. No one ever saw anything more terrible or beautiful."[50] Growing up in Calormen, Shasta hadn't heard "the true stories about Aslan," son of the Emperor-over-the-sea. "But after one glance at the Lion's face he slipped out of the saddle and fell at its feet."

> The High King above all kings stooped towards him. Its mane, and some strange and solemn perfume that hung about the mane, was all round him. It touched his forehead with its tongue. He lifted his face and their eyes met. Then instantly the pale brightness of the mist and the fiery brightness of the Lion rolled themselves together into a swirling glory and gathered themselves up and disappeared. He was alone with the horse on a grassy hillside under a blue sky. And there were birds singing.[51]

The episode shimmers with allusions to Moses' encounter with God and Paul's with Jesus and, as in every book in the Chronicles, another instance of the Beatific Vision. As with Emeth in *The Last Battle*, though he had the greater disadvantage of growing up with false teaching and Tash worship, one glance at Aslan, and he knew his Savior. This is the moment of salvation for Shasta.

To reassure Shasta that the appearance was not a dream, Aslan leaves a paw print that presently fills with water and then overflows into a stream from which Shasta drinks, then dips his face and splashes his head. The stream is "clear as glass, and refreshed him very much."[52] On the literal level, this is another evidence of Aslan's care in supplying Shasta's need, both for belief and for sustenance. But for those familiar with the Bible, the rich symbolism of water imagery floods our memories. We recall

Moses again, who brought water from a rock in God's name; Jesus who described himself as the "living water"; the command of baptism, which follows belief in him and itself symbolizes Jesus' death, burial, and resurrection; the river ("the river of the water of life, as bright as crystal, flowing from the throne of God and of the Lamb") that flows through Heaven and waters the trees whose leaves bring healing to the nations.[53] Though only a few of the allusions are directly to Heaven, taken on the whole, the informed reader will bring to the encounter of Aslan the rich backdrop of salvation history that so enriches our thinking about Heaven as home and shows us the way there.

Other great moments of Beatific Vision in this book are Aslan's appearance to Aravis, the Calormen aristocrat destined to become the wife of Shasta, who becomes King Cor; to Hwin, the mare; and Bree, the warhorse. Bree is still smarting over hurt pride in his failure of courage in the lion attack and has foolishly said of Aslan that "it would be quite absurd to suppose he is a real lion. . . . He'd have to be a Beast just like the rest of us."[54] At this moment, two things are happening. Translated into our world, Bree is denying both the humanity of Jesus and his divinity. Second, Aslan has appeared beside him. In a scene reminiscent of Jesus' challenge to doubting Thomas to test his bodily resurrection by feeling his wounds, Aslan urges Bree to touch and smell him and know that he is "a true Beast."

Not so with Hwin. She instantly recognizes Aslan and loves him as her deepest heart's desire. In a humorous yet touching response, Hwin spontaneously offers herself to be eaten by Aslan. Hwin has died to herself. She abandons herself completely to Aslan, which is the beginning of true selfhood and the way to deepest fulfillment.

The atmosphere of *The Horse and His Boy* wonderfully complements the theme of spiritual transformation: from black night to blue sky, from fog to clear skies, from silence to birds' song, from lost to found, from danger to safety, from sorrow to joy. Lewis evokes the numinous, the sense of something or someone totally "other," a mode of existence unlike our own, which hangs about Aslan. It is the feeling we get from sensing the presence of a ghost or a spirit being, like an angel. It is the ultimate fear of the unknown, but when associated with Aslan, to the good who love him, the fear is replaced by awe.

The Horse and His Boy is blessedly awash with biblical allusion attendant upon Aslan. Along with the natural lore about majestic lions, Aslan is "the lion of Judah," and like Jesus, he is always with us (both seen and unseen), our goal and the means to reaching it. There are the intangible qualities of Christ that appear throughout the Old Testament prophecies and the New Testament fulfillment—omnipotence, omniscience, and omnipresence—plus the actions bringing peace, comfort, and joy. Aslan, like Jesus/God, is the eternal and only self-existent one. Aslan answers Shasta's question, "'Who *are* you?'" with the reply, repeated three times, "'Myself,'" at once reminding us of the triune God and recalling God's words to Moses in the burning bush encounter.[55] God sends Moses to Israel to deliver them; so Moses asks, "'Who shall I say sent me,'" to which God replies: "Say this to the people of Israel, 'I AM has sent me to you.'"[56]

The "shining whiteness" Shasta sees on meeting Aslan is the Shekinah glory that accompanies manifestations of God in the Old Testament and Jesus at the Transfiguration. Aslan's appearance to the traveling Shasta in his near despair recalls Jesus' appearance to two of his followers on the road to Emmaus as they are confused and downhearted following the Crucifixion. Like Shasta, they didn't know who he was until much conversation and several familiar actions by Jesus. Just as Jesus disappeared at the moment of recognition, so does Aslan. Aslan's refusal to answer questions about events involving other characters recalls Jesus' rebuke of Peter. Jesus had just foretold Peter's suffering, and the disciple asked about John, to which he received the admonition: "What is that to you? You follow me."

In meetings with Aslan, several characters ask about others, and Aslan responds by instructing them all, "I am telling you your story. . . . I tell no one any story but his own."[57] Aslan tells us only the meaning of our own lives. How groundless our fears are about losing ourselves in either conversion or reaching Heaven, when in reality we find ourselves in Christ. "Be sure that the ins and outs of your individuality are no mystery to Him; and one day they will no longer be a mystery to you," Lewis says of Heaven in *The Problem of Pain*. "Blessed and fortunate creature, your eyes shall behold Him and not another's. All that you are, sins apart, is destined, if you will let God have His good way, to utter satisfaction. . . . Your place in heaven will seem to be made for you and you alone, because you were made for it."[58] In having Aslan explain everyone's own story and not another's, Lewis shows that Jesus' goal with each of us is a personal relationship, not impersonal religion. The personal stories further link to the promise in Revelation that Jesus will give each of us "a white stone" that will have our new name on it, known only to him and to ourselves.[59]

PRINCE CASPIAN: ACQUIRING A TASTE FOR HEAVEN

Another way of keeping Heaven in view is recognizing that Narnia and earth are not forever—neither the place itself nor our place in it. At the end of *Prince Caspian,* Aslan tells the two older Pevensie children, Peter and Susan, that they will not be coming back to Narnia. Though Susan deserts Aslan along the way, Peter will be faithful and will find himself in the New Narnia (Heaven). This is another kind of initiation, as the children grow toward adulthood and learn to know Aslan by another name (Jesus) in their earthly home. One of many instances will serve to illustrate the common theme of growing in our knowledge of Christ—an activity that will engage eternity as we will know more and more and want to know more yet, while never getting to the end of him. On seeing Aslan after a long time away in our world, Lucy receives Aslan's greeting and expresses her surprise at how big he seems, the opposite of most childhood recollections in which things are smaller than memories make them out to be.

> "Welcome, child," he said.
> "Aslan," said Lucy, "you're bigger."
> "That is because you are older, little one," answered he.
> "Not because you are?"
> "I am not. But every year you grow, you will find me bigger."[60]

Could it be otherwise in Heaven itself? We find here another key point about Heaven never far away in any of Lewis's work: that Heaven is a choice we make by means of a series of small choices; through these choices we turn ourselves into persons who would like Heaven or wouldn't like it in the end, even if it were offered. For Lewis, to be damned means to be so separated from God that his presence is no longer desired even in the midst of Hell's misery. In *The Great Divorce,* this idea takes the form of people from Hell visiting the outskirts of Heaven, being urged in by earthly family or acquaintances, and *choosing* (almost universally) to return to Hell.

In *The Magician's Nephew,* Aslan says of Uncle Andrew, the dabbler in black magic who is fearful of Aslan and enamored of the White Witch, that he "has made himself unable to hear my voice." So here, "more than half" the Telmarines who were "important under Miraz" choose to leave the restored Narnia as a place no longer desirable. Aslan has a messenger announce that "any who chose to stay under the new conditions might do so; but for those who did not like the idea, Aslan would provide another home." The worst of the Telmarines "had no desire to live in a country where they could not rule the roost," especially, "with that awful Lion and all."[61] This reminds us again of Satan in *Paradise Lost*, who thinks it "Better to rule in Hell, than serve in Heav'n."[62]

"Men of Telmar," said Aslan, ". . . I will send you all to your own country. You do not belong to this world at all," to which the Telmarines retort to each other, "There you are. Might have guessed we didn't belong to this place with all its queer, nasty, unnatural creatures."[63] By contrast, the Pevensies are sad to leave Aslan and Narnia and would not have done so, except for their wish to obey his order to return to their world, knowing that it is temporary and that obedience prepares them for the time when they will never leave his presence. Prince Caspian's old nurse provides another example of longing for Aslan's permanent presence. Banned from court by the usurping king Miraz for telling stories of Aslan, she is now "at death's door." The scene is highly evocative of Jesus' bringing Lazarus back from the dead. When Lewis himself recovered from a coma, he lamented having to do his dying all over again and sympathized with Lazarus for the same reason. Though Lewis's lament for himself came late in life and after the Chronicles were written, he with prescience puts the sentiment into this scene. The Nurse looks into the lion's face, saying, "Oh, Aslan! I knew it was true. I've been waiting for this all my life. Have you come to take me away?" "Yes, dearest," said Aslan. "But not the long journey yet."

Here, again, the long view, with Heaven grasped by faith, is at the heart of the deepest human longing. Lewis's life was dominated by longing for God, even when he was an atheist and didn't know what the longing he came to call "Joy" was all about. In a letter to former pupil Dom Bede Griffiths not many years after his conversion, Lewis confides his heart's desire.

> What state of affairs in this world can we view with satisfaction? If we are unhappy, then we are unhappy. If we are happy, then we remember that the crown is not promised without the cross and tremble. In fact, one comes to realise, what one always admitted theoretically, that there is nothing here that will do us good: the sooner we are safely out of this world the better. But "would it were evening, Hal, and all well."[64]

THE VOYAGE OF THE "DAWN TREADER": JOURNEY TO THE UTTER EAST

Reepicheep and the Quest for Heaven

Lewis said in a letter to one of his young correspondents that *The Voyage of the "Dawn Treader"* is chiefly about the spiritual life and that Reepicheep is its chief example.[65] Reepicheep's aim is to sail to "the very eastern end of the world," where he expects "to find Aslan's own country," because "it is always from the east, across the sea, that the great Lion comes to us."[66] For Reepicheep, it is not an initiation story, as it is for Eustace, but a revelation archetype. He is on a sacred quest, couched in chivalric terms, with the irony and paradox that he is a courageous mouse. Mice run by instinct when threatened; Reepicheep stays to fight. He is devoted to Aslan. The total effect illustrates two biblical paradoxes: 1) the least among us shall be the greatest, the servant the master of all, and 2) in our weakness Christ is strong. Reepicheep also embodies the Pauline commitment expressed in Philippians 1:21: "To live is Christ, and to die is gain." He has, like Paul, already died to personal gain. Reepicheep is ready to give his life for another's safety or honor, and he will not be deterred from his goal of reaching Heaven: "Aslan's country," the "utter east."

Nowhere is such wholehearted dedication better expressed than in Reepicheep's resolve to fulfill his quest and his destiny: "'My own plans are made. While I can, I sail east in the *Dawn Treader*. When she fails me, I paddle east in my coracle. When she sinks, I shall swim east with my four paws. And when I can swim no longer, if I have not reached Aslan's country, or shot over the edge of the world in some vast cataract, I shall sink with my nose to the sunrise.'"[67]

Reepicheep's commitment is like that of Shadrach, Meshach, and Abednego when faced with imminent death in the fiery furnace for refusing to worship the golden image of Nebuchadnezzar. "'Our God whom we serve is able to deliver us from the burning fiery furnace. . . . But if not, be it known to you, O king, that we will not serve your gods or worship the golden image that you have set up.'"[68] And Reepicheep reminds us of Job's stirring words: "though he slay me, I will hope in him."[69]

For these, as for Reepicheep, the chief value is not preserving earthly life, but living and dying with the greater glory in view, the King of Kings' "well done." What drives Reepicheep is what drove Lewis: "Joy," a deep longing that is constantly stirred up by creation and has its fulfillment only in the Creator. That the longing or desire called "Joy" is the holy haunting that has hung over Reepicheep's life from its beginning is clear in the verse spoken over his cradle by a Dryad (serving in the role of a guardian angel):

> *Where sky and water meet,*
> *Where the waves grow sweet,*
> *Doubt not, Reepicheep,*
> *To find all you seek,*
> *There is the utter East.*[70]

Though Reepicheep is not a missionary, he has the missionary spirit. He wishes to take the knowledge of Aslan and the pursuit of him to the end of the world. Jesus' last words to his disciples before ascending to Heaven were: "ye shall be witnesses unto me both in Jerusalem, and in all Judea, and in Samaria, and unto the uttermost part of the earth."[71] The last words of Matthew's Gospel record Jesus' Great Commission to his apostles: "Go ye therefore, and teach all nations . . . teaching them to observe all things whatsoever I have commanded you: and, lo, I am with you alway, even unto the end of the world."[72] Lewis uses the language of the King James Version of the Bible, most familiar to Bible readers of his day, combining key terms "utter" and "end of the world" in characterizing Reepicheep's quest.

Following Lewis's clue in suggesting that *The Voyage of the "Dawn Treader"* is about "the spiritual life (especially in Reepicheep)," we see a model of how life is lived when Heaven is in view. He is "the most valiant of all the Talking Beasts of Narnia."[73] Before discussing his heroism and leadership, let it be said that he is also the object of mock-heroic fun. Reepicheep's courage is sometimes foolhardy and his sense of dignity often laughable, but always endearingly so. For example, in playing chess, his imagination wanders, and he moves his knight as if in war, not in game logic. Despite the humor, he is still the heroic center of the story. "Reepicheep's courage is," as Paul Karkainen says, "the wind that keeps the sails of the ship filled and moving forward."[74] As such, he is the first to approach the dragon, gives wise counsel to Lucy about Coriakin's book of spells, saves the ship from the sea serpent, answers the voice of the terrified Lord Rhoop in the Dark Island, is not tempted by treasure, and is first to eat of Aslan's table on the island at "the beginning of the end of the world." And he is the one who alone sails in his coracle (a small boat of sticks and animal skin) over the last wave into Aslan's country, thus breaking the sleeping spell of the last three lost Lords of Narnia. As Lewis says, it is those who care most for the next world who do the most for this.[75]

Learning to Love

Eustace is a stinker. He's the kind of kid you want to introduce to the paddle, perpetually in need of a good spanking. In one of the best starts in fiction, Lewis opens: "There was a boy called Clarence Eustace Scrubb, and he almost deserved it."[76] Eustace always has something against everyone: His shipmates are "fiends in human form," Reepicheep a "dangerous little brute," Caspian an "idiot." Nothing is ever done to suit Eustace; nothing is ever his fault. He whines and shirks his way through several adventures until his rotten nature gets him in a fix so bad that only the grace of God can get him out. When a violent storm blows twelve days straight (thirteen according to the others, "who can't even count right"), and the exhausted party finally gets ashore, where there's more work to do, Eustace slips off to have his selfish rest. In a fog that symbolizes his spiritual state, he slips down a narrow ridge to a valley, sees a dragon expire, and discovers the dragon's lair full of treasure. In his greed, he fantacizes about the good times he will have in the evil land of Calormen, puts a golden bracelet on his arm, and turns into a dragon. The judgment Eustace gets is perfect because dragons are legendary for their greed. He has no choice but to go back to the others, hoping for help and not a dragon-slaying.

From the beginning of his predicament, Eustace is shown love far beyond his deserts and, many of us might think, beyond what we would have given in the same circumstance. But we have, truth to tell, either all been a Eustace or been plagued by one, or both. What keeps Eustace from despair while still a dragon is the new pleasure of "being liked and, still more, of liking other people."[77] He learns this chiefly from Lucy and Reepicheep. On first entering the camp and before the others realize it is Eustace in dragon form, he sheds boiling hot dragon tears. Lucy, though warned of a possible trick, compassionately and at risk of her own life, moves instinctively forward to comfort him. Besides the frustration of his new identity, Eustace is in pain from the golden, diamond-studded bracelet he has put on his arm. (The bracelet had belonged, it turns out, to Lord Octesian, one of the seven lost Lords of Narnia whom Caspian is journeying to find.) Lucy tries her magical healing cordial, which can only help but not solve the problem.

But it is Reepicheep, the one Eustace taunted most and even injured, who cares most effectively for Eustace's wounded spirit. "Greatly to his surprise, Reepicheep was his most constant comforter."[78] He tells Eustace stories of men from every walk of life whose fortunes fell low but "lived happily ever afterwards."[79] This love and that of others, along with the efficacy of suffering and the new joy of serving others' needs by bringing food and warming them when cold, all help prepare Eustace for his coming metamorphosis. These are all Aslan's people who have been doing Aslan's work. The payoff is that "Eustace realized more and more that since the first day he came on board he had been an unmitigated nuisance and that he was now a greater nuisance still. And this ate into his mind, just as that bracelet ate into his foreleg."[80] Still, he can't undragon himself; nor can others do for him what only Aslan can do. That Eustace is in the grip of sin and in need of salvation, we cannot doubt, especially if we remember that the Bible calls Satan both "serpent" and "dragon."[81]

The Salvation of Eustace

In *The Voyage of the "Dawn Treader,"* the adventurers encounter temptations typical of those that distract our own pursuit of Heaven, temptations falsely promising the fulfillment our souls' desire. For the Narnians as for us, the lure of riches threatens their ruin. The gold at Deathwater Island provokes, not peace, plenty, and pleasure, but the first instance of power-grabbing between Caspian and Edmund, whom Lucy describes as "swaggering, bullying idiots."[82] Similarly, the dragon's treasure trove turns Eustace into a dragonish embodiment of greed itself. At the end of these episodes, when their eyes have been opened by suffering, the characters want nothing to do with the treasures and are happy to leave them behind to pursue their quest for Aslan's country.

At the point of Eustace's deepest despair, Aslan tells Eustace he will have to undress before going into the pool of water that Eustace believes will ease his pain. He is undragoned, thrown into the pool, then dressed—all three by Aslan. Each is highly symbolic. The undragoning is emblematic of sin being removed to the extent that Eustace's whole nature is changed. The first tear of the lion's claw seems to go all the way to his heart. Eustace had become a dragon by his selfishness: slinking away to rest and avoid work, putting on the gold and diamond bracelet, and stuffing his pockets with diamonds. He believes with these riches he can "have quite a decent time here—perhaps in Calormen," the country of Narnia's enemies.[83] Dragons, the narrator tells us, are only found singly because in their greed they eat their rivals. Eustace has become his sin.

Of course, he is not in Hell yet; so there is still hope for him. The first step is to despair of helping himself. In *Mere Christianity*, Lewis says that Christianity is a religion of despair before it is one of comfort. We must realize that there is nothing we can do for ourselves. Only then can God in Christ give us as gift what we cannot earn. When Eustace pulls off his scales and a layer of skin, which he does three times before he sees the futility of his own efforts, he is still a dragon underneath: more scales and dragonish hide. But when Aslan claws him to the heart, the Lion reveals the person beneath that by grace he was making Eustace into by this whole horrific and yet necessary experience.

After his undragoning, Eustace is thrown into the pool. This reminds us of the healing of the man at the Pool of Siloam and also of baptism, emblematic of dying to sins, being buried with Christ, and rising to a new life, mirroring Christ's resurrection as we come up from the water. The clothing metaphor is a common one in the Chronicles as in the Bible. The undressing and nakedness symbolize exposure of our sin before God, as with Adam and Eve, who also had to be dressed by God after their sin. The reclothing or covering of nakedness is emblematic of the forgiveness of sin, as it is covered through forgiveness, purchased for us by Christ's blood and in Narnia by Aslan's blood on the Stone Table.

After Eustace tells the story of his transformation to Edmund, the latter's response is both humorous and poignant: "Between ourselves, you haven't been as bad as I was on my first trip to Narnia. You were only an ass, but I was a traitor."[84] Such humility is one of the hallmarks of those redeemed by Aslan; no more of "the great sin," pride, which had kept Eustace from submitting to Aslan's claims on him and made him, with a great pun, "pretty beastly."[85] Edmund underscores the fact that the transforming initiative is Aslan's. Eustace asks: "'But who is Aslan? Do you know him?' 'Well—he knows me,' said Edmund. 'He is the great Lion, the son of the Emperor-Beyond-the-Sea, who saved me and saved Narnia.'"[86] As there is great rejoicing over one sheep that was lost and is found, so the circle is completed with the celebration that follows Eustace's return as a human. "Great was the rejoicing when Edmund and the restored Eustace walked into the breakfast circle round the camp-fire."[87]

More Undragoning

As Michael Ward explains, the undragoning of Eustace is a microcosm of the whole novel.[88] The *Dawn Treader* is the only such Narnian ship, the others being ordinary, unornamented vessels. It was built by the boy king Caspian and symbolizes his need to grow spiritually out of his own drag-onish character. From his first Christian work (*The Pilgrim's Regress*) on, Lewis refers often to dragons and always negatively, except in unfallen Perelandra. Caspian's sin is not so obvious and therefore requires such clues as the dragon ship. When Edmund, Lucy, and Eustace fall through the picture and into Narnia at the opening of the story, they hear from Caspian that he has left Narnia in the care of a regent and gone on adventures. You could say that the quest to find the seven lost Lords of Narnia is legitimate, but is the job for him?

We can think of other examples of characters ill-advisedly leaving their responsibility to reign. It happens when things are going well, and rulers want to take their leave. Orual, in *Till We Have Faces*, is the Queen of Glome. She says, "I resolved to go on a progress and travel in other lands. We were at peace with everyone. Bardia and Penuan and Arnom could do all that was needed while I was away; for indeed Glome had now been nursed and trained till it almost ruled itself." But she is the rightful authority of Glome, and the responsibility is hers. She is to learn on her journey that the most personal part of her kingdom is still out of control: She hasn't yet learned to rule herself. Shakespeare's King Lear foolishly decides to take his ease, putting authority into usurping hands, only to learn that he, too, had need of self-governance.

This is Caspian's situation. His sin of greed comes out on Deathwater Island where he and Edmund are both seduced by gold. His greater and more subtle sin, though, emerges at the end of the journey when he wants to go unbidden into Aslan's country as though he can dictate the terms. We would all like to go to Heaven on our own terms, pretend that we are good enough for God to take us as we are and when we choose. But this is not the case. None is worthy; all are dragons. And as with Eustace, we can not undragon ourselves. Both Eustace and Caspian must submit to Aslan and his process of undragoning. It won't be easy. Aslan, like God, "has paid us the intolerable compliment of loving us," and love "demands the perfecting of the beloved."[89]

Dufflepuds: The Case of the Hard to Reach

Prince Caspian's party lands on an island controlled by the old magician Coriakin, who, we later learn, is a retired star. He also oversees the Dufflepuds, a one-legged, slow, but rational species that move like pogo sticks. They have made themselves invisible and want to be restored to visibility. Lucy has the task of looking in the magician's book of spells for one to restore them. She encounters several spells, one "for the refreshment of the spirit."[90] Upon reading the spell, Lucy declares it "'the loveliest story I've ever read or ever shall read in my whole life.'"[91] After wishing she could go on reading it for "ten years," she discovers she can't turn the pages back. After finding and working the spell for making the invisible visible, she sees Aslan. When she thanks him for coming, he informs her that he has "been there all the time." She is already forgetting the story that refreshes the spirit and begs Aslan to retell it. He answers, "'Indeed, yes, I will tell it to you for years and years. But now, come. We must meet the master of this house.'"[92] This episode illustrates three things: 1) Aslan's (Christ's) unseen presence, 2) our longing for satisfaction, and 3) Aslan's promise to fulfill it.

The Dufflepuds are a foolish race to whom even Aslan's representative cannot show himself because they are not prepared. "'I should frighten them out of their senses,'" he says.[93] They don't even know their own good. The magician has to make them tend the garden and raise food. The Duffers imagine that it is for their master when all along it is for themselves. Like the Duffers, we imagine that we are set arbitrary tasks to please God, when they are really essential for our spiritual lives. Lucy and the magician see that the Duffers are "stupid," but we as readers realize before long that their shallow understanding of their relationship to the magician is exactly like ours to God. With the new spell to make them visible again, the Duffers think they and Lucy have outsmarted the old man and caught him off guard, while the old man was listening and permitting it all along. Lucy wonders:

> "But do they dare to talk about you like that?" said Lucy. "They seemed to be so afraid of you yesterday. Don't they know you might be listening?"

"That's one of the funny things about the Duffers," said the Magician. "One minute they talk as if I ran everything and overhear everything and was extremely dangerous. The next moment they think they can take me in by tricks that a baby would see through—bless them!"[94]

We call out to God in distress or plead our case to God whenever we have need, assuming that he will hear and that he has all the power to grant the request. The next moment we may sin with some absurd rationalization as though he were irrelevant and impotent to give us our just punishment. The Dufflepuds have a bad habit of listening to a misguided leader that makes their progress under the magician even slower. They are amusing, and, just a little, we laugh at ourselves reflected in their inability to know their own good. They are at the far end of the continuum in their longing for God.

Voyage to the End of the World

The writer of Hebrews, speaking of the heroes of the faith, says: "they desire a better country, that is, a heavenly one. Therefore God . . . has prepared for them a city."[95] This could well serve as a summary of the quest running through the Chronicles of Narnia, which begins with the creation of Narnia and ends with a "Farewell to Shadowlands" in the New (or "real") Narnia, Heaven. The nearest approach to Aslan's country apart from the conclusion of *The Last Battle* (though every meeting of Aslan is an encounter with the essence of Heaven) is in the concluding chapters of *The Voyage of the "Dawn Treader."* Even the chapter titles resound with otherworldliness: "The Beginning of the End of the World," "The Wonders of the Last Sea," and "The Very End of the World." These chapters shimmer with images of the Resurrection, which is our earnest of Heaven.

At Ramandu's Island, the adventurers find Aslan's Table, which is replenished daily by birds, to suggest the marriage feast of the Lamb. Aslan placed the table there for the refreshment of travelers who have journeyed so far and neared the world's end. On it lay the Knife of Stone used to kill Aslan in a sacrifice that saved Edmund and Narnia, which takes the place of the cross. There is wine for the Communion cup. Reminiscent of Isaiah, Ramandu has a fiery coal put to his lips every morning by a bird. It makes him younger, but more importantly, it symbolizes purification from sin and preparation to meet Aslan. The allusion is to Isaiah, who sees a vision of the Lord enthroned in glory with attending angels. Isaiah, overawed, cries, "Woe is me! For I am lost; for I am a man of unclean lips, and I dwell in the midst of a people of unclean lips; for my eyes have seen the King, the LORD of hosts!"[96] Then a seraph puts a coal from the altar on Isaiah's lips. Now he can speak for the Lord of hosts and answers the challenge of prophesying to the people with those ringing words of commitment: "Here am I! Send me." As Mrs. Beaver says in *The Lion, the Witch and the Wardrobe*, "'if there's anyone who can appear before Aslan without their knees knocking, they're either braver than most or else just silly.'"[97] Interpreting the parallel strictly, you could say that Ramandu is being prepared to speak for Aslan, which is true. But more generally, he is being purified, becoming suited for service to Aslan.

Nearing Aslan's Country, the crew finds sweet ocean water that satisfies, like the living water or water of life, and lilies associated with the Resurrection. The music and mountains always had associations with Joy in Lewis's mind. After Reepicheep has disappeared over the final wave at the edge of the world, Edmund, Lucy, and Eustace come to the shore for what will prove to be their final moments in Narnia. Aslan, before assuming his lion form, appears as a lamb, preparing a breakfast of cooked fish, thus combining Jesus as sacrifice (the Lamb of God) and the resurrected Lord, who proved his bodily resurrection to his disciples by eating fish with them. Aslan tells the children they are too old for Narnia now, but their lament is not for Narnia itself, even though they were kings and queens there. "'It isn't Narnia, you know,' sobbed Lucy. 'It's *you*. We shan't meet *you* there. And how can we live, never meeting you?'"[98]

These are the words of someone who is ready for Heaven, who has acquired the taste for it, as Lewis says, because Heaven is that place where Christ is preeminent, the all in all. Happily, Aslan informs them that he is in their world, too, but that they must learn to know him by another name. Then Aslan tells the purpose of adventures in Narnia and indirectly of life in our world: "you were brought to Narnia, that by knowing me here for a little, you may know me better there." We were created to know Jesus as Savior and Lord here that we may know and love him forever in Heaven.

THE SILVER CHAIR: CROSSING JORDAN

Most of *The Silver Chair* finds Eustace and Jill in a return adventure to find and free the lost Prince Rilian, a prisoner of the Queen of Underland in a strange subterranean world. The story intersects our theme of Heaven toward the end when Prince Rilian is restored to his people, and the narrator announces what Jill felt and what all will say in Heaven looking back at earth: "Their quest had been worth all the pains it cost."[99]

As Aslan blows them back to his own country, just before returning them to this world, they are allowed a glimpse into Heaven. They had witnessed the return of Caspian X and his reunion with his son Prince Rilian. Only moments after their reunion, the king dies and Rilian weeps. At this point Jill wishes she were home, and Aslan comes to blow them to his country. There in a stream, they see the body of the aged King Caspian. The river is a multifaceted symbol. First, as in the expression "crossing over Jordan," it is a commonplace symbol of death. It is the same river Jill drank from in chapter 2, which there symbolized Jesus as "the living water."

Here it is also a subtle symbol both of the "river of the water of life" flowing through the middle of the heavenly Jerusalem and of baptism, picturing the death, burial, and resurrection of Christ, which his followers will share, as Caspian is about to do.[100] In Narnia Rilian wept at his father's death. Now in Aslan's own country, Eustace and Jill weep, mirroring the scene in Narnia. Aslan also weeps at the sight of Caspian in the river of death, even though (as with Jesus and Lazarus) Aslan is on the verge of raising Caspian from the dead. The narrator says of the "great Lion-tears" that each is "more precious than the Earth would be if it was a single solid diamond."[101] Lewis condenses worlds of meaning into Aslan's tears. First, as with Jesus, there is love and compassion. In *Mere Christianity*, which Lewis was revising for publication as he was composing the Chronicles, we find this haunting sentence that captures at once the demands and compassion Jesus extends to us: "Though our feelings come and go, His love for us does not. It is not wearied by our sins, or our indifference; and, therefore, it is quite relentless in its determination that we shall be cured of those sins, at whatever cost to us, at whatever cost to Him."[102]

These tears capture the love of Aslan (and Jesus) for his creature, the sorrow at his death, and the knowledge that in a very short time, he will take on himself the sin of the world and die that we might live again. The word *solid* reminds us that Jesus is, as Lewis says, "reality himself": Reality at root is not a thing, but a person. It suggests, too, the permanence of the heavenly realm. And finally, it captures the true wealth: in the words of the chorus, "Lord, you are more beautiful than diamonds. Nothing in this world compares with you."

In this marvelously compact scene, Lewis packs in the passion of Christ, too. Aslan instructs Eustace to pluck a thorn and drive it into his paw, evoking the crown of thorns and the nails in his hands. Then a drop of blood from Aslan's paw falls over Caspian, who is resurrected from the stream full of youth, life, and vigor. The interaction between Caspian and Aslan suggests the central joy of Heaven. Caspian "rushed to Aslan and flung his arms as far as they would go round the huge neck; and he gave Aslan the strong kisses of a King, and Aslan gave him the wild kisses of a Lion."[103] This is truly to love and be loved.

Caspian expresses a desire for a glimpse of the children's world, asking if it would be wrong. Aslan's answer suggests another of the glories of Heaven: "You cannot want wrong things any more, now that you have died, my son."[104] Lewis's characters show us what it means for sin to be vanquished. The truest freedom in the universe or the eternities is freedom from sin and the unimpeded freedom to love. In Heaven we may then act on every impulse because every impulse will be pure. None of them will harm either ourselves or others; nor will we fear rejection. This is another way of saying that in Heaven our obedience to God will be perfect.[105] At the end of his purification in *The Divine Comedy*, which is a major literary backdrop for much of Lewis's fiction, Dante is similarly told that he may now do whatever he likes because his capacity to love has been perfected.[106] What concludes *The Silver Chair* may be described as a mini-millennium. Aslan comes to earth with the resurrected Caspian to establish justice and the reign of righteousness at Experiment House. As Caspian joins Eustace and Jill in disciplining the bullies, the episode also suggests the biblical truth about the hereafter that we will have meaningful and fulfilling work, which will be our joy to perform.

THE LAST BATTLE—THE NEW HEAVEN AND WHO GOES THERE

The artist's role, as Coleridge and Shelley remind us, is to "strip the veil of familiarity from the commonplace," to bring back wonder in the everyday. Even the grand themes of cosmic history can be dulled by repetition and familiarity, quenching if not the belief, at least the emotion and the joy. Lewis's gift through these stories is a return to glorious wonder. In *The Last Battle*, the children see their beloved Narnia unmade as the sun blackens and the landscape freezes. But sorrow soon turns to joy as they walk into Aslan's country where, to their surprise, everything seems strangely familiar. Lord Digory solves the puzzle, exclaiming that all the good from Old Narnia is preserved in the new as in waking from a dream.[107]

We are not surprised at most of what is pulled in through the magic door to Aslan's country, the Narnian Heaven: mountains, waterfalls, pastures, Reepicheep and the Pevensie kids, and all the talking animals and people who love Aslan. But there is one big surprise. A member of the enemy Calormene camp makes the cut. The troublesome part is not so much that he fought the Narnians as that he gave allegiance to a false god. The big theological question of this book centers on Emeth's admission to Heaven; so we will take it up at once. The case of Emeth puzzles and troubles many and will require some explanation. At issue is whether Lewis believed that some will go to Heaven apart from knowledge of and belief in Jesus. It puzzles us because Emeth has grown up worshiping Tash, who is clearly evil and plays the role of Satan in claiming the damned. Emeth says, "Gladly would I die a thousand deaths if I might look once on the face of Tash."[108]

To Emeth, Aslan is the hated name of the foreign God of the Narnians, political enemies of the Calormenes. At the end of time, Aslan and Tash are in a stable where all enter, the good going to Aslan's side and paradise, the evil to Tash and destruction. On Aslan's side are the good characters who have died before, both from earth and Narnia, and Aslan claims the newly arrived characters who have sided with him and called on his name, like Tirian, the last King of Narnia, who had announced when all looked lost that it was better to serve Aslan and die than give up or go to the other side. When other Calormene characters enter the stable for judgment, especially Rishda Tarkaan, Tash claims them as he does Shift the Ape and all others who have embraced Tash and evil or who have refused to believe in the supernatural at all. Emeth is the sole Calormene exception.

"Emeth" means in Hebrew "faithful" or "true," to which Lewis added the further definition, "intrinsic validity, rock bottom reality, something rooted in God's own Nature."[109] A foreshadowing of Emeth's good end comes from one of the most faithful Narnians, Jewel the Unicorn, special friend of King Tirian. Jewel emboldens his comrades with a positive view of dying for Aslan's name when defeat seems imminent: "It may be for us the door to Aslan's country and we shall sup at his table tonight."[110] But when Jewel sees the courage and dedication of Emeth, the Unicorn whispers in King Tirian's ear, "By the Lion's Mane, I almost love this young warrior, Calormene though he be. He is worthy of a better god than Tash."[111]

A Calormene Tarkaan, or nobleman, Emeth has wanted to serve Tash from his youth and will risk everything to see him face to face. To the point of entering the stable, Emeth hasn't yet figured out that Tash is a false god, but the truth is further foreshadowed to us in the derivation of the word. *Tash* is from the Scottish dialect, meaning "blemish, stain, fault, or vice."[112] When Emeth meets Aslan in the stable instead of Tash, he needs no explanation but recognizes Aslan instantly as the true God of his universe and the one he has really been seeking all his life. Emeth values Aslan rightly as not only the most important thing in life, but more important and valuable than everything else combined. He says, in words worthy of a Narnian king, "It is better to see the Lion and die than to be Tisroc [king] of the world and not to have seen him."[113] Emeth also recognizes his error in mistakenly pursuing Tash and hating the name of Aslan, as he was taught from boyhood. Emeth pronounces his own unworthiness for having been a servant of Tash, but Aslan, knowing his heart, receives the service rendered to Tash as rightfully his own. We could say that Emeth was faithful to the light he had received.

There are several points to make about Emeth. First, he seems to have broken the first commandment: "You shall have no other gods before me."[114] Admittedly, the ground here is close to quicksand, and I have often wished that Lewis had kept the speculation in a footnote somewhere out of the books so much read by children. But there it is. In Lewis's view, Emeth had actually kept the first commandment in his heart, though the externals look like false religion. The reverse is also true. As Jesus warned, what offers itself as worship to the true God may be false in the heart of the pretender or the self-deceived.[115] Instead of death, Emeth receives a welcome, and not from Tash but from Aslan, who greets him as "Son" with a Lion's kiss. The surprised Emeth asks if it is true after all that Tash and Aslan are equal, as the cynical Shift had claimed. In answer, Aslan growls and the earth shakes. He explains that he and Tash are "opposites" and that anything that is truly good belongs to Aslan, whatever name is used, and anything bad belongs to Tash, even if done in Aslan's name. Emeth had been a seeker after God, even though he didn't know his name or much about him.

Second, Emeth is saved by Aslan, not any other. On this point Lewis never wavered: All salvation comes through Jesus, without exception. Third, Emeth is not dead when he meets Aslan. Some suggest that the stable door symbolizes death, which is indeed a primary function, but that doesn't account for all the facts of the story. Ginger the Cat is the first to pass through the stable door after Tash has entered it unknown to the crowd outside. Upon seeing Tash, Ginger jets out the door in terror, having lost rationality, but alive. The evil Calormene soldier, who is a plant by Ginger and Rishda, is alive within the stable. The soldier is killed by Emeth and his body thrown out. Part of the importance of recognizing that entering the stable door is not necessarily to die is in interpreting what happens to Emeth. It needn't be seen as a second chance for salvation after death. In fact, Lewis did not believe such a thing possible. Even if Emeth were dead, this would not be a second chance; rather, it would be the culmination and completion of choices already made (see the section on Purgatory for more on this).

There are passages in Lewis's writing that might seem to contradict this idea. One such letter, written "To a Lady" in the same year he composed *The Last Battle*, refers her to 1 Timothy 4:10 and the passage in Matthew 25 on the separation of the sheep and goats (the good and evil, respectively) on the apparent basis of good or bad deeds.[116] He also mentions the doctrine of "Christ's descending into Hell (i.e. Hades, the land of the dead; not Gehenna, the land of the lost) and preaching to the dead," explaining that Jesus would be outside of time so that he could be preaching not only to those who died before his crucifixion, but all who died (in earthly time) after him.[117] This is also worked out fictionally in *The Great Divorce* (chapter 13), where MacDonald explains that "All moments that have been or shall be were, or are, present in the moment of His descending. There is no spirit in prison to whom He did not preach."[118] Lewis alludes here to a little understood and diversely interpreted passage, 1 Peter 3:18-20, where Jesus after his resurrection proclaims his truth to spirits in prison from the days of Noah. (We aren't told how they responded and if they were released.)

In these cases, as with Emeth, hearing the gospel would be the completion of choices made on earth that had already set their eternal destination. This, of course, is speculation, as Lewis knew and makes clear in several letters.[119] Lewis says of those who haven't been given an opportunity to hear that we do not know how God will deal with them. But if some who haven't heard are saved, they will be few (narrow is the way even in societies where Christ is preached), and it will be in Jesus' name and by his death on the cross, not by their own goodness.[120]

Fourth, it is not enough to be sincere. Admittedly, it is a fine distinction in Emeth's case. He sincerely looks to Tash, but to sincerity Emeth adds a love of truth and goodness. Anything that is good, Aslan explains, is truly of him, whatever the human attribution. Conversely, anything evil is of Tash (the Devil), even if names are ignorantly reversed. Rishda Tarkaan sincerely believes in Tash at the end, but his response is fear and attempted appeasement of a destructive power, and he is damned. Emeth was not simply culturally religious; he was a true seeker after God: "'Beloved,' said the Glorious One [Aslan], 'unless thy desire had been for me thou wouldst not have sought so long and so truly. For all find what they truly seek.'"[121] When he sees Aslan, the true God, he recognizes him immediately. The implication is that if he had learned the truth about him earlier, he would have both recognized it and accepted it. Lewis also intends through this episode to caution us in judging the heart.

Finally, a closely related point, the Emeth episode is not a case for universalism, which Lewis consistently disavowed. In the book's judgment scene, many are rejected by Aslan (because they have rejected him); those go to Tash. The whole point of having Shift claim that Tash and Aslan are the same, then conflating the two names to Tashlan, is to show that such a claim is only made by usurpers and false prophets. In the end, we see that the difference in characters' choices determines nothing less than their eternal destiny. Lewis often demonstrates in his books that objective truth exists and that no amount of subjective belief can make a thing legitimate. All religions do not lead to God. As Lewis insisted in the Preface of his early book, *The Great Divorce*, there can be no Blakean marriage of Heaven and Hell. We can take nothing of Hell into Heaven.

In a survey of letters on the fate of those who haven't heard, Lewis characteristically makes these points, which are close to his handling of the Emeth episode: 1) that he did believe that some who didn't know of Christ in this life will be saved; 2) that we don't know the fate of all who haven't heard, and some may be saved who don't fit our formulas; 3) that his own ideas are speculations based primarily on Matthew 25:31-46;[122] 4) that all salvation, however it happens and to whomever it is granted, is from Jesus and by his grace; 5) that our duty, out of concern for those who haven't heard, is not to speculate but to tell them about Christ.[123] These key points are summarized in a letter "To a Lady" of November 8, 1952:

> I think that every prayer which is sincerely made even to a false god or
> to a very imperfectly conceived true God, is accepted by the true God
> and that Christ saves many who do not think they know Him. For he is
> (dimly) present in the *good* side of the inferior teachers they follow. In

the parable of the Sheep and Goats (Matt. XXV. 31 and following) those who are saved do not seem to know that they have served Christ. But of course anxiety about unbelievers is most usefully employed when it leads us, not to speculation but to earnest prayer for them and the attempt to be in our own lives such good advertisements for Christianity as will make it attractive.[124]

The belief that Christ may save some who haven't heard is sprinkled here and there in Lewis's writing, but it does not bulk large. His emphasis was on the orthodox view that salvation comes by hearing the Word (the good news of salvation in Christ and placing our trust in his death for us), and that works of righteousness flow out of a changed heart. The consequence of putting too much weight on speculation about those who haven't heard of Christ is to miss the biblical gospel, the emphasis Lewis places on that gospel, and our possible failure to act on it ourselves or lose the urgency to tell others.

By contrast, those who have once believed can, in Lewis's view, turn their backs on Christ and Christianity and be lost, though this also seems rare. When King Tirian, remembering the old stories of Narnia before his time, asks if there is not a fourth Pevensie, Queen Susan, Peter explains that she is "no longer a friend of Narnia," while Eustace, Jill, and Polly flesh out her rebellion as a love of the world and a desire to be grown up. This alludes to Jesus' explanation of faith as being like that of a child, in total dependence on another for its well-being. Susan's apostasy is here as a warning, but in her case we may hope that she will yet repent and return. Since Narnian time does not square with earthly time, and she was not killed in the train wreck, it may not be too late for her.

The Emeth episode has taken some time to explain. It belongs to the sifting tribulations that will shake the whole world and test every belief before the end has come. *The Last Battle* is a twice-told tale, a fresh presentation of Revelation, the last book of the Bible, the Apocalypse. Events prophesied that lead up to the end of the world are sketched in here, including the coming of false prophets, the Antichrist, the deception of even some of the elect, and the oppressive control of the world by evil forces. "The Ape and Puzzle," Lewis explains to a young correspondent, "are like the coming of Antichrist before the end of our world."[125] Shift represents Satan and employs his only mode of operation: He apes Jesus. Satan cannot create, stands for nothing positive, and is only anti-Christ. He is a fraud and a counterfeiter. Shift presents a counterfeit lion as a counterfeit Aslan in a counterfeit stable (true worshipers were drawn to the true Son of God when Jesus came in a stable). As G. K. Chesterton observed, when people stop believing in God, they don't believe nothing; rather, they will believe in anything. Even in Tash; even in a costumed donkey.

The Last Battle also reenacts the Last Judgment. "Millions" of creatures from all creation "ran up to the doorway where Aslan stood."[126] They all look directly into Aslan's face with one of only two results. One group looks on him with "fear and hatred"; these go off to Aslan's left, into his shadow—that is, to Hell—and are never seen again. The other group looks on his face with love and go to his right—that is, to Heaven. This, of course, parallels the biblical separation Jesus makes into goats on his left (the lost) and sheep on his right (the saved). And here again is the Beatific and Miserific Vision rolled into one, where to look on the face of the divine is to be judged, to know within ourselves what we are to him (that is, as we are in reality), to know him as rightful Lord of all, and to have our destinies confirmed in separation from or in union with him. It will be bounty beyond deserving or imagining, or horror beyond nightmare.

There is no description of Hell in *The Last Battle*. The imaginative work of presenting damnation is done by describing the grotesque figure of Tash, his association with all things evil, and his actions. Tash has roughly the body of a human, four arms with clawed fingers, and the head of a vulture. He moves like a shadow, fouls the air with a nauseating smell, oppresses the spirit, and kills the grass beneath him. The selfish and manipulative characters like Ginger the Cat, Shift the Ape, and Rishda Tarkaan invoke his name, though at first they don't believe in him or Aslan either. In the Last Judgment at the stable door, Tash picks up Shift and downs him in a single gulp, echoing the eating/consuming metaphor for Hell's destruction at the end of *The Screwtape Letters*. When Tash tucks Rishda under his arm and is told by Aslan to depart with his "lawful prey," we assume that a similar fate awaits the Tarkaan.

As Lewis and many of his characters often point out, neither human life nor worlds nor universes are intended to last forever. They must all submit to death in order to be remade, free from sin and its consequent scarring. Everything good from the old creation will be preserved and perfected in the new. Though it would be marvelous in itself, the new will not simply be the old without flaws, but a new order of things beyond our present powers of imagination. The relation of the old to the new, in one of Lewis's common analogies, will be like that of a line incorporated into a square, the square incorporated into a cube, and the cube into a building with dimensions now unknown. The wisest of the Narnians knew it couldn't and shouldn't last. Jewel the Unicorn says to Jill, "'All worlds draw to an end, except Aslan's own country.'"[127] Lord Digory explains to Peter that the Narnia they had known "'was only a shadow or a copy of the real Narnia'" that had always been and will always be.[128] Turning to Lucy, Digory assures her: "'You need not mourn over Narnia, Lucy. All of the old Narnia that mattered, all the dear creatures, have been drawn into the real Narnia through the Door. And of course it is different; as different as a real thing is from a shadow or as waking life is from a dream. . . . It's all in Plato, all in Plato: bless me, what *do* they teach them at these schools!'"[129]

Colin Manlove puts the topsy-turvy events of *The Last Battle* in the right perspective, showing how Aslan and his Father were never really out of control: "The larger idiom of the book is paradox and reversal. In trying to perpetrate a lie, the ape and the others 'call down' ultimate truth. By setting a false god in a stable, the ape serves to put a true one there. . . . In destroying Narnia, Aslan makes it far more real." Night turns to morning, and a world that had "a beginning and an end has become one which has always been here and always will be here . . . in Aslan's real world."[130]

After all the mighty contests of wit and weaponry, the battle belongs to the Lord. The Narnians' delivery this time is not from mortal enemies but from mortality itself. The denouement is more of a crescendo as Lewis unfurls one of the most soaring conclusions in literature, giving us the exhilaration rightly belonging to a vision of Heaven. Instead of retiring to mansions, the party of talking beasts and Narnian lords and ladies rush like the wind up sheer cliffs and waterfalls. Jewel the Unicorn, on arriving in Aslan's country, proclaims what all are feeling: "'I have come home at last! This is my real country! I belong here. This is the land I have been looking for all my life, though I never knew it till now. The reason why we loved the old Narnia is that it sometimes looked a little like this.'"[131]

At the end of the world, the apostle Peter tells us, "the heavens will pass away with a roar, and the heavenly bodies will be burned up and dissolved."[132] So in Narnia, the stars are called home, the sun and moon extinguished, and the Narnian Peter at Aslan's command shuts forever the door of Heaven on the old world. But what sticks in everyone's imagination with perpetual delight is Lewis's vision of Aslan's country, the New Narnia or Heaven. Then "the earth trembled. The sweet air grew suddenly sweeter. A brightness flashed behind them. All turned. Tirian turned last because he was afraid. There stood his heart's desire, huge and real, the golden Lion, Aslan himself. . . . Tirian came near, and the Lion kissed him and said, 'Well done, last of the Kings of Narnia who stood firm at the darkest hour.'"[133]

The discoveries of the new place come at a fast pace. All look at the fruit growing profusely in the New Narnia, fruit so beautiful that everyone feels at first "it can't be meant for me." "'It's all right,' said Peter. 'I know what we're all thinking. But I'm sure, quite sure, we needn't. I've a feeling we've got to the country where everything is allowed.'"[134] The taste is so heavenly that even the best of former tastes are like "medicine" by comparison. Heaven, like Aslan's country, is the place where everything is allowed. Because sin has been banished and we love everything and everyone as we ought, there will be no impulse that needs restraint. "Love God and do what you want" will truly be the order of the day. Our earthly prayer "thy will be done" is reality in Heaven, which Lewis describes in a letter as "not merely submission" but enablement "to do God's will *as* (in the same way as) angels and blessed human spirits do it, with alacrity & delight like players in an orchestra responding spontaneously to the conductor."[135]

The more common expectations of Heaven are also met in Aslan's country. Edmund's sore knee is healed; Lord Digory no longer feels old or stiff. All the older people (in earthly years) have youthful vigor and hair no longer gray. All good-byes forever over, the characters from *The Last Battle* who enter the New Narnia are greeted by those who loved Aslan in earlier stories: parents; kings and queens of Narnia who had died (including the three Pevensie children of the first books); centaurs and the like; and talking animals, preeminently Reepicheep, who had traveled successfully to Aslan's country in *Voyage of the "Dawn Treader."* We have learned to love these characters and enter into one of the promised joys of Heaven: reunion with all we know who also love Jesus.

The new bodies match the New Narnia in wonder. Lewis unfolds a landscape breathtaking in its height, range, and beauty. As the company encourage each other with new discoveries and the cry of "further up and further in," they encounter gigantic waterfalls, which they swim up vertically at great speed, mountains higher than clouds they run up without loss of wind. They have come to the real Narnia, the real England, the heavenly original of all earthly shadows, of worlds within worlds. As with the stable, everything is bigger on the inside than the outside. In the exhilaration of discovery and physical virility, we lose the old fear that Heaven will be boring. But all of this wonder is instantly forgotten as "Aslan himself was coming, leaping down from cliff to cliff like a living cataract of power and beauty."[136] Lewis says of Aslan in the last paragraph that "He no longer looked to them like a lion."[137] Here we are gently nudged back to Aslan's original: Jesus, whose presence will be our deepest joy, the very definition of Heaven itself.

In earth every beauty is tinged with sorrow because we know it must decay or we must move on or die and leave it. Because they had had to leave Old Narnia so many times before, Lucy laments, "'We're so afraid of being sent away, Aslan.'" "'No fear of that,'" Aslan reassures them. And in a few words the sting of death, the fear of the unknown, is whisked away. "'Have you not guessed?' Their hearts leaped and a wild hope rose within them. 'There *was* a real railway accident,' said Aslan softly. 'Your father and mother and all of you are—as you used to call it in the Shadowlands—dead. The term is over: the holidays have begun. The dream is ended: this is the morning.'"[138]

The longing behind every story, that it might end "happily ever after," has its true fulfillment. On first arriving, Peter wonders that he is in Narnia, since Aslan has told him he was too old and would never come back. Lord Digory explains, "'Listen, Peter. When Aslan said you could never go back to Narnia, he meant the Narnia you were thinking of. But that was not the real Narnia. That had a beginning and an end. It was only a shadow or a copy of the real Narnia which has always been here and always will be here.'"[139] They have, as Jewel announced, "come home" to their "real country." In words we love to hear again and again: "For them it was only the beginning of the real story. All their life in this world and all their adventures in Narnia had only been the cover and the title page: now at last they were beginning Chapter One of the Great Story which no one on earth has read: which goes on forever: in which every chapter is better than the one before."[140]

7

WHEN SEEING IS
NOT BELIEVING:
Till We Have Faces

I am the bread of life; whoever comes to me shall not hunger, and whoever believes in me shall never thirst. But I said to you that you have seen me and yet do not believe.[1]

JESUS

The theme that runs like a golden thread through all of Lewis's work is longing. Lewis identified even in childhood a stab of desire for something beyond his reach that promised to open into vast, unexplored territories. It came to him through memories of fond experiences, through books, music, and beauty. In addition to *longing* and *desire*, Lewis sometimes used the German word for longing, *Sehnsucht*, but in the end settled for a term he found in Wordsworth: *Joy*. Confusingly, it does not mean, in this special sense, happiness or fulfillment, but quite the opposite. as Joy is not a "having" but a "wanting," though to have the longing is more desirable than any earthly satisfaction.

It was a mistake, Lewis came to see, to think that the longing was in the books or music or landscape. Pursue them, and they prove to be "cheats." They are only conduits of longing for another world: "acceptance by God . . . and welcome into the heart of things."[2] Any earthly good may enrich and give a momentary sense of satisfaction, but we always want something more. At their core, Joy and all other desires are for Heaven, signposts along the way to guide the pilgrim home.

When Lewis discovered that his deepest imaginative experiences were linked with what his intellect pushed him to acknowledge—that God in Christ is creator of all, source of the moral law and guarantor of our eternal home—he was profoundly converted to Christianity, heart and soul, body and mind, to the last fiber of his being.[3] He stopped his vain pursuit of Joy as an end in itself, but never stopped writing about it. Lewis's books are so magnetic because they either explain such things as Joy or, more often, set us to longing for them. Whether apologetically or imaginatively, his books are signposts to Heaven. The poet (and later friend) Ruth Pitter comments on Lewis's writing that "one's homesickness for Heaven finds at least an inn there; and it's an inn on the right road."[4]

Lewis's remythologizing reached its zenith in the novel *Till We Have Faces*, the book that Lewis and most critics judge his best. With wonderful irony, in using pagan myths to retell the Christian story, Lewis is demythologizing our stereotypes and remythologizing Christianity. To moderns, especially skeptics, agnostics, and atheists—but even Christians for whom familiarity has bred contempt or dulled wonder—the setting of classical myth puts us off our guard. It is yet another way of slipping "past the watchful dragons" of assumption and prejudice. This coupled with Orual as a skeptical narrator enables us, in turn, to enter into a world creatively operating at two levels simultaneously, pagan story and Christian story. The biblically uninformed reader will never know that this is the true Christian myth in another form because none of the names or precise events are given. For instance, Psyche, the Christ-figure, is not crucified, but she is chained to a tree, "tree" being a common alternate for the cross in Christian circles. The advantages of this approach are two: The person antagonistic to Christianity is imaginatively prepared for the Christian story by having an attractive model in mind, and the Christian will get a fresh view of old beliefs by interpreting the numerous biblical allusions and echoes.[5]

To discern what *Till We Have Faces* has to say about Heaven will require some interpretation of these symbols and allusions. This retelling of the Cupid and Psyche myth touches on our theme in these ways: longing for Heaven (Psyche directly and from childhood, Orual indirectly in her unwillingness to let go of questions about the gods); Psyche's heavenly habitation; the necessity of faith to gain Heaven; and the related theme of love.

Psyche (beautiful and spiritually attuned), along with her sisters Orual (ugly and intelligent) and Redival (lovely and vain), are daughters of the king of Glome. The book is cast as Orual's complaint against the gods for perversely hiding both their reality and will, and for taking Psyche from her as a sacrifice for the troubled city. This and the relationship between believing Psyche and doubting Orual is the focus of the novel. The local mystery religion centers around Ungit, who requires blood sacrifice and is represented by a shapeless but suggestive stone. The priests of Ungit determine that the city's disease and infertility will be appeased only by a perfect sacrifice and that Psyche is the one. She had gone through the city like a messiah, her touch bringing healing. The crowds bow before her, kiss her feet, and, as with Jesus, touch the edge of her robe. She is worshiped as Ungit incarnate. Then, also as with Jesus, in the space of a mere week, the crowd turns on her. Some townspeople die, problems persist, and the priest of Ungit lies deathly ill, for which they now blame Psyche. As parallels with Jesus multiply, the priest determines that Psyche must die.

Now we come back to Joy, in the sense of longing. Psyche is a willing sacrifice. From her earliest days, she has looked with longing to the Grey Mountain sacred to the gods. So with Lewis, the Castlereagh Hills of Northern Ireland seen from his childhood home, distant and "unattainable," taught him longing. From his first book as a Christian, the allegorical *Pilgrim's Regress*, to *Till We Have Faces*, the last work of fiction published in his lifetime, the image of mountains connected with longing is a central symbol. Think, for example, of Aslan's country in the unattainable mountains of Narnia—blessedly attained by Aslan's gift. Like Lewis himself, the child Psyche associates the distant mountains with her heart's desire. "Psyche, almost from the beginning (for she was a very quick, thinking child) was half in love with the Mountain. She made herself stories about it. 'When I'm big,' she said, 'I will be a great, great queen, married to the greatest king of all, and he will build me a castle of gold and amber up there on the very top.'"[6]

Psyche connects her longing with the divine and welcomes her role as sacrifice to the god of the mountains because it means also her marriage to him—recall the marriage feast of the Lamb promised in Revelation and Jesus' terming the church his bride. Psyche is not Pollyanna about what lies ahead: "it means death. Orual, you didn't think I was such a child as not to know that? How can I be the ransom for all Glome unless I die? And if I am to go to the god, of course it must be through death. That way, even what is strangest in the holy sayings might be true. To be eaten and to be married to the god might not be so different." Alluding to Greeks their teacher the Fox does not follow, Psyche believes in opposition "that death opens a door out of a little, dark room (that's all the life we have known before it) into a great, real place where the true sun shines."[7]

In the event, what Psyche longs for, she gets beyond her fondest imaginings. When Orual goes to find her remains or rescue her if living, she finds her sister robust in mind and body, basking in the love of her divine husband, relishing the soaring mansion and ambrosial food. Psyche invites Orual in, but she cannot enter this Heaven for two reasons. First, unbelief blinds Orual to the reality before her, just as it had the Dwarfs who were surrounded by Aslan's country (Heaven) in *The Last Battle* but would not acknowledge even the possibility of it for fear of being taken in. They had turned in upon themselves in a profound self-centeredness signified by their repeated motto, "The Dwarfs are for the Dwarfs."

Orual has brought her own Hell with her to the very threshold of Heaven. She cannot see the mansion, food, or noble dress of Psyche, but only the dirt, grass, and stones of the windswept mountainside. Those who want to see can; those who refuse to believe can't. As Augustine said, "Faith precedes understanding." Even the evidence Orual is given she explains away to suit her predetermined beliefs. From the beginning, the god is thought of from two radically different perspectives: Where the majority foresee only a devouring Shadowbrute (emblem of death), Psyche foresees the greatest King. Orual sees Psyche's sacrifice as death, devouring, and desecration, but Psyche, with the eyes of faith, sees new life, reality, and light.

As Michael Ward has pointed out, we find an excellent gloss on this truth in Lewis's "Five Sonnets":

> *Of this we're certain; no one who dared knock*
> *At heaven's door for earthly comfort found*
> *Even a door—only smooth, endless rock. . . .*

> *Pitch your demands heaven-high and they'll be met.*
> *Ask for the Morning Star and take (thrown in)*
> *Your earthly love. . . .*

> *If we once assent*
> *To Nature's voice, we shall be like the bee*
> *That booms against the window-pane for hours*
> *Thinking that way to reach the leaden flowers.*

"If we could speak to her," my doctor said,
"And told her, 'Not that way! All, all in vain
You weary out your wings and bruise your head,'
Might she not answer, buzzing at the pane,
'Let queens and mystics and religious bees
Talk of such inconceivables as glass;
The blunt lay worker flies at what she sees. . . .'
We catch her in a handkerchief (who knows
What rage she feels, what terror, what despair?)
And shake her out—and gaily out she goes
Where quivering flowers stand thick in summer air,
To drink their heart. But left to her own will
She would have died upon the window-sill."[8]

Until Orual opens herself to Heaven, she will puzzle hopelessly over things temporal and eternal. Even what is plain before her eyes, like the flowers beyond the window to the bee, will make no sense. *Why can Psyche see what I cannot? Is it even possible for things to be two ways at once? Is Psyche someplace where I cannot reach her, though I've held her in my arms, or is she mad?* On her way to salvation from this Hell of self-doubt and doubt about ultimate things, Orual reaches bottom, preferring to judge Psyche both mad and cruel, willing to kill Psyche and herself, rather than admit to the unthinkable reality beyond her grasp—but not, as she will learn, beyond gift. Indeed, believing is seeing.

The second reason Orual could not enter Heaven is that, as Lewis says in the Preface to *The Great Divorce*, you can't take even the least bit of Hell into Heaven, and Orual was hanging onto the Hell of perverted and selfish "love" for Psyche.[9] Orual is like the wife of Robert and like Pam, the mother of Michael, both characters in *The Great Divorce*, who would rather have their husband and son in Hell where they could dominate them with a devouring "love" than to change themselves and enter Heaven.[10] Orual would rather have Psyche in her constricted world than to share Psyche's love with her husband. She can't believe what Psyche claims, that loving the god first, she actually loves Orual even more. Throughout Lewis's work and as the primary theme of *The Four Loves*, we find the principle of ordinate loves, that loving God first and everything in its priority below that results in loving everything more than if you loved the lesser thing or person exclusively. Conversely, love anything before God and it turns into an idol and a demon that will destroy you. This line from *The Great Divorce* sums up the core truth aptly: "There is but one good; that is God. Everything else is good when it looks to Him and bad when it turns from Him."

Here is one of many such statements that belie the selfishness that Orual passes off as love: "She [Psyche] made me, in a way, angry. I would have died for her (this, at least, I know is true) and yet, the night before her death, I could feel anger. . . . The parting between her and me seemed to cost her so little."[11] A little later Orual can say of the gods, blaming them for her own projection, "finding me heart-shattered for Psyche's sake, they made it the common burden of all my fantasies that Psyche was my greatest enemy. All my sense of intolerable wrong was directed against her. It was she who hated me; it was on her that I wanted to be revenged."[12] This hardened into "a settled sense of some great injury that Psyche had done me, though I could not gather my wits to think what it was. They say I lay for hours saying, 'Cruel girl. Cruel Psyche. Her heart is of stone.'"[13]

The solution for Orual is radical and profound, as it is for us all. After she has her day in court with the gods and ends up self-condemned, her eyes are opened, and she repents her soul-consuming self-centeredness. "Die before you die," she concludes in words reminiscent of Jesus' words in the Gospel of John: "unless a grain of wheat falls into the earth and dies, it remains alone; but if it dies, it bears much fruit. Whoever loves his life loses it, and whoever hates his life in this world will keep it for eternal life."[14] This point of release does not come for Orual without great struggle and her own demythologizing, and a great sacrifice from Psyche, who leaves her own Heaven for Orual's sake and rescues her from the Law in the form of tasks impossible for her but easy for Pysche. Orual doesn't deserve it and can't achieve it: It is grace.

In her greedy, possessive love, Orual had sabotaged her own true identity, symbolized by the veil she wears to hide her ugliness. Her grotesqueness was to her at first only outer, but later she discovered it to be truly on the inside also. It is God's desire to give us our true selves, which only he can do. The process culminates in Heaven, but begins here on earth, as indeed it must, as the only place we can "die before we die." In the symbolism of the novel, Orual says, "I saw well why the gods do not speak to us openly, nor let us answer. Till that word can be dug out of us, why should they hear the babble that we think we mean? How can they meet us face to face till we have faces?"[15] Orual's words to Psyche near the end bespeak her healing: "'Oh Psyche, oh goddess,' I said. 'Never again will I call you mine; but all there is of me shall be yours. . . . I never wished you well, never had one selfless thought of you. I was a craver."[16] She has passed from need-love to gift-love, and this, Lewis has said, is the very pattern of Heaven, where everyone gives and, therefore, everyone receives. Now that Orual's soul is healed, she has ordinate loves. "Though I loved her [Psyche] as I would once have thought it impossible to love, . . . if she counted (and oh, gloriously she did) it was for another's sake. . . . And he was coming. The most dreadful, the most beautiful, the only dread and beauty there is, was coming."[17] Orual has learned to love God first, and her reward is the Beatific Vision—to see God face to face.

HELL

PART I

DEMYTHOLOGIZING HELL:

THE NONFICTION

8

THE MYTHS OF HELL EXPOSED

"O Jerusalem, Jerusalem, the city that kills the prophets and stones those who are sent to it! How often would I have gathered your children together as a hen gathers her brood under her wings, and you would not!"[1]

JESUS

MYTH #1: A GOOD GOD WOULDN'T SEND ANYONE TO HELL

I willingly believe that the damned are, in one sense, successful, rebels to the end; that the doors of hell are locked on the inside.[2]

—C.S. LEWIS

"Hell," alas, like "God" (as in the loathsome phrase, "O, my God"), has largely become a figure of speech, a convenient way of letting people know we wish them ill. As for Hell as a literal place, an eternal destination for those disapproved by God, it is dreadfully out of fashion. Even though two-thirds of Americans "believe in hell and the devil, hardly anybody expects that they will go to hell themselves."[3] In most minds, Hell is only a place where the Hitlers of the world go. Apparently, not many believe Jesus' warning: "The gate is wide and the way is easy that leads to destruction, and those who enter by it are many. For the gate is narrow and the way is hard that leads to life, and those who find it are few."[4] The thought of such destruction as Jesus described in very grim terms is apparently too painful for many to consider seriously.

Hell, though not a pleasant subject, is a necessary and instructive one. We surely agree with Lewis when he says of Hell, "there is no doctrine which I would more willingly remove from Christianity than this, if it lay in my power. . . . I would pay any price to be able to say truthfully 'All will be saved.'"[5] But neither Lewis nor anyone else who takes the Bible seriously can sidestep the issue because the authority for its existence is Jesus himself, creator of all that is and our exclusive hope for Heaven. As has often been pointed out, Jesus had more to say about Hell than about Heaven.[6] That is because Hell is the human default: It is where we go unless we deliberately turn off that road onto the only other alternative. Why should this be so when Heaven is what we were created for and the only place where we are fully ourselves?

As Lewis states in *The Problem of Pain*, if it were simply an issue of "assigning" selected people to Hell, we would have not the Christian problem, but the Muslim. Christianity presents a more complex claim: "a God so full of mercy that He becomes man and dies by torture to avert that final ruin from His creature, and who yet, where that heroic remedy fails, seems unwilling, or even unable, to arrest the ruin by an act of mere power. . . . So much mercy, yet still there is Hell."[7] Why? Attempts to answer this question are scattered through the remaining sections on Myths of Hell, but the short answer to "Why Hell?" is sin—because "the wages of sin is death," which is separation from God, which is Hell. For Lewis, the issue turns on free will. If our greatest good consists of freely surrendering ourselves to God, he cannot without contradiction make us choose him. If human beings have choice, and Heaven is the presence of God, then Hell must exist by definition as the place apart from God.

Lewis asks us to imagine a man who lives a dissolute life, relishing evil to the end and mocking goodness: Perhaps such persons as Paul describes in Romans chapter 1 who have lived so long in cruelty and debauchery, suppressing the truth, that their minds have come under the judgment of a deadened conscience. They no longer know right from wrong. Over such hangs the awful, thrice-repeated pronouncement, "God gave them up." Given what he has become, justice demands that such a person should not continue in perverted happiness and forever think he's had the last laugh. Lewis asserts that "a truly ethical demand" requires that a flag of truth be planted in his soul, that the man come to acknowledge evil as evil, to know he is wrong.[8]

The question is not whether God will forgive. There is no evil, even crucifying the Lord of life, which will not be forgiven, but the sin must be acknowledged, and the sinner must repent. Otherwise, says Lewis, God is merely asked to condone the sin, which he cannot do. Neither evil nor goodness are arbitrary rules laid down by a capricious God. They cannot be waived as though they don't really matter, because goodness and morality flow out of the character of God. All that opposes that character is evil. To overlook sin would require God not to be God. This is the meaning of the cross: Our own sin could not be overlooked. It had to be repented and paid for when we were in a state of bankruptcy.

For those who will not accept the payment, who "love darkness rather than light," the pains of Hell, whatever they be, bring the clarity that darkness is not light, evil is evil. If we balk at the idea of either Heaven or Hell, it is because we fail to see the character of God in its grandeur, trivializing both his holiness and the sin that cannot live in his presence.

The danger in choosing such a stark case is thinking ourselves safe because "I'm not anywhere near as bad as all that; at worst, I only want to be left alone." This ignores our elemental nature as creatures. We were created for a relationship with God. We can see this pictured in children who are dependent on us for life, whatever they may say or think. To leave an infant alone is to kill it. So with us. Separated from God, we die, both physically and spiritually.

We may change the perspective without violence to the concept of judgment, Lewis suggests, and see damnation as a person being what he has chosen to be. "He has his wish—to live wholly in the self and to make the best of what he finds there. And what he finds there is Hell."[9] Lewis also reminds us that there are degrees of punishment in Hell, just as there are degrees of reward in Heaven. An all-knowing God can determine how much and what kind of pain will "plant the flag of truth." Or, if we prefer, we may think of even the degree of punishment as self-inflicted by the hardness of the heart.

Another common complaint against the biblical view of Hell is that temporal sin does not merit eternal punishment. Lewis suggests several useful ways of thinking about this issue. For one, it doesn't require a very profound faith to think that an omniscient God knows whether or not more time will make a difference to a person's choice. If an evil person were given a million years, he may be all the worse and subject to greater judgment. Lewis believes that if more time or second or multiple chances would do any good, they would be given.

Similarly, we only know one way to think about time: as a succession of moments stacked one on another in linear fashion. But what if time in the hereafter is thick as well as long? We think of destruction as an end, but it may be in some sense a beginning. "That the lost soul is eternally fixed in its diabolical attitude we cannot doubt: but whether this eternal fixity implies endless duration—or duration at all—we cannot say."[10] May not the punishment of the damned be experienced as a moment, perhaps a perpetual moment? When we come to eternal matters, our categories quickly fail us.

All this said, Hell is still "a detestable doctrine." That is why God spared no price in purchasing our salvation. The extent of his love and the depth of the sacrifice will take all eternity to explore. Lewis helps us begin to understand it in *The Four Loves*:

> He creates the universe, already foreseeing—or should we say "seeing"? there are no tenses in God—the buzzing cloud of flies about the cross, the flayed back pressed against the uneven stake, the nails driven through the mesial nerves, the repeated torture of back and arms as it is time after time, for breath's sake, hitched up. If I may dare the biological image, God is a "host" who deliberately creates His own parasites; causes us to be that we may exploit and "take advantage of" Him. Herein is love. This is the diagram of Love Himself, the inventor of all loves.[11]

And when we look to ourselves as the recipients of that love, we see that "God loves us; not because we are loveable but because He is love, not because he needs to receive but because He delights to give."[12] Lewis believed "the detestable doctrine." He had found in his own heart such as would suit him for Hell. When he looked within, he found what we all find. As related in his autobiography, "for the first time I examined myself with a seriously practical purpose. And there I found what appalled me; a zoo of lusts, a bedlam of ambitions, a nursery of fears, a harem of fondled hatreds. My name was legion."[13]

"Legion" not only means a large number, but alludes to a man who called himself "Legion," possessed of many demons and delivered by Jesus.[14] After healing him, Jesus commanded him: "Go home to your friends and tell them how much the Lord has done for you, and how he has had mercy on you." Lewis knew the judgment he was under. He had received mercy and spent the rest of his life laboring to tell others. He would have preferred a stay-at-home life of books and friends, but he delivered on the radio the talks that would come to be known as *Mere Christianity*; wrote books for those who were, as he had been, skeptics; carried on a massive daily correspondence with inquirers after faith, though the task was physically painful (due to a thumb defect) and emotionally draining; and traveled far and wide to speak to the Royal Air Force about hope and deliverance from "the detestable doctrine." Such deeds are the most charitable thing one person can do for another.

MYTH #2: A PHYSICAL HELL WOULD BE CRUEL

God in His mercy made
The fixed pains of Hell.[15]
—C. S. LEWIS

When Lewis was an atheist, he was also a materialist and annihilationist, believing that the mind and personality died with the body, and nothing else survived. While this idea terrifies some, as it did Samuel Johnson, for example, it was great comfort to Lewis. As he says in his spiritual autobiography, *Surprised by Joy*, he wanted more than anything else to be in control of his destiny and most of all not to be interfered with. He took comfort in believing that if life got to be too much for him, suicide was always the ultimate escape. Many are taking a similar comfort in our generation. Even in Christian quarters, some high-profile theologians are embracing a Christian version of annihilationism, claiming that the soul of the lost is destroyed in Hell. This solves the problem of a God cruelly punishing the lost forever. It also salves some consciences about not evangelizing those who haven't heard the gospel.

But we are back again to the issue of biblical authority. In analyzing what Scripture has to say about the fate of the damned, Lewis cautions against confusing the doctrine of Hell with the symbols used to characterize it. He notes that Jesus uses three symbols: "punishment"; "destruction"; and "privation, exclusion and banishment," along with the "prevalent image of fire."[16] The problem with the annihilationist view is in ignoring the other symbols. In looking for an interpretation that takes into account the obvious horror Jesus intends and yet accommodating all of the images, Lewis reaches for an analogy. When we burn a log, we don't get nothing; rather, we get heat, gases, and ash. To be these three things means "*to have been* a log." Similarly, what is cast into Hell is "remains," something subhuman, infinitely less than its created potential, excluded from its "natural" state in Heaven. "The saved go to a place prepared for *them*, while the damned go to a place never made for men at all.[17] To enter heaven is to become more human than you ever succeeded in being in earth; to enter hell, is to be banished from humanity. What is cast (or casts itself) into hell is not a man: it is 'remains.'"[18]

But Lewis is not content to give pleasure and pain the last word. Even if the damned suffered no pain as we know it and lived with such dark pleasures as the damned enjoy, if these were presented to someone in Heaven, the response would be to run the other way in horror. And if the pleasures of Heaven were to be offered the damned, they would likewise recoil. Lewis quotes a saying, "'hell is hell, not from its own point of view, but from the heavenly point of view.'" Perhaps "it is only to the damned that their fate could ever seem less than unendurable."[19] As Lewis observes in a letter to his brother, "even here on earth there seem to be two kinds of people: not just the happy and the unhappy, but . . . those who *like* happiness and those who, odd as it seems, really don't."[20] Lewis thinks it will be the same way between those in Heaven and those in Hell.

Lewis has another important perspective on pain in a physical Hell. We have seen in the previous chapter that justice demands Hell. It may be surprising to hear that mercy demands it, too. One of the best answers to the charge that God would be cruel and unloving to create a place like Hell comes in the very first book Lewis wrote after becoming a Christian, *The Pilgrim's Regress*. In this allegory the fictional traveler, John, wrestles with the character and deeds of the Landlord (God), who has created a "black hole" (Hell) for those who reject him. John asks his Guide how "anyone can refute the charge of cruelty" aimed at the Landlord. The Guide explains that this common slander of the Landlord's enemies is easily refuted. The stronger charge would be to call him a gambler, since he takes the risk of giving his tenants freedom to choose. The only alternative would be to make them slaves, restraining them from going into places where they might eat forbidden fruit (here the "mountain-apple"). The Guide explains:

> "A man can go on eating mountain-apple so long that *nothing* will cure his craving for it: and the very worms it breeds inside him will make him more certain to eat more. You must not try to fix the point after which a return is impossible, but you can see that there will be such a point somewhere."
>
> "But surely the Landlord can do anything?"
>
> "He cannot do what is contradictory: or, in other words, a meaningless sentence will not gain meaning simply because someone chooses to prefix to it the words 'the Landlord can.' And it is meaningless to talk of forcing a man to do freely what a man has freely made impossible for himself."[21]

The only thing the Landlord can do for those who have finally rejected him in favor of sin is to stop the proliferation of sin. "Evil is fissiparous": that is, it produces ever more evil in an endless cycle, for "Form and Limit belong to the good."[22] Left alone, the godless would find no black hole—only bottomless and wall-less evil, the darkness that God did not create that was already present in the evil heart. It "could never in a thousand eternities find any way to arrest its own reproductions' of evil.[23] The black hole, or "the fixed pains of hell," are the last and only remaining mercy God may bestow on them.[24] Hell was created as a "tourniquet on the wound through which the lost soul else would bleed to a death she never reached."[25] And, finally, we know that even on earth physical pain can be so debilitating that it would stop even the strongest urge to harm another. It may be that the physical pains of Hell further limit evil from reaching others. There would be no good person, no advocate for the wronged. All that is good will have been garnered into Heaven.

MYTH #3: HELL IS JUST A STATE OF MIND

The mind is its own place, and in itself
Can make a Heaven of Hell, a Hell of Heaven.[26]
—MILTON

For those who might wish to take comfort in thinking of Hell as a mental state only, Lewis wonders if they know what they are asking for. In the dream-journey fantasy *The Great Divorce*, Lewis's inquiring traveler misunderstands his guide, MacDonald, who says that those in Heaven will remember earth as part of Heaven, while those in Hell will remember earthly experience as part of Hell. The traveler questions whether both are states of mind. He is rebuked for blaspheming when saying such a thing about Heaven, which is Reality itself, the earth only Shadowlands by comparison. But about Hell, MacDonald has a different view: "'Hell is a state of mind—ye never said a truer word. And every state of mind, left to itself, every shutting up of the creature within the dungeon of its own mind—is, in the end, Hell. But Heaven is not a state of mind. Heaven is reality itself. All that is fully real is Heavenly.'"[27]

As we have seen, "God in His mercy made/The fixed pains of Hell" to staunch the flow of evil. In a letter to his lifelong friend and correspondent Arthur Greeves, we find another kind of mercy in a physical Hell:

About Hell. All I have ever said is that the N.T. [New Testament] plainly implies the possibility of some being finally left in "the outer darkness." Whether this means (horror of horror) being left to a purely *mental* existence, left with nothing at all but one's own envy, prurience, resentment, loneliness & self conceit, or whether there is still a world or a reality, I wd. [would] never pretend to know. But I wouldn't put the question in the form "do I believe in an *actual* Hell." One's own mind is actual enough. If it doesn't seem fully actual *now* that is because you can always escape from it a bit into the physical world—look out of the window, smoke a cigarette, go to sleep. But when there is nothing for you *but* your own mind (no body to go to sleep, no books or landscape, no sounds, no drugs) it will be as actual as—as—well, as a coffin is actual to a man buried alive.[28]

T. S. Eliot agrees, in this characterization of Hell from *The Cocktail Party*:

> *What is Hell? Hell is oneself,*
> *Hell is alone, the other figures in it*
> *Merely projections. There is nothing to escape from*
> *And nothing to escape to. One is always alone.*[29]

If, as Lewis and Eliot suggest, Hell is largely within, a condition of the spirit that infects the mind and personality, it would be no mercy to be consigned to a bodiless, mental Hell. It may be a question of which ward of the hospital you prefer. Anyone who has had a serious look at the dark reaches of the psych ward would take the trauma ward for escape in a heartbeat. If Hell is a physical place, which is the plain implication of Jesus' words, then we may be as sure of his mercy as of his wisdom and justice, even in that.

MYTH #4: ALL THE INTERESTING PEOPLE WILL BE IN HELL

As for the cowardly, the faithless, the detestable, as for murderers, the sexually immoral, sorcerers, idolaters, and all liars, their portion will be in the lake that burns with fire and sulfur, which is the second death.

—REVELATION[30]

From George Bernard Shaw, Oscar Wilde, and Groucho Marx to more contemporary comedians, we have heard the rationalizing quip that Hell is where the fun is, with all the really interesting people. This has some of zip of stolen pleasure in it, but we know that this sort of pleasure is a barbed hook and a cheat. So it is with the imagined social life of the "liberated" in Hell, where righteousness quells no libido. Even a moment's thought unveils the greed and self-centeredness behind lust, for example. Since Hell is the place where human potential is dried up—a place filled with remains of what were once humans but are now mere shells or ghosts, if you like—it is the last place to seek companionship. Sprinkled throughout Lewis's work, we find characters who typify the constriction into self and sin that is Hell. We will see Hell imagined in its true colors in the consideration of fictional pieces to follow. A few snapshots will give the right hue to our consideration here.

Think of *The Great Divorce* where the occupants of Hell are forever moving farther out because they can't get along. Clarence Dye explains Lewis's notion aptly: "His concept of hell is the total alienation of man from God, nature and his fellow man. And this is dramatically portrayed by this image of hell . . . as individuals frantically trying not to be neighbors."[31]

In *Perelandra* the possessed Weston, so unlike a human that he is called the Un-man, descends to unspeakably childish banality, endlessly calling Ransom's name, responding to each reply with "Nothing." From *That Hideous Strength*, the very names of Wither and Frost belie their lost humanity. When there is intelligence, it is always warped and in the service of evil, doing someone in. For these early deconstructionists, even language becomes a tool for confusing and manipulating, not for communication and truth. It is all politics and savage abuses of power with this lot. To end up in Hell with these and with Screwtape, Jadis the White Witch, Rishda, and Shift would be to enter a nightmare without the hope of waking. Jean-Paul Sartre in his play *Huis Clos* is closer to the truth than G. B. Shaw when he says, "Hell is other people."[32] But actually Hell is much worse than even the company of the damned suggests. It is having no company at all. It is, as Harry Blamires suggests, "the self, the confined, invulnerable, incommunicable, inescapable self."[33]

Satan gives us the supreme example of created potential shriveling into boredom. He was the archangel Lucifer, second only to God before his own fall. Lewis analyzes his constriction in his study of Milton's *Paradise Lost* and contrasts him with the newly created Adam:

Adam, though locally confined to a small park on a small planet, has interests that embrace "all the choir of heaven and all the furniture of earth." Satan has been in the Heaven of Heavens and in the abyss of Hell, and surveyed all that lies between them, and in that whole immensity has found only one thing that interests Satan. It may be said that Adam's situation made it easier for him, than for Satan, to let his mind roam. But that is just the point. Satan's monomaniac concern with himself and his supposed rights and wrongs is a necessity of the Satanic predicament. Certainly, he has no choice. He has chosen to have no choice. He has wished to "be himself," and to be in himself and for himself, and his wish has been granted. The Hell he carries with him is, in one sense, a Hell of infinite boredom. . . . Satan *wants* to go on being Satan. That is the real meaning of his choice "Better to reign in Hell, than serve in Heav'n."[34]

God could not be just or good without punishing evil, if we take punishment to mean in any way exclusion from Heaven. If he allowed people with evil bents to run free in his Kingdom, then Heaven itself would cease to be good.[35] Because evil descends to the banal and self-centered, Hell is monotonous. Heaven, where each person forever grows into the distinct personality God designed for unique and ever-expanding roles, is the place with all the interesting personalities. To explore the mind of our Creator, who knows the history and future path of the electrons at the farthest reach of the cosmos and numbers the particles of plankton strained through the baleens of every whale and guides the flight of every comet—*that* will be interesting company.

MYTH #5: A TOLERANT GOD WOULD LET ME CHOOSE

Choose this day whom you will serve.[36]

—JOSHUA

If desire or longing is the golden theme in Lewis's work, choice is the silver. If the character of God and the sacrifice of Christ are the bedrock of his thinking on Heaven and Hell, God-given human freedom of choice is the superstructure. Lewis reasons that if the ultimate happiness of created beings comes from the willing surrender of the self to God, then the will must be free. If we have free will, it must be possible for us to reject God. In *The Great Divorce*, the narrator's heavenly guide, MacDonald, instructs him:

There are only two kinds of people in the end: those who say to God, "Thy will be done," and those to whom God says, in the end, "*Thy* will be done." All that are in Hell, choose it. Without that self-choice there could be no Hell. No soul that seriously and constantly desires joy will ever miss it. Those who seek find. To those who knock it is opened.[37]

MacDonald checks the narrator's alarm at inferring that all human actions are predetermined, by challenging his time-bound logic. You can't understand eternal verities, he asserts, from within the framework of time—the only lens we have for viewing eternity. The danger of making the logical leap from within time is that it destroys our understanding of free will. From where we reside in time, we can't sort out how our actions and God's actions both freely consort. Reformed theology is vibrant and thriving in Christian academic circles, and many from this camp are uncomfortable shifting the focus from God's sovereignty to an Arminian emphasis such as Lewis's.[38] But Lewis does not reject predestination per se and certainly not God's sovereignty. What he rejects is a definition so narrow that it excludes human choice. Any honest reading of the Bible must acknowledge that God's sovereignty and human choice exist side by side in the same biblical books, even the same sentences.

In the end, we are in the same situation as with the Trinity: God is one and at the same time Father, Son, and Holy Spirit. All analogies fail us, and we must confess that our minds are finite and will not comprehend very much of the infinite. Lewis's major contribution to resolving the paradox is in asserting God's independence from time. To God, all times are always present, including our past and future. He *sees* (present tense) us choosing next year and next decade and so on to the end of earthly time. He therefore takes every choice into account from the foundation of the world. This resolves the problem some have with God answering millions of prayers at once and giving an answer tomorrow that involves events set in motion six months ago. Space and time are, like humanity itself, God's creation, and he is not trapped inside his creation.[39]

Lewis portrays the coexistence of sovereignty and choice dramatically in *Perelandra* when Ransom must decide whether God has ordained that he fight the Un-man hand to hand and whether he has a choice in the matter. "The whole distinction between things accidental and things designed, like the distinction between fact and myth, was purely terrestrial."[40] Ransom realized that the pattern was so large that he could only see bits of it with his own eyes. In language reminiscent of Lewis's conversion to Christianity after a long struggle, Ransom's final choice has little emotion: "Without any apparent movement of the will, as objective and unemotional as the reading on a dial, there had arisen before him, with perfect certitude, the knowledge 'about this time tomorrow you will have done the impossible.'" God's will or man's? "You might say, if you liked, that the power of choice had been simply set aside and an inflexible destiny substituted for it. On the other hand, you might say that he had [been] delivered from the rhetoric of his passions and had emerged into unassailable freedom. Ransom could not for the life of him, see any difference between these two statements. Predestination and freedom were apparently identical. He could no longer see any meaning in the many arguments he had heard on this subject."[41]

The importance of this belief to Lewis in thinking about Heaven and Hell cannot be overstated. He sees, of course, that we can talk of God judging and sending people to Hell. Lewis would not argue against that. But in explaining why God would make such a judgment, Lewis shifts the focus to human choice. Earlier, we talked about the logical sequence Lewis laid out in *The Problem of Pain* and *Mere Christianity*. God loves his human creations and wants a relationship with them. If God were to force our response, he would effectively make robots of us. By definition, love, in any way we understand it, involves free selves making choices. We use terms like rape and lust for forced "intimacy," never love. Anyone who makes such unloving demands is sick. God's willing sacrifice to win us is such that no one will ever plumb the depths of divine humility, but he cannot in his nature force us. This, to Lewis, is one of the most astonishing of God's miracles: making creatures with free wills who are independent of himself and may even reject him.

Our only good, the hope of fulfilling our personalities and eternal destinies, requires submission of our will to his. If we do not, we are forever separated from him by our own choice. It makes no difference whether we live good lives in the eyes of others. Heaven is by definition connection to life in God through Christ. It will make no difference what we have put before him if we do not put him first. He cannot bless what we do not give him; therefore, in love, he demands all. "To be a complete man means to have the passions obedient to the will and the will offered to God: to *have been* a man—to be an ex-man or 'damned ghost'—would presumably mean to consist of a will utterly centered in its self and passions utterly uncontrolled by the will."[42] In Lewis's view, and surely this is true, those in Hell choose it, by whatever name they call the choice that excludes God or whatever else they put ahead of him.

For this reason, not to mention biblical authority, Lewis rejects universalism, the belief that all will be saved in the end. Lewis owed and acknowledged a great spiritual, imaginative, and intellectual debt to George MacDonald, whose books nourished and mentored him from age sixteen on. But Lewis did not agree with him at all points. He has MacDonald (a universalist in real life) reject in *The Great Divorce* the idea that all will be saved in the end. If God overrules human choice to the extent that all will be saved whether they will or no, we are stuck with the same problem, the impossibility of love. In *The Pilgrim's Regress* Lewis sounds the theme of choice: God "has taken the risk of working the country with free tenants instead of slaves in chain gangs: and as they are free there is no way of making it impossible for them to go into forbidden places and eat forbidden fruits."[43]

The process of choosing is the business of a lifetime, and the individual choices of a day or even a whole year may seem insignificant. That's the way the Devil likes it, as Screwtape advises his apprentice tempter. Time can be an ally of Hell:

> The long, dull, monotonous years of middle-aged prosperity or middle-aged adversity are excellent campaigning weather. . . . Prosperity knits a man to the World. He feels that he is "finding his place in it," while really it is finding its place in him. His increasing reputation, his widening circle of acquaintances, his sense of importance, the growing pressure of absorbing and agreeable work, build up in him a sense of being really at home on Earth, which is just what we want. You will notice that the young are generally less unwilling to die than the middle-aged and the old.
>
> The truth is that the Enemy, having oddly destined these mere animals to life in His own eternal world, has guarded them pretty effectively from the danger of feeling at home anywhere else. That is why we must often wish long life to our patients; seventy years is not a day too much for the difficult task of unraveling their souls from Heaven and building up a firm attachment to Earth.[44]

Lewis's fiction is full of characters making choices that determine their destiny. They range from the starkly evil, like Weston and Wither, to the green professional like Mark Studdock in *That Hideous Strength*, who is seduced nearly to his ruin by the desire to be an insider at work and in a daring new social experiment. Whatever form the temptation away from God may take, it is always a means of choosing something for self over

God, and at its heart choosing self and choosing Hell are synonymous. Wanting to be God (or our own god) is the root of all evil. The mature sorn Augray, in *Out of the Silent Planet*, explains to younger sorns that the cause of sin on earth is that "every one of them wants to be a little Oyarsa [ruler of a world] himself."[45]

Sometimes we get a glimpse of damnation in characters who have made wrong choices for so long that the cry of conscience and longing for God have died. Here are two examples, one early and one late. In *Out of the Silent Planet*, the Oyarsa of Malacandra, speaking of Satan, says:

> He has left you [Weston] this one [lesser law of loyalty to one's kind] because a bent *hnau* [creature with a soul] can do more evil than a broken one. He has only bent you; but this thin One who sits on the ground [Devine] he has broken, for he has left him nothing but greed. He is now only a talking animal and in my world he could do no more evil than an animal. If he were mine I would unmake his body for the *hnau* in it is already dead. But if you were mine I would try to cure you.[46]

For a later example, Aslan says in *The Magician's Nephew* that he can't help Uncle Andrew, whom he calls "an old sinner," nor can he comfort him because Uncle Andrew "has made himself unable to hear my voice. If I spoke to him, he would hear only growlings and roarings. Oh Adam's sons, how cleverly you defend yourselves against all that might do you good!"[47] Uncle Andrew has muffled the voice of conscience so long that he is now deaf to it and no longer discerns good from evil. His mind is darkened. He is damned. The only thing Aslan can do for him in all his store of mercy is put him to sleep.[48] Richard Cunningham observes that this condition, perhaps rare on earth, is the rule in Hell: "Their wills are so fixed inward that a second chance after death would be of no avail."[49]

There is, of course, a solemn warning in this. It is human nature to rationalize sin. In fact, the principle of cognitive dissonance demands it. We cannot live comfortably with a discrepancy between what we believe and what we do; therefore, we must justify what we do to be easy with our conscience. Put another way, we pervert good into evil, evil into good. Every bad choice, however small, is telling. Richard Cunningham sums up the principle and the stakes this way: "One's future state is only a mimicry of choices made on earth—which is the beginning of heaven or hell—and is an eternal attainment of his earthly desires."[50] In *God in the Dock*, Lewis cautions: You may "be sure there is something inside you which, unless it is altered, will put it out of God's power to prevent your being eternally miserable. While that something remains there can be no Heaven for you, just as there can be no sweet smells for a man with a cold in the nose, and no music for a man who is deaf. It's not a question of God 'sending' us to Hell. In each of us there is something growing up which will of itself *be Hell* unless it is nipped in the bud. The matter is serious: let us put ourselves in His hands at once—this very day, this hour."[51]

In a very poignant poem, Lewis reflects on the knife-edge of decision on which eternity may hinge:

> *Nearly they stood who fall;*
> *Themselves as they look back*
> *See always in the track*
> *The one false step, where all*
> *Even yet, by lightest swerve*
> *Of foot not yet enslaved,*
> *By smallest tremor of the smallest nerve,*
> *Might have been saved.*
>
> *Nearly they fell who stand. . . .*
> *The choice of ways so small, the event so great. . . .*
>
> *Therefore, oh man, have fear*
> *Lest oldest fears be true,*
> *Lest thou too far pursue*
> *The road that seems so clear,*
> *And step, secure, a hair's*
> *Breadth past the hair-breadth bourn,*
> *Which, being once crossed forever unawares,*
> *Denies return.*[52]

MYTH #6: NO ONE COULD BE HAPPY IN HEAVEN KNOWING SOME ARE IN HELL

He [God] will wipe away every tear from their eyes, . . . neither shall there be mourning nor crying nor pain anymore, for the former things have passed away.[53]

—REVELATION

Lewis's best answer to the objection that no one could be perfectly or justly happy in Heaven knowing some were in Hell, especially if our loved ones are among them, appears in *The Great Divorce*. The scene at issue involves a woman named Sarah Smith and her husband, Frank. Sarah, now glorious in her resurrection body, comes from Heaven to its threshold to meet Frank, who has come up from Hell. The wise guide, MacDonald, explains to the watching narrator that "already there is joy enough in the little finger of a great saint such as yonder lady to waken all the dead things of the universe into life."[54] She is Sarah Smith from Golders Green, which is like saying Jane Doe from the slums, a "nobody" by the world's standards, but a "saint" by Heaven's, and in appearance, a goddess to the narrator.

Next, the narrator sees a figure looking like a "Tragedian" in a bad play, holding a string as though he had an "organ-grinder's" monkey on the end. The monkey turns out to be Frank, and the Tragedian a projection of his besetting sin, pity. By pity Frank manipulated everyone around him in his earthly life, striking the pose of a man injured or about to be injured by another's words or acts. The Tragedian is large and Frank a small ghost because there is more sinful pity than human soul by now. Though Sarah addresses Frank directly, he is so fully controlled by his sin that the Tragedian does his speaking for him. Frank has come to the edge of Heaven only to enjoy the self-gratifying feeling of having been missed and to see Sarah's misery at her loneliness. He discovers that there are no needs in Heaven and that Sarah has now learned what love really is because she is "in Love Himself," that is, in Christ.

When she says her love for him on earth was mostly the need to be loved, though having some of the real thing, she only says what is true of all of us, but for Frank it is another opportunity to wallow in his hurt feelings. He announces that he had rather see her dead at his feet than to hear he is not needed. All the while "merriment danced in her eyes," and joy poured from her countenance. To Frank's surprise and dismay, she is cheerful throughout the conversation in which she attempts to persuade him to give up his manipulating ways long enough to think of something besides himself and thereby move toward Heaven. She speaks of the joy she has entered and exudes, and issues an invitation for him to join her. Frank prefers the misery of his pet sin to abandoning it for the fullness of joy. In the end, the Ghost disappears, and only the Tragedian sulks back to Hell; he becomes the sin he has chosen.

To the narrator's surprise, Sarah goes rejoicing on her way, singing a psalm of praise to God, who "fills her brim full with immensity of life" and "leads her to see the world's desire."[55] The narrator, as usual, asks his guide the question that brews in our own minds: How is it possible that she could be happy when her husband languishes forever in Hell? MacDonald, giving always Lewis's view, distinguishes the "action of Pity," which is ever ready to sacrifice for another's good and is eternal, and the "passion of pity," which is used as a weapon to blackmail others for supposed personal gain. Such passions have led statesmen to betray their countries and women to give up their virginity. This weapon, used by the evil against the good, "will be broken."[56] Hell will not be allowed to blackmail Heaven. "Every disease that submits to a cure shall be cured: but we will not call blue yellow to please those who insist on still having jaundice."[57] The logic and justice of Lewis's position hinges on choice. God will not force someone to choose Heaven. In other words, he will not force someone to love him because love must be given. It always involves surrender, which force would annihilate.

The case of Frank and Sarah Smith—along with several other relational situations in *The Great Divorce*, like the mother who would rather have her son in Hell than lose control of him and the manipulative wife whose life was lived on earth vicariously and possessively through control of her husband—illustrates the necessity of a very hard biblical doctrine that Lewis understands. In *God in the Dock*, he cites the words of Jesus directly: "If any man come to me, and hate not his father, and mother, and wife, and children, and brethren, and sisters, yea, and his own life also, he cannot be my disciple."[58] Family is newly defined in the New Testament, and in Heaven it will be radically altered, where the redeemed are characterized by images like friends, brothers and sisters, joint heirs with Jesus, and the bride of Christ. In other words, the closest we can get to these new heavenly relationships is with categories describing our earthly dearest.

Even on earth, Jesus creates a new priority that transcends family. It places him first and family allegiances second. As we have seen, Lewis shows that such realignment is the only way to love any others truly and most deeply. But if it comes to being disowned, following Jesus is still our first priority, though we must still sacrificially love even our enemies. Further, there is a closeness fellow believers have that transcends family ties as they are "born again" with a new life from Christ. If this is true on earth, how much more in Heaven? In *The Great Divorce*, we see family members like Sarah Smith joyfully "in Love Himself," though apart from earthly family. In the Bible, when the Sadducees tried to trick Jesus by posing the situation of a woman marrying, as the law required, seven successive brothers who each had died, asking whose wife she would be in the resurrection, Jesus exploded their earthly categories by saying that we would be like the angels: that is, there will be no marriage in Heaven.[59] The reason is easy to infer, as Lewis suggests. Something even greater engulfs our earthly best. Our closest earthly relationships are but shadows of the intimacy awaiting us.[60]

In the end, what else is to be done with or for those who refuse Heaven? Lewis concludes:

> I willingly believe that the damned are, in one sense, successful, rebels to the end; that the doors of hell are locked on the *inside*. . . . In the long run the answer to all those who object to the doctrine of hell is itself a question: "What are you asking God to do?" To wipe out their past sins and, at all costs, to give them a fresh start, smoothing every difficulty and offering every miraculous help? But He has done so, on Calvary. To forgive them? They will not be forgiven. To leave them alone? Alas, I am afraid that is what He does.[61]

If we doubt the wisdom and love of God in consigning some to Hell, we imply that we are more merciful and loving than he. But look at what such a position requires:

> "What some people say on earth is that the final loss of one soul gives the lie to all the joy of those who are saved. . . ."
>
> "That sounds very merciful: but see what lurks behind it. . . ."
>
> "The demand of the loveless and the self-imprisoned that they should be allowed to blackmail the universe: that till they consent to be happy (on their own terms) no one else shall taste joy: that theirs should be the final power; that Hell should be able to *veto* Heaven."[62]

In fact, we may state it the other way around: God, in his mercy and justice, will not allow those who have chosen Hell to manipulate those who have chosen Heaven. Even on earth, we see that our sorrow for the suffering needn't expel love, joy, and security from a healthy home. We must remind ourselves that it is impossible to outlove God, and all that can be done, will be done. In that we may rest; God has promised that one day we will.

HELL
PART II

REMYTHOLOGIZING HELL:
THE FICTION

In remythologizing Hell, Lewis develops five major themes through a great variety of characters and circumstances: 1) Those in Hell are consumed with self; 2) As a consequence, Hell is the drying up of human potential in separation from Christ, in whom we find all fulfillment or not at all; 3) Hell and evil cannot create and are reduced to counterfeiting good; 4) Those who go to Hell choose it by choosing something other than Christ; and 5) Hell is destined for ultimate defeat. The works of fiction are treated in chronological order, but it might be useful to read *That Hideous Strength* after *The Screwtape Letters* since they match so well in their emphasis on Hell, both presenting it as a thoroughly nasty bureaucracy. The themes interconnect, but each piece may be read independently as familiarity and interest direct.

THE PHILOSOPHY OF HELL:

The Screwtape Letters

Be sober-minded; be watchful. Your adversary the devil prowls around like a roaring lion, seeking someone to devour.[1]
1 PETER

〜⚜〜

Perhaps few things in our mental landscape are as dominated by stereotypes as Hell. If you ask people to describe what they imagine about Hell, you will likely get flames and red devils with pitchforks—just think of what came to your door last Halloween. If you ask someone to imagine a sermon about Hell, it will likely be a "fire and brimstone" rant. Even the educated fall under the spell of literary and artistic stereotypes.

In Lewis's judgment, we get from literature a dangerous view of Satan, ironically, from the Christian Milton. His Satan makes grand speeches in soaring language and emerges as a hero of sorts, who will venture all against great odds, defying God even in defeat. From Goethe, Lewis suggests, we get the most dangerous image of all: Mephistopheles, the suave, "humourous, civilized, sensible, adaptable" being who strengthens the "illusion that evil is liberating." The Devil is, in truth, more like Faust: "ruthless, sleepless, unsmiling concentration upon self which is the mark of Hell."[2] Lewis found evil in reality far less human and far more menacing, though at the same time inane. When confronting the Un-man of *Perelandra*, the possessed body and soul of Weston, Ransom feels that "a suave and subtle Mephistopheles with a red cloak and rapier and feather in his cap, or even a somber tragic Satan out of *Paradise Lost*, would have been a welcome release from the thing he was actually doomed to watch.

It was not like dealing with a wicked politician at all: it was much more like being set to guard an imbecile or a monkey or a very nasty child."[3] Here the demon regards intelligence only as a weapon and lapses into banality whenever it is not at war.

Anthropomorphic projections about evil are just as misleading when making them about God and the good angels. From art we get perhaps the most insidious stereotypes of all. In Lewis's analysis, angelic representations have "steadily degenerated" from Raphael's "chubby infantile nudes" to the nineteenth century's effeminate creatures with swanlike wings and flowing robes. In Scripture, Lewis reminds us, angels struck such awe and fear into human beholders that they needed reassurance to keep from fainting away. Before the angels could deliver their message, they would often say, "Fear not." But these Victorian angels look as if they "were going to say, 'There, there.'"[4] The problem Lewis faced was how to tell about the spiritual assault on our souls in such a way as to avoid the accretion of error and win a hearing for the truth.

A person in possession of these stereotypes would have little interest in reading a theology book on Hell. Lewis could have written straightforward theology, of course, and did so brilliantly in a short chapter entitled "Hell" in *The Problem of Pain*. But in *The Screwtape Letters*, Lewis slips past all the stereotypes and lands us in the world of Monday morning at the office reading someone else's mail. With a shock, we recoil from the mildly voyeuristic pleasure of reading this intercepted correspondence when the subject turns out to be our own destruction—mediated through the unnamed "patient," who is an everyman character. The writer of these hateful epistles, one Screwtape, turns out to be a sort of middle manager in the "lowerarchy" of Hell, with the title "His Abysmal Sublimity Undersecretary Screwtape."[5]

Lewis chose for his chief symbol the efficient, modern bureaucracy, complete with a touch of nepotism in the uncle-nephew relationship. It is a perfect choice for saying a few essential things about the character of Hell at the deepest level. A certain amount of bureaucracy is necessary to every group, but the tighter the control and the stronger the emphasis on "the state," the more deadly the effect on its people, as dictatorships past and present amply show. Like any bureaucracy, Hell chews up individuals in favor of the abstract collective. The collective good, as it turns out, is a convenient excuse or philosophical cover for the selfishness and greed of those capable of seizing power. Collectives breed self-serving individualists for the simple reason that one survives in such environments only by domination—using the system that would otherwise use you. A person gets ahead, or gets anything, only by subverting the system and subverting others. "We must picture Hell," says Lewis, "as a state where everyone is perpetually concerned about his own dignity and advancement, where everyone has a grievance, and where everyone lives the deadly serious passions of envy, self-importance, and resentment."[6]

In his *Preface to "Paradise Lost,"* Lewis captures perfectly the mean-spiritedness of Hell in his description of the devils. They are fallen angels, newly ejected from Heaven, awakening in Hell, dazed by a thunderous defeat that is painful to recall. Their state of mind is like a traitor who has sold out his country "and knows himself to be a pariah" or a man who has "just quarreled irrevocably with the woman he loves. For human beings there is often an escape from this Hell [a way to avoid going there in the first place], but there is never more than one—the way of humiliation, repentance, and (where possible) restitution."[7]

But for those in Hell there is no exit: only pouting, rage, and endless regret. Knowing they can neither escape Hell nor hurt God, they purpose to hurt the human creation God loves: "Perhaps you cannot harm your own country; but are there a few black men somewhere in the world owning her flag whom you could bomb or even flog? The woman may be safe from you. Has she perhaps a young brother whom you could cut out of a job—or even a dog you could poison? This is sense, this is practical politics, this is the realism of Hell."[8]

Following the branch to the root, Lewis doesn't see concentration camps and the like as places where the worst evil is done. The camps are only the end result of what happens in more respectable places: "it is conceived and ordered (moved, seconded, carried, and minuted) in clean, carpeted, warmed, and well-lighted offices, by quiet men with white collars and cut fingernails and smooth-shaven cheeks who do not need to raise their voice. Hence, naturally enough, my symbol for Hell is something like the bureaucracy of a police state or the offices of a thoroughly nasty business concern."[9] The demons operate under a thin veneer of formal respect and deference, but we easily see the impersonal and selfish cogs chewing up even the devils within it.

This "world of 'Admin'" provides a perfect stage for playing out the philosophy of Hell, which Screwtape explicitly describes in Letter 18:

The whole philosophy of Hell rests on recognition of the axiom that one thing is not another thing, and, specifically, that one self is not another self. My good is my good, and your good is yours. What one gains another loses. Even an inanimate object is what it is by excluding all other objects from the space it occupies; if it expands, it does so by thrusting other objects aside or by absorbing them. A self does the same. With beasts the absorption takes the form of eating; for us, it means the sucking of will and freedom out of a weaker self into a stronger. "To be" *means* "to be in competition."[10]

Readers of *Mere Christianity* may see in Screwtape an idea Lewis unfolded in that later book. In his masterful chapter on "Pride," Lewis suggests that all sins come from this one. Pride is at the bottom of other sins because "it is the complete anti-God state of mind" and is "in competition with everyone else's pride."[11] Paul, in Romans 1 agrees, stating that all sin, including the "big" perverted sexual sins, is the result of failing to honor God—that is, of putting ourselves in the place of preeminence. And when Jesus condensed the requirements of Scripture to their essence, he named two things: Love God and love others as ourselves. This means that God is in the center, and we put the needs of others before our own.[12] Pride puts self in the center and sacrifices others for its preeminence.

Since only God can create, Satan and his demons can only pervert.[13] Since only God is love, the powers of Hell can only counterfeit the original. Instead of love, which gives, they have desire, which consumes. Screwtape explains to Wormwood in Letter 8 that "to us a human is primarily food; our aim is the absorption of its will into ours, the increase of our own area of selfhood at its expense," with the final aim that "Our Father Below," Satan, draws "all other beings into Himself." This he contrasts with God's aim:

> One must face the fact that all the talk about His love for men, and His service being perfect freedom, is not (as one would gladly believe) mere propaganda, but an appalling truth. He really does want to fill the universe with a lot of loathsome little replicas of Himself—creatures whose life, on its miniature scale, will be qualitatively like His own, not because He has absorbed them but because their wills freely conform to His. We want cattle who can finally become food; He wants servants who can finally become sons. We want to suck in, He wants to give out. We are empty and would be filled; He is full and flows over.[14]

As this suggests, the philosophy of Heaven rests on love, which an uncomprehending and frustrated Screwtape continually claims to be an impossibility and a sham on God's part. In explaining the opposing philosophy of Heaven to Wormwood, in which the Enemy is God, we sense that Screwtape is grappling with a puzzle himself.

> Now the Enemy's philosophy is nothing more nor less than one continued attempt to evade this very obvious truth [the above philosophy of Hell]. He aims at a contradiction. Things are to be many. yet somehow also one. The good of one self is to be the good of another. This impossibility He calls *Love*, and this same monotonous panacea can be detected under all He does and even all He is—or claims to be. Thus He is not content, even Himself, to be a sheer arithmetical unity; He claims to be three as well as one, in order that this nonsense about Love may find a foothold in His own nature. At the other end of the scale, He introduces into matter that obscene invention the organism, in which the parts are perverted from their natural destiny of competition and made to cooperate.[15]

Screwtape just doesn't get it because he has internalized the Nietzschean "will to power," with himself at the center as his only "good." Those in Hell believe in a zero-sum game: My gain is your loss; your loss is my gain. There must always be winners and losers, unlike Heaven, where all are winners. To Screwtape, love is an illusion and self-sacrifice an outrageous and irrational puzzle. His inability to understand the case of married love occasions many hilarious moments. "The patient" falls in love with a wholesome Christian girl. Not only does Screwtape hate what she is, but what difficulty this will create in tempting both, now that they have each other for mutual support. As the demon's scalding hatred boils over into Letter 22, we see his total failure to comprehend love and the role of sex, as well as his own hurt pride in being laughed at. Here Hell shows its true colors, loathing all that is good, nurturing, and legitimately pleasurable.

> I have looked up this girl's dossier and am horrified at what I find. Not only a Christian but such a Christian—a vile, sneaking, simpering, demure, monosyllabic, mouselike, watery, insignificant, virginal, bread-and-butter miss! The little brute! She makes me vomit. She stinks and scalds through the very pages of the dossier. It drives me mad, the way the world has worsened. We'd have had her to the arena in the old days.

That's what her sort is made for. Not that she'd do much good there, either. A two-faced little cheat (I know the sort) who looks as if she'd faint at the sight of blood and then dies with a smile. A cheat every way. Looks as if butter would melt in her mouth, and yet has a satirical wit. The sort of creature who'd find ME funny! Filthy, insipid little prude— and yet ready to fall into this booby's arms like any other breeding animal. Why doesn't the Enemy blast her for it, if He's so moonstruck by virginity—instead of looking on there, grinning?[16]

In a crowning humorous touch, Screwtape's response to seeing this scene of goodness and to being himself the potential subject of ridicule is a spasm of anger, ending in his metamorphosis into a centipede.[17] He simply cannot stand it. Not only is the young woman morally tough and her manner genteel, but her whole family and its habitation remind Screwtape of Heaven, leading him to conclude that God is "vulgar" and "bourgeois," a "hedonist" for filling "his world full of pleasures." This is a masterpiece, as is the whole book, of verbal irony: saying one thing and meaning another. The humor works because the violence of the language swells out of all proportion to the innocence and goodness of the girl. At the same time, it shows Screwtape to be humor*less*. This, too, plays a part in revealing the character of Hell because humor requires not only a sense of proportion, but the awareness of a standard from which a character deviates. Without a sense of right and wrong, jokes, satire, and irony would not be possible. Our ability to laugh at this shows that we are still in God's territory.

Screwtape's struggle to understand love gets him in trouble and provides us with a glimpse into his relationship with Wormwood. On the surface, the uncle claims affection for his nephew and habitually closes each letter, "Your affectionate uncle, Screwtape." This thin veneer of family love cracks when Wormwood rats to the secret police that Screwtape has broken ranks with the party line in suggesting heretically that God may actually "love the human vermin," wishing their freedom and fulfillment. Realizing his heresy and personal danger, Screwtape tries to sweet-talk his nephew into overlooking it.

I hope, my dear boy, you have not shown my letters to anyone. Not that it matters, of course. Anyone would see that the appearance of heresy into which I have fallen is purely accidental. By the way, I hope you understood, too, that some apparently uncomplimentary references to Slubgob were purely jocular. I really have the highest respect for him.

And, of course, some things I said about not shielding you from the authorities were not seriously meant. You can trust me to look after your interests. But do keep everything under lock and key.[18]

Just three letters later, it becomes apparent that Wormwood has used his uncle's slips to press his own advantage with the authorities. Of course, Wormwood's motivation in betraying his uncle is suggested in nearly every letter from his senior, as he relentlessly criticizes, belittles, and threatens. In the very first letter, Wormwood is called "a trifle *naïf.*" After his patient becomes a Christian, he is assured he will not "escape the usual penalties." Then he is "disappointing," "alarming," "very bad," and so on. Screwtape speaks with an invariably condescending tone, and even when he praises something, it is followed with "now for your blunders."

After Wormwood reports his uncle to the secret police, Screwtape, in Letter 22, brings their hostilities out into the open. He laments first that "we fight under cruel disadvantages. Nothing is naturally on our side." Good is self-existent; evil is only a perversion of the good, a parasite like mold on bread. Then this: "Not that that excuses *you.* I'll settle with you presently. You have always hated me and been insolent when you dared."[19] Both survive this storm, and Screwtape resumes the charade of "affectionate uncle" as long as he has something to gain from Wormwood's potential success in damning his patient. Just nine letters later, the thirty-first and last, we learn that the patient has died in a wartime bombing in Christian belief, lost to Wormwood, Screwtape, and the combined powers of Hell. Now that Screwtape can gain nothing personally from his nephew, he turns on him to rationalize his own failure as a manager and to consume the only self now available to him. The demonic desire to totally dominate or consume others again takes on the symbolic form of eating. "Rest assured," Screwtape writes, "my love for you and your love for me are as like as two peas. I have always desired you, as you (pitiful fool) desired me. The difference is that I am the stronger. I think they will give you to me now; or a bit of you. Love you? Why, yes. As dainty a morsel as ever I grew fat on."[20] He now signs himself "Your increasingly and ravenously affectionate uncle."

Before consuming him, Screwtape taunts Wormwood with one of the forms suffering takes in Hell: watching their victim escape to see the spiritual world as it truly is, with the resulting humiliation to the hellians. Their patient now sees clearly in an instant the evil arrayed against him, including Wormwood, with the knowledge that it can never influence him again. To the demons' consternation, the patient not only sees evil in its true colors, but also the glories of Heaven. First, "all his doubts became, in the twinkling of an eye, ridiculous."[21] This is no small thing. Lewis himself had wrestled his way through intellectual puzzles for half his life, to age thirty-two. From then on, as Walter Hooper says, he was "the most thoroughly converted man I ever knew."[22] Because Lewis knew the other side, he sympathized with every struggler, as his massive correspondence attests. His view on Heaven answering our doubts is brilliant: It is not that we will finally have all our questions answered; rather, the questions will no longer seem important. Why not? Let us return to the patient's encounter with Heaven. His doubts fall away because he sees reality. From Screwtape's diabolical point of view:

> As he saw you [Wormwood], he also saw them. I know how it was. You reeled back dizzy and blinded, more hurt by them than he had ever been by bombs. The degradation of it!—that this thing of earth and slime could stand upright and converse with spirits before whom you, a spirit, could only cower. . . . He had no faintest conception till that very hour of how they would look, and even doubted their existence. But when he saw them he knew that he had always known them and realized what part each one of them had played at many an hour in his life when he had supposed himself alone, so that now he could say to them, one by one, not "Who *are* you?" but "So it was *you* all the time."[23]

Finally, the doubts fall away when the Christian sees Truth Himself, the one who said, "I am the way, and the truth, and the life."[24] Screwtape again:

> He saw not only them; he saw Him. This animal, this thing begotten in a bed, could look on Him. What is blinding, suffocating fire to you, is now cool light to him, is clarity itself, and wears the form of a Man.[25]

He sees Jesus. This is the Beatific Vision. As intended, this account gives direction to the lost and hope to the believer. It is also a valuable corrective to thinking about Hell, a warning to avoid it, and an inverted guide to Christian living. Eternity is always in view; after all, the goal of Screwtape and Wormwood, like all devils, is to spite God and puff up themselves by damning human souls to Hell. Of Hell as a destination, then, we have plenty, but of Hell as a place we have nothing. There is no physical description. But from the interaction of these two devils and their attitudes toward God and humanity, we have the character of Hell as brilliantly drawn as anywhere. In the mix, we also learn how to live in the home and office (the two chief settings of the temptations) to thwart the devils' schemes.

The philosophy of Hell embraces a perverted love that seeks to enlarge the self by consuming other selves, which requires separating souls from God. Since God has made us free moral agents, the demons can only achieve their aim by tempting humans into making bad choices. And since all choices are ultimately for God or the self, even the most mundane choice matters greatly. When Wormwood commits the novice tempter's error of being overeager to "report spectacular wickedness," Screwtape must remind him of "the only thing that matters," which is to "separate the man from the Enemy [God]." In fact, "murder is no better than cards if cards can do the trick. Indeed, the safest road to Hell is the gradual one—the gentle slope, soft underfoot, without sudden turnings, without milestones, without signposts."[26]

Lewis quotes William Law: "'If you have not chosen the Kingdom of God, it will make in the end no difference what you have chosen instead,'" then questions. "Will it really make no difference whether it was women or patriotism, cocaine or art, whisky or a seat in the Cabinet, money or science? Well, surely no difference that matters. We shall have missed the end for which we are formed and rejected the only thing that satisfies. Does it matter to a man dying in a desert by which choice of route he missed the only well?"[27]

As this list implies, virtually anything can be the occasion for sin. Nothing created is intrinsically bad, including sex, drugs, drink, politics, and money. Rather, it is preferring any of these to God, which usually takes the more subtle form of using the creation to bolster the ego in an implicit defiance of God. The idea of a priority of loves has its roots in the oldest portions of Scripture—for example, in the first of the Ten Commandments: "you shall have no other gods before me."[28] It means that "our deepest concern should be for first things, and our next deepest for second things, and so on down to zero—to total absence of concern for things that are not really good, nor means to good, at all."[29] Lewis often uses St. Augustine's term "ordinate loves" and employs the concept frequently in his writing, giving it fullest treatment in a valuable book I sometimes include with a wedding present, *The Four Loves*. The following passage illustrates the concept with romantic love, showing how it cannot take first place in our lives and rooting love finally where it belongs—not in the feelings, but the will:

> It is probably impossible to love any human being simply "too much." We may love him too much *in proportion* to our love for God; but it is the smallness of our love for God, not the greatness of our love for the man, that constitutes the inordinacy. . . . But the question whether we are loving God or the earthly Beloved "more" is not, so far as concerns our Christian duty, a question about the comparative intensity of two feelings. The real question is, which (when the alternative comes) do you serve, or choose, or put first? To which claim does your will, in the last resort, yield?[30]

The consequence of loving ordinately, putting God first, is to experience as much of Heaven on earth as is possible. One of the most liberating aspects of Heaven will be that our loves are purified so that we may act with confidence on every impulse, because it will be right. Conversely, whenever any second thing takes priority in our love, it becomes a demon, destroying all loves, including the thing put first. The failure of love is the hallmark of Hell. As we will see, Lewis's fiction gives many examples of inordinate, destructive love.

A Postscript on Names and Name-Calling

One of the great contributions of Lewis's fiction is to train our affections so that we love what is good and hate what is evil. Lewis's biographer George Sayer sees *The Screwtape Letters* doing just that: "The effect of the book is to clarify thought, to sharpen our knowledge of the distinctions between good and evil, to increase our desire to be virtuous, and through much practical advice to make it easier for us to become so. It is truly a devotional work."[31] A good deal of this work on clarifying good and evil gets done through names and name-calling. The devils' names suggest, as Lewis says he intended, unpleasantness and meanness. "Screwtape" reflects bureaucratic imagery suggesting "red tape" and the nastiness of the bureaucrats with suggestions of torture in "thumb screw." Similar qualities could be mentioned for the other demons' names. But the demons' names for us, for humanity, are the most alarming. In following up the food metaphor and the devils' desire to consume us, we are called "cattle" and "human sheep," and, in the "Toast," some are a "Lukewarm Casserole of Adulterers" and others "Sound old vintage Pharisee." Even worse, we are "trash," "disgusting little human vermin," and "hairless bipeds." Wormwood's patient is "fool," "booby," "earthborn vermin," "thing of earth and slime."[32]

Screwtape, being only a spirit and not willing to trust God's creation as good, is a Gnostic who can't stand or understand the physical, either God's creation of it or humanity's enjoyment of it. Screwtape sees us as inferior because we have bodies like animals. "Nor is his contempt reserved only for humans." as David Clark says. "One can almost taste Hell's disgust at a God who stoops so low as to create, love and even die for a puny creature of dust. The overall impression of cattle herded around while being fattened for the kill should be enough to drive us to God."[33] Screwtape uses the name "Enemy" for God or Jesus 149 times in the thirty-one letters and another nine in the "Toast," for an average of five times per letter. This, says Clark, keeps us reminded of "the underlying hostility between Heaven and Hell."[34]

10

EVIL IN PARADISE:
Perelandra

By man came death.[1]
1 CORINTHIANS

Perelandra casts a new vision of an unfallen world teeming with life and goodness, a process begun in *Out of the Silent Planet* but brought to new heights here, in the second book of the space trilogy. For me, the distinct gift of *Perelandra* is feeling for the first time what I knew to be theologically true: the glory of a world where Christ reigns supreme and the terrible loss to that world when invaded by sin. As I explored the planet of Perelandra along with Ransom, I came to love its floating islands, yellow fruit that introduced "a new *genus* of pleasure," bubble trees with their enchanting and refreshing liquid, the innocence of the Green Lady, and the dolphins who joyfully serve their human masters.

Then: enter evil. When Weston's spacecraft splashed down, and he began to wantonly destroy the beauty and harmony of this unfallen world, I felt almost physically ill. When out of sight of the Green Lady, Weston, having given himself to demonic possession, delights in destroying what God has made. In a surprisingly heart-wrenching episode, Ransom discovers one of the brightly colored frogs of Perelandra with a ghastly wound from the back of its head to its nearly severed hind legs. He tried to put the frog out of its misery, but it took an hour to kill. Though he had seen the horror of war, Ransom felt this first death in the otherwise unspoiled world as an "intolerable obscenity" and "shame" from the remembered evil of our world. It was worse, in a way, than the evil that degenerates into apocalyptic nightmare in *That Hideous Strength*. Then he discovers a whole trail of mutilated frogs leading to the Un-man in the act of emotionlessly ripping apart another. Ransom (and the reader) feels sick.

Lewis here achieves what the Puritans rightly advocated: training the affections to love the good and, by seeing sin in its true colors, to hate evil. "The wages of sin is death," and here we begin to sense in microcosm how much the wage is.[2] What kind of person could do such a thing? In Weston's case, the person has been replaced, of his own free will, by a demon. "Weston himself was gone."[3]

The first mark of Hell upon him is self-centeredness. Weston, the monomaniac, views himself as "Chosen. Guided. . . . a man set apart."[4] He has come to believe in "emergent evolution" surging forward through the inorganic to the organic and himself the chief conduit at the present time for its forward progress to pure spirit. This belief is unfolded more fully in the next volume of the trilogy, *That Hideous Strength,* and its prose antecedent, *The Abolition of Man.* Weston announces, "I am it," in a parody of God's answer, "I am," to Moses' question, "Who shall I say sent me?" With the hubris of a Walt Whitman, Weston proclaims, "I *am* the Universe. I, Weston, am your God and your Devil. I call that Force into me completely."[5] His face contorts as though in a deathly vomit, and he writhes on the ground like a madman. To be consumed with self is very madness; it is antithetical to a creature made for relationship with God, a creature who finds freedom in submission. Except for a horrifying reemergence to bespeak the horror of Hell, Weston's potential as a human being has dried to nothingness. He has been, à la Screwtape, consumed.

His goal is to corrupt the Green Lady, as yet unfallen, by pretending to bring her good in the form of knowledge beyond what Maleldil (God) has given her. This knowledge she must gain by asserting her independence and violating Maleldil's command not to spend a night on the Fixed Land. Except for Ransom and Weston, the Green Lady, whose name is Tinidril, and her momentarily absent husband, Tor, are the two lone persons as yet on the planet, its Adam and Eve. Weston tempts the Green Lady with a withering barrage of argument and emotional appeal to vanity and ultimately to pride. He redefines vanity as her natural due, death as life, disobedience as a subtle form of submission to Maleldil's secret will, and sin as service to God and Tor.

Though he has truth on his side, Ransom cannot compete with the sleepless, demon-animated body of Weston. Weston has become the monomaniacal sin he chose, claiming the role of savior of his own race, which he will achieve by annihilating this one and all others and by sending his own descendants from planet to planet. To his horror, Ransom realizes that there is only one option for defeating the Un-man: He must kill the physical body that has become home to sin and has completely usurped the place of God.[6] Like other characters in Lewis's works and some still on earth, Weston has willed his own damnation in claiming independence from God. In this and other portraits of those who have abandoned God and have in turn been abandoned by him, we glimpse the horror that is Hell.

Assuming the role of Satan, Weston suffers the fate of Satan. Ransom kills him once by choking him. In a strange twist, the Un-man returns in an underground cavern that has a pit of fire in one end. The reanimated body of Weston drags itself toward Ransom, who crushes his head with a stone and then throws him into the lake of fire. "This is the second death," in biblical terms. Ransom as the Christ-figure has vanquished the Satan-figure for the final time. Hell was, after all, created for the Devil and his angels. Ransom has both taken the epic voyage to the underworld and enacted the words of the Apostles' Creed in which Jesus "descended into Hell."

After he emerges through a watery slide, signifying both baptism and rebirth, Ransom determines that his body is only sore and exhausted from the fight, except for a bleeding wound in the heel, caused by Weston's teeth. Here again the defeat of Hell is suggested by allusion to the very first Messianic prophecy from Genesis 3:15. God promised a Messiah from Eve's offspring that would "bruise" (or "crush") Satan's head, but that Satan would "bruise his heel." We have seen again the major themes Lewis elaborates about Hell: Those in it are consumed with self; it is the drying up of human potential; evil is a counterfeit of good; those who go there choose Hell by choosing something other than Christ, and Hell is destined for ultimate defeat.

11

THE SOCIOLOGY OF HELL:
That Hideous Strength

They did not honor him as God or give thanks to him, but they became futile in their thinking, and their foolish hearts were darkened. Claiming to be wise, they became fools.[1]

ROMANS

All of Lewis's fiction has theological heft, blended with imaginative reach and a sure grasp on world history and human nature. These stories also, each in their own way, stir up our insatiable longing for our true home. This explains why so many find them so nourishing. As Thomas Howard points out, nearly all of Lewis's fictional books feature an alternate world his characters can escape to, sometimes Heaven itself (*The Great Divorce*), sometimes made up worlds that resemble our own but breathe a heavenly air (like Narnia), and sometimes places in our universe endowed with pre-Fall goodness and harmony (like Malacandra and Perelandra in *Out of the Silent Planet* and *Perelandra*).[2] Alone among these works, *That Hideous Strength* has no alternate world, no Heaven-like place our imaginations and spirits aspire to. Of the fourteen fictional books, only this one do I reread with reluctance. It portrays a world where evil has had its head and turned into Hell. It is our world.[3]

Before we look into this portrait of Hell, it must be said that Heaven's forces are represented, too, and the narrative ends with the redemption of its main characters, Mark and Jane Studdock. The chief representative of Heaven—Elwin Ransom, the unwitting but willing hero of *Out of the Silent Planet* and *Perelandra*—heads a small company of believers who battle the powerful National Institute of Co-ordinated Experiments (N.I.C.E.) and win only because God intervenes. Of course, in all our lives we are outnumbered and doomed if God doesn't intervene—but, then, he always does when we, too, are willing.

In this book, Ransom has become the Pendragon of Logres, head of the mythical Arthurian realm with utopian dreams of justice, mercy, and goodness.[4] This links Ransom with Merlin, the magician from Arthur's court fifteen centuries ago, who reappears with miraculous powers, coveted by both sides. Ransom, aided by a spiritually awakened Mark Studdock, succeeds in getting to Merlin before the forces of evil do.

As several have pointed out, the narrative also features the two cities, of Heaven and earth (here St. Anne's-on-the-Hill and Edgestow, represented by their opposing mansions St. Anne's and Belbury), one of many ways Lewis makes use of St. Augustine's writing.[5] In contrasting these two cities, Augustine recognizes, as Dante had before him, that what we have called the "philosophy of Hell," as of Heaven, hinges on love.[6]

> We see then that the two cities were created by two kinds of love: the earthly city was created by self-love reaching the point of contempt for God, the Heavenly City by the love of God carried as far as contempt of self. In fact, the earthly city glories in itself, the Heavenly City glories in the Lord. The former looks for glory from men, the latter finds its highest glory in God. . . . In the former, the lust for domination lords it over its princes as over the nations it subjugates; in the other both those put in authority and those subject to them serve one another in love, the rulers by their counsel, the subjects by obedience. The one city loves its own strength shown in its powerful leaders; the other says to its God, "I will love you, my Lord, my strength."[7]

As with the vision of Hell in *The Screwtape Letters*, relationships in the N.I.C.E. operate on fear and greed. Underlings like Mark Studdock are manipulated by appeals to their desire to be in the "inner ring": to have the Gnostic's pleasure of having special, inside knowledge and belonging to an exclusive coterie that looks down on the uninitiated. As with all of Hell's appeals, this one is counterfeit: It never keeps its promise. So the victim either comes to his senses or keeps up the futile search for yet another set of relationships elsewhere or further in. But of love that looks to benefit another, even at personal sacrifice, Hell and its manifestation in Belbury know nothing.

Conversely, Ransom and the community at St. Anne's-on-the-Hill thrive on love, which is always looking away from the self to God and others. In adding "on-the-Hill" to the name, Lewis deliberately echoes Jesus' charge to all Christians in building community. In his Sermon on the Mount, which inaugurated Jesus' public ministry, he said, "A city set on a hill cannot be hidden. . . . Let your light shine before others, so that they may see your good works and give glory to your Father who is in heaven."[8] The light of St. Anne's illumines the darkened minds of those like Jane, who seeks shelter there in her distress, and ends by overcoming the dark vision of Belbury.

Like Belbury, St. Anne's is hierarchical, but its leaders serve their willing subjects, and here Jane Studdock learns to love. The book opens with the word *Matrimony*, elaborating Jane's disillusionment with her recent marriage and growing estrangement from Mark. Her husband is eagerly and unwittingly pursuing his own destruction by currying favor at his college and the N.I.C.E., which takes ever more of his time. Jane, a thoroughly modern "liberated" woman, pursues illusive fulfillment in earning a doctorate. Her ironic topic is Donne's concept of "the triumphant vindication of the body." Jane, however, has no children and wants none, and she even has serious doubts about her own sexuality. The minor characters play their role in her healing.

The Dennistons, one of the well-adjusted couples at St. Anne's, take Jane on a picnic. This seems innocent enough, but not from the perspective of Hell. Remember that the demon Screwtape scolds Wormwood for letting his patient read a book just because he liked it, not so he could show off his learning. Further, Wormwood's victim took a walk in the countryside just for enjoyment. God invented all the pleasures, as Screwtape laments, and anytime we take them as intended by God, we are in his territory. We move out of ourselves, a first step toward God himself. The Dennistons have all of Lewis's own sense of gusto in weather of all kinds and in the manifold riches of nature.

Jane suggests that they escape the cold and fog of the picnic site into a restaurant, but Frank counters, "don't you like a rather foggy day in a wood in autumn?" and suggests that he and Camilla got married because they "both like weather" of all kinds. Jane asks how to learn such a thing. Frank replies that children find it natural to play in rain and snow. We have to unlearn it as adults. The suggestion is clear: The Dennistons have simultaneously kept their healthy curiosity and gained the spiritual virtue of becoming childlike. As Christ commanded, we must learn to have a childlike dependence and trust in him. The cure has begun, and Jane will eventually learn submission to all proper authorities—God, Ransom, and Mark—finding there the freedom that comes in discovering what it means to be a creature with a purpose, design, and role with eternal implications. Hell has no such healing elements, no creation redolent of God to aid in escaping the imprisonment of self. And, of course, dying to self is the prerequisite of life in Christ. Mark's conversion comes only when he has gotten so tangled in the Institute's web that he has no hope of escape and faces his own death.

That Hideous Strength joins several of Lewis's other books in powerfully unfolding the key idea that Heaven is the fulfillment of human potential and Hell its drying up. We see the culmination of both: positively in the St. Anne's community and in the protagonists Mark and Jane Studdock; negatively in the chief antagonists, Wither and Frost, even in their very names, each turning himself into a virtual parody of human nature. They represent and advocate the denial of everything utterly real and eternal, along with everything redemptive and enriching in this earthly life. They are anti- God, humanity, nature, matter, and mind. Under the deceptive and seductive ruse of saving humanity by dominating it and reshaping it in their own vision, with painful irony, Wither and Frost destroy even themselves and their co-conspirators. Had they not been stopped, the apocalyptic destruction visited on Belbury would have ravaged the world.

Though the forces of good ultimately prevail and the main protagonists, Mark and Jane Studdock, come to recognize their sinful self-centeredness and are converted, the book has a very dark tone. Just as *Out of the Silent Planet* and *Perelandra* breathe a heavenly air and show us not only what might have been on earth but what will be regained in Heaven, *That Hideous Strength* shows us what may well happen on earth and gives us a foreshadowing of the final horror that is Hell. That horror is nearly as unimaginable as the glory of Heaven, but getting our imaginations moving in the right direction is very important because what we really believe and have trained ourselves to feel about our ultimate destiny and that of others will also determine both the contours and details of our daily lives. Understanding consequences is a hallmark of wisdom. Lewis helps us gain a healthy fear of Hell and hellish human behavior in two chief ways: first, through symbolic names, objects, and actions; second, through presenting the nature of Hell.

The most obvious symbols are the names. As noted earlier, the novel's controlling idea is suggested by the chief antagonists' names, Wither and Frost. Whatever they control by cold calculation withers and dies. They have become mere remnants of human nature with all that is good removed, and they plan the same for the whole world. The organization the two lead is ironically referred to by the acronym N.I.C.E. (National Institute of Co-ordinated Experiments). Embracing a state of pure mental existence, the organization hates the physical and works for its elimination. This philosophy is symbolized by secretly maintaining a head detached from the body. The Saracen's Head, Alcasan, explains Dimble, "is a criminal's brain" experiencing a mode of consciousness unknown to them but likely "of agony and hatred."[9]

To a lesser extent, at first, all the brains at Belbury are "criminal" and occupy a private Hell. Mark says of John Wither, the Deputy Director, that "he was so far from listening that Mark felt an insane doubt whether he was there at all, whether the soul of the Deputy Director were not floating far away, spreading and dissipating itself like a gas through formless and lightless worlds, waste lands and lumber rooms of the universe."[10] Shortly after this, Mark "loses his nerve" and bolts from Belbury for home and Jane.

Second, the actions of the antagonists result in the destruction of the N.I.C.E. and the community that embraced it. *That Hideous Strength,* as Lewis says in the Preface, is the outworking of ideas in *The Abolition of Man.* In this book, Lewis demonstrates the necessity of governing life on the basis of absolute moral standards. When we step outside the moral law (which he designates in the deliberately neutral term "Tao"), we invite the destruction of human nature itself. In *Mere Christianity,* Lewis shows how this law, far from being arbitrary, grows out of the character of God the Creator. When we lose our connection with him, the very source of life and meaning, we are marooned in the void of moral chaos. I won't repeat the arguments of either book here.[11] *That Hideous Strength* shows what a world might look like when taken over by people substituting their own values for those given by God.

What does the new world order of the N.I.C.E. look like? Wither and Frost run a bureaucracy like that implied in *The Screwtape Letters.* All here are opportunists, clawing their way into the illusive inner circle, using and manipulating each other until the last trace of human decency is gone. Inside the N.I.C.E., the new world they have made looks like a house of horrors. Fairy Hardcastle, a lesbian sadist, heads the Institute's Gestapo-like police. Filostrato, described as a eunuch, wishes to sterilize the earth of every organic thing—from human bodies to vegetation, leaving pure mind, as he imagines, conquering death through the creation of "the artificial man."[12] In a kind of Frankenstein's monster revisited, Filostrato and the scientists at Belbury have learned how to keep the guillotined head of the murderer Alcasan alive by technological means. The drooling head, clearly in some otherworldly pain, links them to the world of the "macrobes," who speak through the head. The macrobes are of another species, all right, but not the purely intellectual species that will save the human race. The mad scientists of the N.I.C.E. have opened themselves to the demonic. Their hope for the future becomes instead the destiny of the damned.

The new world without God also looks like the apostate priest Straik, who believes they have discovered immortality in the Saracen's Head. "The resurrection of Jesus in the Bible was a symbol," he exults. "Tonight you shall see what it symbolized. This is real Man at last, and it claims all our allegiance."[13] Worse than pagan idolaters, they have descended to worshiping the god they have made with their own hands, but they add blasphemy of Jesus to their curse. Straik says to Mark, "we are offering you the unspeakable glory of being present at the creation of God Almighty."[14] And they hope themselves to be in line as the next Chosen Head.

Of Belbury, where the policies of the N.I.C.E. are fully deployed, Thomas Howard says simply and truly, "this is Hell."[15] Here everything good, rational, and life-giving is either destroyed or perverted. The agenda calls for the elimination of the physical world, which God created and declared good, to the extent of replacing living vegetation with metal and separating the head from the body. The enterprise of releasing the spirit from its imprisonment in the body, controlled by an elite with special knowledge who usurp the role of God, is aptly symbolized by the gruesome, bodiless Head. The Head drools and sputters idiocy. Similarly, language in Wither's mouth becomes a tool for obfuscation, not communication, as he responds to questions with political non-statements. All traditional values are swept away to clear the ground for rebuilding human society and the very definition of human. This is symbolized by Mark's brainwashing, where everything is at deceptive angles so that his very sense of up and down is as confused as the Institute's ideas of right and wrong.

At the apocalyptic end, reenacting the confusion of languages at

Babel, no one in the Institute understands anyone else, resulting in nearly total isolation. Humanity, remade in this vision, is no longer human. The logical outcome of Frost's life-denying commitments is suicide for himself and destruction for Belbury and the neighboring town. Animals used in cruel experiments are now let loose to trample their masters. In the end, the Great Chain of Being has been turned on its head with humans as gods, animals over humans, and nature over all. What Lewis had predicted as the result of jettisoning absolute moral values has come to pass in this fictional narrative. The frightening aspect of this story is that we are seeing so many of these ideas gaining acceptance in Western society. The cynicism, backstabbing, and confusion of *That Hideous Strength* is what we may expect of Hell, and Hell on earth, with all potential for goodness and fellowship deadened.

Wither and Frost have bought the Devil's line, and they can be fruitfully examined for ideas and consequences. Both illustrate another of Lewis's major themes on Heaven and Hell: that by our own free choices we turn ourselves into creatures fit only for one of these two destinations. Lewis recognizes that God is sovereign and makes choices in detail about his creation. But Lewis also recognizes as one of the mysteries, like the Trinity and Incarnation, the coexistence of predestination and free will. Which one you emphasize depends on whether you look from God's eternal, timeless perspective or from your own experience in time.

Lewis emphasizes freedom of choice, both for his apologetic aim and because it is so difficult, even dangerous, to even attempt a finite, rational explanation of the eternal perspective. The character George MacDonald in *The Great Divorce* cautions the sojourning narrator: "Every attempt to see the shape of eternity except through the lens of Time destroys your knowledge of Freedom. Witness the doctrine of Predestination which shows (truly enough) that eternal reality is not waiting for a future in which to be real; but at the price of removing Freedom which is the deeper truth of the two."[16] Apropos of Wither and Frost, "A man can't be *taken* to hell, or *sent* to hell: you can only get there on your own steam."[17]

As the destiny of Frost draws near, we see again two dominant themes about Hell, which reverberate throughout Lewis's writing, reach a crescendo here: Hell is the drying up of human potential, and it is self-chosen. Frost has conditioned himself, in the philosophical skeptic's way, to deny the existence first of reliable knowledge, then of reality itself. He embraces the view that life is an illusion. He had followed a train of humanistic philosophy "into the complete void. . . . He had long ceased to believe in knowledge itself. . . . He had willed with his whole heart that there should be no reality and no truth, and now even the imminence of his own ruin could not wake him."[18] In rejecting a final act of grace, Frost "became able to know (and simultaneously refused knowledge) that he had been wrong from the beginning, that souls and personal responsibility exist. He half saw: he wholly hated"; so "with one supreme effort he flung himself back into his illusion."[19] With that, Frost throws himself into the fire, willing his own destruction. This may remind us in a way of the Tragedian in *The Great Divorce*, whose pattern of choosing self-pity and living by manipulating others' pity results in his becoming the sin he chooses: a constriction that culminates in his physical disappearance.

The leaders of the new world's rush to perdition are Wither and Frost, whose careers we follow through a full-orbed descent to damnation. They have experienced the judgment of a reprobate mind, which Paul lays out so frighteningly in Romans 1—that is, they have sinned their consciences into total and irrevocable silence. They no longer know the difference between good and evil, having perverted reason by rationalizing their evil commitments. Here is a major theme with intimations both of Heaven and Hell: these are destinies of choice. The characters become the sin they have chosen, thereby constricting their human potential into monomania. They have, in a sense, gone to Hell before they died because they are impervious to the voice of God. Like Weston, called the Un-man in *Perelandra*, they have lost their humanity and are possessed. What the Head is, they will be forever.

The nightmare conclusion is awash with the blood demanded by the dark forces whose power the directors had sought to tap for their own ends. Within the N.I.C.E., there are demons asking for another head, self-immolation, bear mauling, guillotining, and knife-fighting mutilation as bad as any gang war in an alley. Without, the town of Edgestow is racked by earthquakes, avalanches, and fire: "the valley seemed to have turned into Hell."[20] The dark eldila did what they always do: They counter God, substituting hatred, destruction, and death for his love, creativity, and life. The forces turned loose at the Institute are such that "'No power that is merely earthly will serve against the Hideous Strength,'"[21] as Ransom proclaims.

But we know the power that can defeat the human and diabolical forces such as the N.I.C.E. unleashed, and prevent the calamity in the first place. Clearly, the solution is to choose God and the values that flow from his character, which have redeemed human behavior wherever they have been embraced throughout human history. It is not a question of how to be nice; it is not ultimately a question of how to live the good life; it is a question of first principles and eternal destiny. To choose God in Christ is to choose love, goodness, and life.[22] It cannot be gotten the other way around. We can't get to God by our goodness because we can't be good without him. Without him, humanity's best utopian efforts are every bit as hideous as these portrayed by Lewis—as examples from the "civilized" world of the twentieth century attest in abundance.

12

HELL IS A CHOICE, TOO:
The Great Divorce

We can understand Hell in its aspect of privation. All your life an unattainable ecstasy has hovered just beyond the grasp of your consciousness. The day is coming when you will wake to find, beyond all hope, that you have attained it, or else, that it was within your reach and you have lost it forever.[1]

C. S. LEWIS

The technique of using contrasts is central to Lewis's success in portraying Heaven as desirable and Hell as repulsive. From the beginning, even before we learn that *The Great Divorce* has opened in Hell, we find the place to be dreary, drab, and literally hollow, since it is largely an unoccupied shell. The people we encounter are peevish, self-centered, grasping, and unpleasant. In this story, we never enter Deep Hell or Deep Heaven: We are only on the outskirts of each. Lewis's opening vision of Hell is people standing in line, waiting for a bus that will take them to Heaven. None of the stereotypic flames in this portrayal. If we think of a foggy, drippy winter evening in London after the shops have all closed, we wouldn't be far off.

To the narrator's surprise Hell is deserted. It's deserted because in Hell you can have anything you want by just wishing for it. Of course, the whole point of Hell is that you don't wish for the right things. People there are always getting into arguments with the folks next door and wishing new houses into existence farther away from their nettlesome neighbors, so that Hell is ever expanding. Napoleon is the nearest of the old rogues of history, and it took a visiting party 15,000 years to get to his place, only to discover him pacing back and forth. They watched him for a year, and all he ever did was pace and mutter, "It was Soult's fault. It was Ney's fault. It was Josephine's fault," and so on, endlessly.[2]

We may be tempted to think that Hell will be an entertaining place because it will have so many colorful people—a bully social club. That's the glimmer of fool's gold. Like Napoleon, all in Hell have become the sin they have chosen, unillumined by the common grace of God liberally dispensed on the earth but absent in Hell. Nothing is more boring than the tawdry and unrelieved self. What a deception we are under when we fear that Heaven will be boring, when all along it is Hell we should fear. In Lewis's *Great Divorce*, we see that Hell is a boring place peopled with bores.

It should not surprise us that there are no pleasures in Hell. Remember Screwtape's lament that the research and development arm of Hell never succeeded in inventing a pleasure. Besides, Hell only uses pleasure to entrap and then steadily reduces the enjoyment while increasing the desire. We call such ill-gotten pleasures vices. But when pleasure is taken God's way, the enjoyment sweetens the memory and brings us closer to him. Hell is the absence of God, and God is the author of all the pleasures, as the Bible claims and as Augustine, Dante, Milton, and Lewis illustrate at length.

As we have seen in the Heaven section on *The Great Divorce*, the signal contribution of this book is to make us feel as well as think that Heaven is the one *real* place in the universe, and by comparison, earth a Shadowland. What, then, is Hell? It is the ultimate unreality of being "so nearly nothing."[3] Hell exists, but everything there is the debris from what was human (or spirit in the angels' case) with the potential for true reality and fulfillment in Heaven squandered. The problem in depicting Heaven and Hell is one we have already considered: creating something believable when their glories or horrors are so beyond our human experience. What happens when we die? The spirit leaves the body. In our space-bound, time-bound existence, we imagine ghosts rising like steam. It's just the way our imaginations work, devoid as they are of a sense category for spirit.

What Lewis does to make our imaginations better fit reality is turn the widespread but mistaken idea about spirit around: In *The Great Divorce* the people from Hell are ghosts; the people from Heaven are solid. Lewis's friend Owen Barfield observed that, paradoxically, "Lewis employs not only material shapes but *materiality itself* to symbolize immateriality."[4] The hellians appear in Heaven as greasy smoke and smudgy stains on the air. The narrator remarks: "One could attend to them or ignore them at will as you do with the dirt on a window pane."[5] As mentioned earlier, when the folk from Hell step on the grass in even the hinterlands of Heaven, it pierces their feet like spikes. Even the grass is more real than they. By contrast, the grass bends normally beneath the feet of the Solid People from Heaven. When the narrator, fresh from Hell himself, gets the bright idea that the water will be solid to him like the unbending grass and that he could therefore walk on it, he gets swept off his feet and bumps along on top of the swiftly moving stream, badly bruising his ghostly body. And the spray from a waterfall goes through him like a bullet.

When the narrator asks his heavenly guide, MacDonald, why the people in Heaven don't go down to Hell to try to salvage the hellians, he learns that they can't because those in Heaven are so large and substantial. The bus from Hell had entered Heaven through some tiny crack in the soil. He is told that if a butterfly from Heaven were to swallow all of Hell, it would make no more difference to the butterfly than swallowing a single atom. The hellians are ghosts because they are blown up from their nothingness to the size of the Solid People in Heaven. From the hellians' perspective, Hell looked vast, though empty. By contrast, Heaven is so spacious that it seems to exist in a different dimension. The narrator remarks, it "made the Solar System itself seem an indoor affair."[6]

If we stop to think a minute, we can see why the spirit must be *more* real. God is spirit. God created the cosmos, the whole physical universe. God is not trapped in his own creation. He is bigger than what he made. Like the heavenly butterfly in *The Great Divorce*, if God were to swallow the whole universe, the effect would be no more than our swallowing an atom. Or if the whole thing were to suddenly collapse upon itself and evaporate into nothing, God would be no less than he is now, and he could make it all over again if he wished. That is, in fact, what will happen at the resurrection: The present Heaven and earth will pass away, and he will make a new Heaven and a new earth. Spirit is more real and more powerful than flesh. Even in the case of our own persons, we see that it is our spirits that animate our bodies. When the spirit leaves, the flesh rots. The spirit will remain to reanimate our imperishable, heavenly bodies.

As the characters from Hell exit the bus on the outskirts of Heaven, they are met by people they knew on earth who have come out of Deep Heaven to invite them in. All but one returns to Hell—for the very reason they went in the first place. It will be instructive to look at a few cases. Lewis's journey motif with its setting in Hell and Heaven makes possible some very effective puns that throw common phrases into a new light. The first visitor to Heaven to get extended treatment is simply called the "Big Man" in Hell and the "Big Ghost" in Heaven. He is met from Heaven by Len, a man who had worked for him and who had murdered a mutual acquaintance named Jack. Upon seeing that Len is a Solid Person and robed in heavenly splendor, the first words out of the Big Ghost's mouth are, "Well, I'm damned."[7] He spoke as he always had on earth, blaspheming to show his surprise, but now it is literally true, which one look at the solid Len confirms by contrast with his ghostly self.

Len explains that the burden of seeing himself as a murderer had driven him to Christ. The Big Ghost merely persists in claiming the unfairness of it all; considering himself a decent chap, he keeps demanding "his rights." Ironically, the Big Ghost and all in Hell have precisely that: their rights. All have sinned; all deserve Hell. As Len urges him to forget about himself and his rights, the Ghost, saying more than he knows, insists, "'I'm not asking for anybody's bleeding charity.'"[8] In Britain, "bleeding" in this usage is a profane oath referring to Christ's blood spilled on the cross, which is literally the Big Ghost's only hope of Heaven. Len replies, "'Then do. At once. Ask for the Bleeding Charity. Everything is here for the asking and nothing can be bought.'"[9]

Language usage has come full circle from concrete heavenly truth to profane abstraction back to literal heavenly truth. We laugh, we see with new insight, we blush, we hopefully repent. Meanwhile the Big Ghost, stubborn as a mule about accepting any Heaven that admits murderers like Len, concludes, "'I'd rather be damned than go along with you. I came here to get my rights, see? Not to go snivelling along on charity tied onto your apron-strings. If they're too fine to have me without you, I'll go home.'"[10] So he goes "home" to Hell.

Another character who prefers Hell is the Episcopal priest (a bishop, no less) who is met by a former colleague. And let us not smugly think that Lewis's target in this satirical portrait is the clergy only. What he says applies to anyone who tries to substitute mere religion for the reality of a personal and vital relationship with the living God. The priest is greatly interested in religion and religious questions. To his chagrin, he discovers that no one in Heaven is the least bit interested in his speculations. They don't need his theology because they all have God himself. The Episcopal ghost prefers questions to answers, questing to arriving, talking about God to meeting him face to face. He has made his choice. In the end, learning that his kind of theology isn't needed in Heaven, he hurries back to Hell and a little Theological Society there to give a paper on "growing up to the measure of the stature of Christ."

The theme that runs through each of the meetings between the Solid People of Heaven and the Ghosts of Hell is choice. As we have seen in so many instances, sin is ultimately the choosing of self over God. Damnation and Hell are receiving that choice of self over God forever. The priest's interests were not really in theology, but in the fact that the views were his. Later on MacDonald, quoting Milton, explains: "The choice of every lost soul can be expressed in the words 'Better to reign in Hell than serve in Heaven.' There is always something they insist on keeping, even at the price of misery. There is always something they prefer to joy—that is, to reality. Ye see it easily enough in a spoiled child that would sooner miss its play and its supper than say it was sorry and be friends."[11]

13

DESCENT INTO HELL: THE CHRONICLES OF NARNIA

"The gate is wide and the way is easy that leads to destruction, and those who enter by it are many. . . . Beware of false prophets, who come to you in sheep's clothing but inwardly are ravenous wolves."[1]

JESUS

THE LION, THE WITCH AND THE WARDROBE: JADIS AND COUNTERFEIT GOOD[2]

A great deal of what can be known of Lewis's views of Hell from Narnia will be glimpsed in its evil characters. The most famous and instructive of these is Jadis, the White Witch, the antagonist to Aslan. Let's look at a few points of contrast. Aslan serves all; Jadis uses all. Aslan lays down his life for the sinful; Jadis preys on the lives of others. Aslan brings worlds into being; Jadis destroys them. Aslan makes heavenly and life-giving music; like Screwtape and Milton's Satan, Jadis hates music and loves noise. Aslan judges, but he rules by love; Jadis is judgmental and rules by fear. Aslan (and representations of the Trinity) is the only original thing that exists and is the originator of all things. Jadis as a derivative being herself can only counterfeit what Aslan has made good. Evil is a false good, a parasite that could not survive if the good were removed.

Jadis makes her appearance larger than life, arrayed in mocking white that parodies purity and at the same time shows her bloodlessness, the whiteness symbolizing death and her lack of humanity. She is powerful, but she uses it for domination, as in turning all who oppose her into stone. She relishes evil and the destruction or embarrassment of the good, as when she destroys Charn—people, plants, and planet—rather than let her sister have it. Though vain to try, she attempts to injure Aslan, first crudely with the rod of iron, later by manipulation of his sinful but beloved creatures. Jadis dupes Edmund, kills Aslan, and plans by deceit to conquer all Narnia. We meet her first as a usurping ruler of Narnia, making it always winter but never Christmas, which is the chief consolation of winter and celebration of the life-giving Christ (Aslan).

Jadis's followers are cruel and grotesque, delighting in evil, laughing at and spitting on the bound and condemned Aslan, as Jesus' murderous mockers did when he walked the Via Dolorosa and hung on the cross. Jadis is even the incarnation herself (or perhaps the sister) of the evil queen in *The Silver Chair*, which makes her the presiding evil presence in Narnia until the coming of the Antichrist in Shift the Ape.[3] Clearly, she is the Satan-figure in Narnia as Aslan is the Christ-figure. If we want a clue to the nature of Hell, we can do no better than to remember that it was created for Satan and the rebellious angels who followed him. Those who follow Satan (Jadis)—that is, choose something other than Christ (Aslan)—will be consigned to this unnatural place, never designed for humanity.

In Lewis's view, it is not humans who go to Hell but grotesque beings, formerly human, who have lost the capacity to respond to God and be transformed by him, and who have become the sin they chose. With his array of evil characters in the Narnian Chronicles, Lewis helps us to imaginatively break free of the myth, usually offered up with salty humor, that all the interesting people will be in Hell. After reading about the deceptive, self-centered, cruel Jadis and her crowd, no one thinks that any place with them would offer hearty fellowship. Jadis's favorite trick is turning Aslan's followers into stone. Not only does this oppose Aslan's action of breathing into them the breath of life, but it also symbolizes the condition of those ultimately in Hell: frozen in the confines of their self-chosen sin.

The secondary evil figures who follow her are an equally gruesome lot that include the wolves who act as her secret police and are as vicious as the hit men in a Hitleresque police state. Then there are those she calls "our people" in *The Lion, the Witch and the Wardrobe*: "Call out the giants and the werewolves and the spirits of those trees who are on our side. Call the Ghouls, and the Boggles, the Ogres and the Minotaurs. Call the Cruels, the Hags, the Spectres, and the people of the Toadstools": all things fearful, savage, bloodthirsty, and grotesque.[4] They, too, lack humanity and goodness. They love evil and encourage those who do it. And when they are not hating goodness, they hate each other.

THE MAGICIAN'S NEPHEW: THE DEPLORABLE WORD

In a spiteful power grab, Jadis speaks "the deplorable word' that destroys the world of Charn, dead now except for her. The world of Charn was about to go to her sister, but Jadis had access to a dark magic, so she thought, *If I can't have it, no one can.* We've seen her budding type, or been it, on the playground: "If I can't be the captain, I'll take my football and go home." It is the ultimate sour grapes allowed to ferment until the whole vat goes bad and must be tossed. Like Satan, Jadis is a great counterfeiter of the true Lord of her world. Having no power intrinsic to herself and being uncreative, all she can do is use her derivative power to thwart and destroy. The universe came into being at Jesus' creative word (*ex nihilo*). *The Magician's Nephew* translates into the Narnian idiom the story of the Creation and Fall, along with the ensuing curse under which we now live.

The significance for Heaven and Hell is to remind us that Hell is part of God's ultimate solution to the sin problem, as Satan/Jadis are consigned to the Hell created for them and those who choose to follow. To whom would it be a mercy if Jadis and her followers entered Heaven? Not for the righteous people, certainly, for what fellowship would they have with this perverse lot? But it would be no mercy for Jadis and company, either, since they hate Aslan, whose presence is Heaven.

On a mission for Aslan, which turns out to be for the fulfillment of his own heart's desire (something to cure his dying mother), Digory approaches the entrance to the mountaintop garden with high golden gates. Written on the gates is this warning:

> Come in by the gold gates or not at all,
> Take of my fruit for others or forbear.
> For those who steal or those who climb my wall
> Shall find their heart's desire and find despair.[5]

When our selfish desires are realized in isolation from God, the result is Hell, whereas even identical actions for the right motive and with others' good in view can be of Heaven. God judges the heart as well as the deed. Digory is tempted by Jadis to eat the fruit and with her "live forever and be King and Queen of the whole world—or of your world."[6] Digory answers wisely, "I'd rather live an ordinary time and die and go to Heaven."[7] That is the true path to immortality.

The Witch's choice to eat the fruit illustrates succinctly the very nature of evil. Having eaten the fruit in disobedience and for perverse reasons, the fruit, itself good, has become hateful to her. Aslan explains:

> "Child," he replied, "that is why all the rest [of the fruits] are now a horror to her. That is what happens to those who pluck and eat fruits at the wrong time and in the wrong way. The fruit is good, but they loathe it ever after."
>
> "Oh, I see," said Polly. "And I suppose because she took it in the wrong way it won't work with her. I mean, it won't make her always young and all that?"
>
> "Alas," said Aslan, shaking his head, "it will. Things always work according to their nature. She has won her heart's desire; she has unwearying strength and endless days like a goddess. But length of days with an evil heart is only length of misery, and already she begins to know it. All get what they want; they do not always like it."[8]

But when Digory plucks the same apple at Aslan's behest and takes it to his mother on his return to the world, it brings her healing. And ultimately the wood from the tree that sprouts from the seeds becomes the magical wardrobe that leads back to Narnia and Aslan.

On the return from Narnia to our world, Polly and Digory must pass through the Wood between the Worlds. There they spy a dry place where a pool had been. Aslan explains that on their last trip it was the very pool through which they entered Charn. But the pool is dry and that world ended "'as if it had never been. Let the race of Adam and Eve take warning,'" Aslan says. Polly asks if their own world is as bad as that one.

> "Not yet, Daughter of Eve," He said. "Not yet. But you are growing more like it. It is not certain that some wicked one of your race will not find out a secret as evil as the Deplorable Word and use it to destroy all living things. And soon, very soon, before you are an old man and an old woman, great nations in your world will be ruled by tyrants who care no more for joy and justice and mercy than the Empress Jadis. Let your world beware. That is the warning."[9]

Just as worlds reach a point of no return and judgment, so with people. Aslan says that he can neither restore nor comfort Uncle Andrew, an occultist who has chosen evil so many times that good and evil are confounded in him. It is not that Aslan won't call to him, but that Andrew has made himself deaf. His conscience is dead. All Aslan can do for him is give him temporary unconsciousness: "Sleep and be separated for some few hours from all the torments you have desired for yourself."[10] Hell is the logical and inevitable result of his own choice.[11]

THE HORSE AND HIS BOY: RABADASH THE RIDICULOUS

The greatest supernatural evil in *The Horse and His Boy* is Tash, the false god worshiped by the Calormenes, and the most hellish place is Tashbaan, the capital of "the land of slaves and tyrants."[12] The chief evil character is Rabadash, who is driven by lust and greed. Several aspects of Hell—or people in Hell—are embodied in Rabadash. As Paul Ford points out, his name indicates his character by combining *rabid* (out of control and dangerous) and *dash* (impetuous).[13] Rabadash has fixed his lust on Queen Susan and will endanger all Tashbaan and ravage Archenland and Narnia to have her. The depth of his evil and self-centeredness comes out most effectively in his personal encounter with Aslan.

All others whose interviews with Aslan are reported have turned from their sin and become believers (if they weren't already) and chastened followers with vastly improved characters. Neither the threats nor the mercies of King Lune and the Narnians can moderate Rabadash's overt hatred and now impotent threats. Surely if Aslan appeared to him bodily and personally, he would reform—but no. Though warned twice that his doom is near, Rabadash lives up to his reckless name, blaspheming Aslan as a "demon." The third time he eschews a warning and mercy, asserting his evil intent, Aslan turns Rabadash into a donkey, which is reversed only in public in the capital city, Tashbaan. The effect is to permanently cast him as the fool he has been, so that even after his death, to do something stupid is to earn the title of a "second Rabadash." His title behind his back and in history becomes "Rabadash the Ridiculous."

Hell is the place, in Lewis's view, where dreams come true. The brash Rabadash is rewarded with his vain wish: He calls on Tash; so he is condemned to live within ten miles of Tash's temple, on pain of being irreversibly turned back into a donkey. Not only is the sinner justly punished, but his evil is mitigated. He can't attack other countries; nor will he allow his armies to do so, for by such valor and acclaim, would-be usurpers might gain a following sufficient to overthrow the king. This brings us back to a theme in Lewis's first Christian book, *The Pilgrim's Regress*, where the fixed pains of Hell are described as the last mercy God can grant the sinner who obstinately opposes him to the end. By turning Rabadash into the embodiment of bestial stubbornness, Aslan has not only spared Rabadash's life for the present and future, but he has saved the lives of countless innocent Archenlanders and Narnians who will now be spared a war with Calormen.

Rabadash is the most extensively developed of the Calormenes. However, we see enough of the others to know that the country abounds in cruel and selfish persons from high to low. There is no affection between Rabadash and his father, or his father and his inner circle, all of whom practice deceit and abuse. Hell is a place where sin is given its head, restrained only by the pain that keeps evil in check. The result is not a company of interesting and exciting people, but the company of the depraved and self-centered. It is not a pretty sight. Tashbaan and the land of the Calormenes is not Hell, but they are hellish places and, as such, a warning. Part of training our affections is to hate what is hateful. Our imaginations are healthier for seeing evil unveiled in all its loathsomeness.

THE VOYAGE OF THE "DAWN TREADER": BECOMING THE SIN YOU CHOOSE

Hell is a choice. The judgment of Hell is becoming the thing you have chosen instead of God. This key idea in Lewis goes back to Dante's detailed imaginative explication of it in the *Inferno*. We will look at two examples from *The Voyage of the "Dawn Treader."* First, there is no clearer example of this principle in Lewis's work than Eustace, who is so self-centered and greedy that he turns into a dragon, the quintessential representative of greed in the medieval stories Lewis loved. "He had turned into a dragon while he was asleep. Sleeping on a dragon's hoard with greedy, dragonish thoughts in his heart, he had become a dragon himself."[14] The depth of Eustace's depravity—he is the very type of the seriously spoiled child—comes out in his first thoughts after being turned into a dragon as a judgment: "In spite of the pain, his first feeling was one of relief. There was nothing to be afraid of any more. He was a terror himself now and nothing in the world but a knight (and not all of those) would dare to attack him. He could get even with Caspian and Edmund now."[15]

Even with pain throbbing in his arm from putting on a gold and diamond bracelet that fit him as a boy but is too small as a dragon, Eustace's first thought is to use his horrible transformation as a weapon to get even for imagined slights from the other boys. He has become in physical reality the spiteful and hideous person he was in personality and spirit before the "dragoning." It should be instructive to us that without the continuing pain, Eustace might have stayed beyond the reach of grace, never seeing his need for anything else.

Eustace's second thought is part of his torment and another image of Hell: He feels the separation. "He wanted to get back among humans and talk and laugh and share things. He realized that he was a monster cut off from the whole human race. An appalling loneliness came over him."[16] The third thought is a further indication that Eustace is not yet in Hell and still has a human nature. His suffering has made him more human, less a spoiled brat. He begins to see the others as less than the fiends he pretended they were and himself as not "such a nice person as he had always supposed."[17] This knowledge will also comprise a part of Hell, in Lewis's view, but without the human capacity to reform.

For the second example, we journey to Dark Island, one of Lewis's powerful images of Hell. *The Voyage of the "Dawn Treader"* employs a great many elements from classical hero and travel narratives. The one most in play here is the journey to the underworld, the place of the dead, visited by heroes both as a trial of courage and an occasion for gaining knowledge. In the Dark Island episode, the normal operation of light overcoming darkness is reversed, and in broad daylight they sail into an area of darkness that has overcome the light. The imagery is meant to reverse the opening metaphors of John's Gospel, where Christ is the light that shines in the darkness. In this darkness, they recover one of the seven lost Lords of Narnia. Lord Rhoop begs for mercy and would rather they haul him on board and kill him than leave him in the enduring darkness where dreams come true. Not dreams as goals, daydreams, and wish-fulfillment, but nightmares. Hell is that place where perverted imagination becomes reality.

The albatross that leads them out of the darkness is Aslan in another form. It evokes biblical imagery associated with the Holy Spirit, though here instead of a dove, we have the bird that is traditionally a good omen for sailors (and that takes the place of the cross around the Ancient Mariner's neck in Coleridge's poem by that name). The albatross whispers encouragement to Lucy and leads the ship from darkness to light. After Rhoop is rescued, Aslan "overcomes" the darkness. Once released from the nightmares and back in the light, following Aslan's appearance, "all at once everybody realized that there was nothing to be afraid of and never had been."[18] Heaven will be thus free of fear and will "work backwards," as we learn in *The Great Divorce*, to free us even from fears of the past.

Daydreams represent unreality, an attempt to have things our way. But truth and Heaven, like the grass and water in *The Great Divorce*, will not bend to the feet or the wishes of visitors from Hell; though "Hell is a state of mind," Heaven is "reality itself."[19] In Dark Island, the travelers are momentarily left to their dreams, their "state of mind," without any influence from the light of truth until Aslan leads them into the light, into reality. Looked at another way, Hell and Dark Island are getting what you wish for, if it is anything other than God himself. Lewis would be comfortable in Christianizing the old saying, "when the gods want to punish us, they give us what we pray for."

THE SILVER CHAIR: JOURNEY TO THE UNDERWORLD

The Silver Chair features the Chronicles' most elaborate image of Hell. Through five chapters, Eustace, Jill, and Puddleglum take, in the terminology of the epic, a "journey to the underworld." Though it is intended to evoke elements of Hell, the underworld is not properly Hell itself, any more than Narnia is Heaven itself. In both cases, there is another state beyond that is permanent and far more pronounced in evil and goodness, respectively. In both, the key figures of Aslan and the various evil witches come and go, the rational characters have moral choices to make, and all decide whether to become a follower of the Satan-figure or the Christ-figure.

As in other books, Lewis will give us characters confirmed in their eternal goodness (Aslan) or evil (Screwtape, the Witches of the Chronicles), but never a portrayal of Deep Hell or Deep Heaven, except for a few glimpses of Aslan's country. We are often taken to the edge of each and make it farther into Heaven than Hell. In *The Silver Chair*, on the way to Narnia and other regions connected to it, the children leave their world and return through "Aslan's country." And in the finale of *The Last Battle*, the characters are in Aslan's country or Heaven but are journeying "further up and further in."

There are at least two reasons for skirting the issue. First, the emphasis is rightly on the moral and spiritual choices we make in this world while choices are possible. Second, any physical portrayal of either final state would fall short. Positioning characters on the outskirts of each and using such devices as the dream motif all help to remind us that our knowledge of the eternal is fragmentary and in many areas provisional. The suggestions of Heaven and Hell are, however, vastly important in helping to train our hearts to love the good and desire it, and hate the evil and turn from it.

With respect to Eustace, Jill, and Puddleglum, the journey to the underworld is not a punishment nor is it owing to their sin; rather, they are on a mission in which their "guide is Aslan," whose instructions and signs they are following, though not well.[20] Their role is the role of all Christians: to save those in the grasp of the Evil One and bring them to liberating submission under Aslan's authority. Here the trio frees Prince Rilian, who takes the throne in Narnia, and the Earthmen who are also under the evil enchantment of the Green Witch.

With these provisos, let us consider the elements of the underworld in *The Silver Chair* that teach us rationally and imaginatively about Hell. It is:

• Under the control ("enchantment") of the Green Witch, a Satan-figure confirmed in evil as the enemy of Aslan (Christ)

• Dark

• Oppressive

• Toilsome

• Intent on conquering the Overworld (Narnia as an image of our world)

• Fiery

• Deceptive

• Home of the grotesque: here irregular Earthmen and the "dozens of strange animals . . . mostly of a dragonish or bat-like sort."[21]

• Futility: "Every gnome seemed to be as busy as it was sad, though Jill never found what they were so busy about."[22]

Evoking Dante's *Inferno*, the "Wardens" of the underworld exchange the repeated phrases: "'Many sink down to the Underworld. And few return to the sunlit lands.'"[23]

The Earthmen call the Underworld "the Shadow Lands," which is Lewis's metaphorical term for our earthly life.[24] The Underworld, while it suggests Hell in many ways, is not the final horror. Nor is Bism, the "Really Deep Land," which is the natural home of the Earthmen. The Underworld, earth, and Narnia are all Shadow Lands in being temporary and under the influence of evil supernatural beings for a time, as our world is under the temporary influence of Satan. We are not yet what we shall be: only shadows. When Jill's and Eustace's quest is finished, Aslan comes in bodily form, "so bright and real and strong that everything else began at once to look pale and shadowy compared with him."[25] All who are in Christ will be like him in Heaven. All who are not will finally be horrors. Jesus said to the Pharisees and others who would not accept him as the Messiah that they belonged to their father, the Devil.[26]

THE LAST BATTLE: HELL AS A STATE OF MIND

In *The Great Divorce*, we saw that "every state of mind, left to itself, every shutting up of the creature within the dungeon of its own mind—is, in the end, Hell."[27] In *The Last Battle*, we find Lewis's most powerful portrayal of this idea in the Dwarfs. They had been taken in by Shift the Ape, believing that Puzzle the Donkey, dressed in a lion's skin and shown only in the dim light of night, was Aslan returned to the land. Shift linked this deception with a half-truth: that Aslan is not a tame lion. It is a half-truth when divorced from the rest of Mr. Beaver's explanation that Aslan is good. With such trickery and manipulation, Shift harnesses the Dwarfs' gullibility to exact slave labor. The effect of unveiling Shift's false Aslan is that the Dwarfs now (with a few exceptions) refuse to believe in even the true Aslan. In their wounded pride, they resolve not to be taken in again. They repeat Adam's and Eve's sin of declaring independence from God, emphasized by the repeated refrain, "the Dwarfs are for the Dwarfs."

The Dwarfs want no authority over them and kill without remorse the forces of Aslan as well as those of Rishda and Tash. Once the Dwarfs realize they have been taken in by Shift, they refuse to believe anyone. They challenge Shift to bring out Aslan, taunting the Ape ironically and mistakenly with the words "seeing is believing."[28] They negatively exemplify St. Augustine's dictum that "faith precedes understanding." Put another way, the axiom "seeing is believing" is false; in truth, as Lewis shows in so many ways (notably in *Miracles* and in discussing answered prayer), it should be "believing is seeing."

The Dwarfs' case is a warning that hypocrites provide agnostics with a rationalization for not believing anything. A pretender once seen through is a more powerful weapon in Satan's arsenal than an outright atheist. Jesus forewarned us of the emergence and destructive force of such hypocrites. In our own day, the politically correct have counterfeited Jesus' command not to judge. He meant for us not to consign someone to Hell in our hearts. Jesus also said that we can judge a tree by its fruit, meaning whether or not someone is legitimate.[29] Paul commands us to judge false teachers by the Word in order to avoid being taken in, as the Narnians were. Judgment in the sense of discerning truth from falsehood is essential; Heaven and Hell hang in the balance.

The Dwarfs enter the same stable that contains Truth himself, along with all those who believe and rejoice. Tender-hearted Lucy, seeing the Dwarfs huddled in a self-absorbed circle, missing out on the delights of Heaven and the presence of the true Aslan, asks if Aslan won't help them. Demonstrating that the real issue is not that Aslan won't help them but that the Dwarfs will not be helped, Aslan places a feast before them. But it is to them only stable food, and the enjoyment of it is further ruined when they fight over the mistaken belief that some have gotten better than others. Where those who believe in Aslan see the glories of Heaven, the unbelieving Dwarfs see only a stinking stable. They have withdrawn into themselves, and what they find there is Hell.[30]

> "You see," said Aslan. "They will not let us help them. They have chosen cunning instead of belief. Their prison is only in their own minds, yet they are in that prison; and so afraid of being taken in that they cannot be taken out."[31]

The other evil characters receive the same judgment, presented with great irony. Like atheistic philosophers of the eighteenth-century Enlightenment, Shift, Ginger, and Rishda Tarkaan do not believe in the supernatural at all—neither Aslan, the God of Narnia, nor Tash, the idol god of Calormen. But to manipulate the culpable, they commit the syncretistic heresy of confounding Aslan and Tash, coining the term Tashlan for the pretended god in the stable. When Rishda emerges with preeminent power, he demonstrates Calormen superiority by setting up their god, calling manipulatively upon Tash.

Lewis supposes that behind all the false gods of mythology are real demons, or that real demons come to exploit such idol worship, performing even supernatural acts, instilling fear and ultimately possessing those who open themselves up by making themselves channels of their diabolical power. In the end, like Weston in *Perelandra*, they become unmen, their humanity consumed by the demons' desire to totally dominate them by supplanting their personhood. Just as Aslan comes when King Tirian calls upon him in great need, so Tash comes at the unwitting behest of Rishda and carries him off into Aslan's shadow.

PURGATORY

14

IS PURGATORY
PLAN B?

Blessed are the pure in heart, for they shall see God.[1]
JESUS

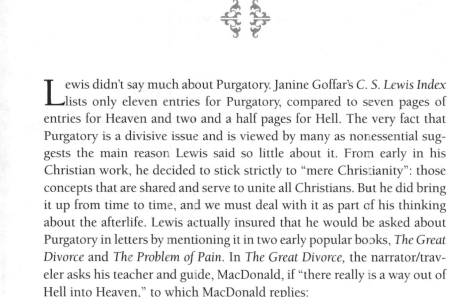

Lewis didn't say much about Purgatory. Janine Goffar's *C. S. Lewis Index* lists only eleven entries for Purgatory, compared to seven pages of entries for Heaven and two and a half pages for Hell. The very fact that Purgatory is a divisive issue and is viewed by many as nonessential suggests the main reason Lewis said so little about it. From early in his Christian work, he decided to stick strictly to "mere Christianity": those concepts that are shared and serve to unite all Christians. But he did bring it up from time to time, and we must deal with it as part of his thinking about the afterlife. Lewis actually insured that he would be asked about Purgatory in letters by mentioning it in two early popular books, *The Great Divorce* and *The Problem of Pain*. In *The Great Divorce*, the narrator/traveler asks his teacher and guide, MacDonald, if "there really is a way out of Hell into Heaven," to which MacDonald replies:

> "It depends on the way ye're using the words. If they leave that grey town behind it will not have been Hell. To any that leaves it, it is Purgatory. And perhaps ye had better not call this country Heaven. Not *Deep Heaven*, ye understand." (Here he smiled at me). "Ye can call it the Valley of the Shadow of Life. And yet to those who stay here it will have been Heaven from the first. And ye can call those sad streets in the town yonder the Valley of the Shadow of Death: but to those who remain there they will have been [in] Hell even from the beginning."[2]

The caution that follows may be worth more than the speculation:

"Son," he said, "ye cannot in your present state understand eternity. . . . But ye can get some likeness of it if ye say that both good and evil, when they are full grown, become retrospective. Not only this valley but all this earthly past will have been Heaven to those who are saved. Not only the twilight in that town, but all their life on earth too, will then be seen by the damned to have been Hell. That is what mortals misunderstand."[3]

To avoid taking sides in this controversial area, Lewis would usually couch his comments in fictional settings, like the dream motif in *The Pilgrim's Regress* and *The Great Divorce*, or put them in the mouths of fictional (Screwtape) or anonymous speakers (*A Grief Observed*). In straightforward prose works, like *Mere Christianity*, the reader must infer the concept of Purgatory from statements on God's intention to perfect us. For example, this one quoted earlier:

Though our feelings come and go, His love for us does not. It is not wearied by our sins, or our indifference; therefore, it is quite relentless in its determination that we shall be cured of those sins, at whatever cost to us, at whatever cost to Him.[4]

But this may be interpreted either as Purgatory or as earthly sanctification. It is a dream within a fantasy whose point is to choose Christ in our earthly life. In the end, however, Lewis does take sides in that he prays for the dead and believes in Purgatory. He also takes a firm position on what Purgatory means. I should clarify at once for someone asking the same question as the narrator in *The Great Divorce*: No, Lewis doesn't believe that Purgatory is a second chance for the lost to go from Hell to Heaven. Purgatory is the process of shedding sin and being purified to meet a holy God in holiness. This preparation is for those already saved.

Lewis made occasional direct mentions of Purgatory in his letters, but usually with one of his favorite analogies (like having a bad tooth pulled—painful but worth it) or in a playful tone, as in the letter to Sister Penelope cited later in this chapter. His first substantial treatment of Purgatory comes with his discussion of Thomas More (of *Utopia* fame) in his *English Literature in the Sixteenth Century*, where he explains that the concept has deteriorated to nothing more than a temporary Hell. Lewis describes More's *The Supplication of Souls* as "a real slough" in which the "last link with Heaven is severed."[5] The only place where Lewis owned his belief in plain language in a work for public consumption was the last book he ever wrote, the posthumously published *Letters to Malcolm*. This is the only book in which he directly took up issues not common to all Christians.

The most definitive statement about Purgatory is in Letter 20, where he links it with praying for the dead: "Of course I pray for the dead. The action is so spontaneous, so all but inevitable, that only the most compulsive theological case against it would deter me. And I hardly know how the rest of my prayers would survive if those for the dead were forbidden. At our age the majority of those we love best are dead. What sort of intercourse with God could I have if what I love best were unmentionable to Him?" Of course, he couldn't pray for them nor would the prayers be beneficial if they were already perfected in Heaven; so Lewis declares flatly, "I believe in Purgatory."[6] Lewis again rejects the pre-Reformation "Romish" doctrine of Purgatory. "If you turn from Dante's *Purgatorio* [or "Purgatory," the middle book of *The Divine Comedy*] to the sixteenth century you will be appalled by the degradation."

The view of Purgatory as punishment, Lewis laments, loses the root meaning of the word, which is to purge, cleanse, or purify. The Reformers were right to reject this, says Lewis, which makes it clear that he does, too. What he accepts as "the right view" is Cardinal Newman's concept of Purgatory, which Lewis paraphrases: "the saved soul, at the very foot of the throne, begs to be taken away and cleansed." Lewis expands on the idea:

> Our souls *demand* Purgatory, don't they? Would it not break the heart if God said to us, "It is true, my son, that your breath smells and your rags drip with mud and slime, but we are charitable here and no one will upbraid you with these things, nor draw away from you. Enter into the joy"? Should we not reply, "With submission, sir, and if there is no objection, I'd rather be cleaned first." "It may hurt, you know"—"Even so, sir."
>
> I assume that the process of purification will normally involve suffering. Partly from tradition; partly because most real good that has been done me in this life has involved it. But I don't think suffering is the purpose of the purgation. I can well believe that people neither much worse nor much better than I will suffer less than I or more. "No nonsense about merit." The treatment given will be the one required, whether it hurts little or much.[7]

To summarize, among theologians who believe in Purgatory there are two views: Purgatory is reserved for those who are already saved as part of their sanctification or preparation for heaven (that's one view), or for those who are in the process of being saved (that's the second). Lewis embraced the first view, which is represented by Dante in *The Divine Comedy* and Newman in *Dreams of Gerontius*.

There is also a range of views about suffering in Purgatory. In Lewis's conception, Purgatory is not a grim thing, as is delightfully clear in the last letter he wrote to longtime correspondent, Sister Penelope, both now old with infirmities, and Lewis under a medical sentence of death. He was blessedly unafraid to die and certainly had no fear of Purgatory. "I was unexpectedly revived from a long coma . . . but it would have been a luxuriously easy passage and one almost . . . regrets having the door shut in one's face. . . . To be brought back and have all one's dying to do *again* was rather hard. If you die first, and if 'prison visiting' is allowed, come down and look me up in Purgatory. It *is* all rather fun—solemn fun—isn't it?"[8] This is not to say that Lewis expected the purging process to be pain-free. He didn't: "that purification must, in its own nature, be painful, we hardly dare to dispute."[9] But the pain is dwarfed by "the joy set before us," and Lewis had the model of Dante's characters in Purgatory happily undergoing their painful tasks to overcome sin by learning to love everything properly.

Why did Lewis believe in Purgatory? One reason may be, as implied above, that it had captured his imagination in Dante's *Divine Comedy*. Lewis's praise for Dante is exalted, and he reworked Dante's material thoroughly in *The Great Divorce*. "The whole thickening treatment [becoming accustomed to Heaven] consists in learning to want God for his own sake," Lewis has a character advise another in *The Great Divorce*.[10] This could be a summary of Dante's *Purgatorio*, and this idea all Christians can embrace. It explains in part why *Purgatorio* is many readers' favorite part of *The Divine Comedy*, including mine—because it says so much about human nature and the role of discipline and sanctification in our earthly lives. It is also a primer on learning to love, the subject Lewis expounded in *The Four Loves*.[11] In other words, the theme of Purgatory and its literary treatment appealed to Lewis's imagination: "A modern tends to see purgatory through the eyes of Dante: so seen, the doctrine is profoundly religious."[12] It appeals to many, but not necessarily as an article of faith.

CRITIQUE OF LEWIS ON PURGATORY

Lewis's views on Purgatory are certainly open to criticism. Lewis accepts the biblical view that only Christ's suffering expiates sin and that his grace is all gift, received by faith, as in Ephesians 2:8-9: "For by grace you have been saved through faith. And this is not your own doing; it is the gift of God, not a result of works, so that no one may boast." The definition of grace is "undeserved favor." If our very salvation is all gift, *a fortiori*, why should our readiness to enter Heaven require "works of righteousness" on our part? Certainly no suffering of ours can add to the efficacy of Christ's on our behalf.[13]

Lewis is open to challenge on the logical fault of begging the question: that is, assuming as true what needs to be proven, here that we will appear before God smelly and dirty with our sin. "Come now, let us reason together, says the LORD: though your sins are like scarlet, they shall be as white as snow; though they are red like crimson, they shall become like wool."[14] While most Protestants do not accept the idea of Purgatory as a place with a lengthy process of continued sanctification or growth in godliness as a preparation for Heaven, all Protestants accept the idea of being purged of sin at death. In the biblical view, "we shall all be changed, in a moment, in the twinkling of an eye, at the last trumpet."[15]

Lewis believed in Purgatory, both because of tradition and because it appealed to his imagination. Lewis's only logical defense of Purgatory (he explains it mostly by analogies) is in *Letters to Malcolm*. His argument goes like this. We are all sinners. We die with a sin nature. The gap between the holiness of God and the sinfulness of the creature is so unimaginably wide and deep that a profound transformation must happen. And, borrowing from Dante's view that the soul in Purgatory willingly and even joyfully undertakes the discipline of each step in learning to love properly (the opposite of sin, which is a failure to love as we ought the right things in the right priorities), Lewis sees Purgatory not as something forced upon us as punishment, but willingly embraced for the good it will do us. Lewis illustrates the concept, as usual, with an engaging analogy:

> My favorite image on this matter comes from the dentist's chair. I hope that when the tooth of life is drawn and I am "coming round," a voice will say, "Rinse your mouth out with this." *This* will be Purgatory. The rinsing may be more fiery and astringent than my present sensibility could endure. But More and [John] Fisher shall not persuade me that it will be disgusting and unhallowed.[16]

For this argument, he assumes that we will continue on in time, though time may have qualities unimaginable now—"thickness as well as length."[17] Praying for the dead is linked with the idea of Purgatory, but what would be the point of praying for a dead person who has already been purified and is already unimaginably "holier" than ourselves? Lewis appears to believe the necessity of Purgatory against his own logic. In salvation, it is not we who seek God, but God who seeks us, as he forcefully argues. It is not our action or goodness that saves us, but God's action and goodness in Christ. For example, in *Mere Christianity* Lewis asserts:

> The business of becoming a son of God, . . . of passing over from the temporary biological life into timeless "spiritual" life, [has] been done for us. . . . We have not got to try to climb up into spiritual life by our own efforts; it has already come down into the human race. If we will only lay ourselves open to the one Man in whom it was fully present, and who, in spite of being God, is also a real man, He will do it in us and for us.[18]

If we can take salvation itself as total gift, why not the final piece of sanctification in which our sin nature drops away? Certainly, Lewis would say, the grace or undeserved favor of God is necessary in either case, whether by a purgatorial process involving time or an instantaneous purging.

Lewis is not entirely consistent on Purgatory in his fictional portrayals either. In *The Last Battle*, as Tirian enters Aslan's country (Heaven), he sees characters from the earlier Narnian tales all regally attired and looking fresh and ageless. But he also sees Jill and Eustace, his companions in these adventures right down to the last battle that ushered them into Aslan's country. Tirian views Jill with astonishment:

> But not Jill as he had last seen her, with her face all dirt and tears and an old drill dress half slipping off one shoulder. Now she looked cool and fresh, as fresh as if she had just come from bathing. And at first he thought she looked older, but then didn't, and he could never make up his mind on that point. And then he saw that the youngest of the Kings was Eustace: but he also was changed as Jill was changed.[19]

At first Tirian feels awkward about being in so august a company, but "next moment" he realizes that he has been likewise transformed and is himself "fresh and cool and clean" and dressed in kingly robes. Here the transformation happens for all of them in "the twinkling of an eye." Similarly, using now familiar imagery, the Episcopal Ghost in *The Great Divorce* is told that he may start over at once, as quickly as yanking a bad tooth.[20] Sabastian Knowles suggests another problem. Lewis's authority figure in *The Great Divorce*, George MacDonald, says: "'I think earth, if chosen instead of Heaven, will turn out to have been, all along, only a region in Hell: and earth, if put second to Heaven, to have been from the beginning a part of Heaven itself.' But if this is the case, then Lewis has the odd situation of earth being a part of heaven, which we leave for purgatory to then return to heaven."[21]

In the final analysis, perhaps the best thing Lewis says about Purgatory and other issues on which the Bible is either silent or merely suggestive is to humbly take stock of our human limitations and trust to an all-wise Providence. The following passage suggests why we cannot fruitfully entertain such questions (because we are limited by being in time) and where our emphasis should go (on making while we may the good choices that affect our eternal destiny). The narrator in *The Great Divorce* asks MacDonald a surprised question after learning that some of the Ghosts from the grey town are saved: "'But there is a real choice after death? My Roman Catholic friends would be surprised, for to them souls in Purgatory are already saved. And my Protestant friends would like it no better, for they'd say that the tree lies as it falls.'" MacDonald replies: "'They're both right, maybe. Do not fash yourself with such questions. Ye cannot fully understand the relations of choice and Time till you are beyond both. And ye were not brought here to study such curiosities. What concerns you is the nature of the choice itself: and that ye can watch them making.'"[22]

A NOTE ON LIMBO

The state known as Limbo also appears here and there in Lewis's work and may need a brief comment. In "Screwtape Proposes a Toast," Screwtape refers to Limbo as a state of "contented sub-humanity forever" and "'failed' humans."[23] The setting here is fictional, and Limbo is used mainly as a way of commenting on the bland state of contemporary belief. The crucial distinction is that Limbo is part of Hell, a place for those already damned, while Purgatory is for the already saved.[24] For Lewis, neither represents a second chance to make a choice after this life. Neither conception—Limbo nor Purgatory—is very important in Lewis's thought; Limbo least of all. He mentions it rarely; the longest treatment is a two-page chapter in his first Christian book, *The Pilgrim's Regress*.[25] In a letter to Joan Bennett, who had inquired about the fate of the "virtuous unbeliever," Lewis says he has no information.[26] We can say with certainty that Lewis believed that all people sin, and none are reconciled to God apart from Christ. The question, then, becomes a form of "What about those who haven't heard the gospel?" treated earlier, especially in the discussion of *The Last Battle*.

15

LAST THINGS: AN EPILOGUE ON WHO GOES TO HEAVEN

He [Jesus] has appeared once for all at the end of the ages to put away sin by the sacrifice of himself. And just as it is appointed for man to die once, and after that comes judgment, so Christ, having been offered once to bear the sins of many, will appear a second time, not to deal with sin but to save those who are eagerly waiting for him.[1]

HEBREWS

Lewis's journey to Christ was long and complex. It followed two paths simultaneously: reason and longing.[2] Lewis traveled these paths for nearly thirty years without seeing their connection. When they came together, he found the high road to Heaven in the person of Jesus Christ. For readers who want to know the twists and turns in Lewis's journey, there are three crucial books. Perhaps the place to start for most would be his spiritual autobiography *Surprised by Joy*, where "Joy" has the special meaning of unsatisfied desire or longing. But this is incomplete without the rational and philosophical part of the quest. While not a conversion narrative, the easiest place to explore his ideas is in the widely read and indispensable *Mere Christianity*. There is a place where the paths of both longing and reason merge into a single account, and that is in the first book he wrote after becoming a Christian: the too-seldom-read *The Pilgrim's Regress: An Allegorical Apology for Christianity, Reason and Romanticism* (longing). However, this book is admittedly not his easiest to understand.[3] Written in an astonishing two weeks, it not only presents his journey to belief in Christ but all of Lewis's major themes for the next thirty years of writing, including Heaven and Hell.

But for now, let us travel back to a major crossroad in Lewis's journey to faith. He was almost thirty when he finally knelt in his Oxford room and acknowledged God.

> You must picture me alone in that room in Magdalen, night after night, feeling, whenever my mind lifted even for a second from my work, the steady, unrelenting approach of Him whom I so earnestly desired not to meet. That which I greatly feared had at last come upon me. In the Trinity Term of 1929 I gave in, and admitted that God was God, and knelt and prayed: perhaps, that night, the most dejected and reluctant convert in all England. I did not then see what is now the most shining and obvious thing; the Divine humility which will accept a convert even on such terms.[4]

But this was only his conversion to theism. Two years would pass before his conversion to Christianity on September 28, 1931, while he was riding in the sidecar of his brother Warnie's motorcycle on the way to Whipsnade Zoo. "When we set out I did not believe that Jesus Christ is the Son of God, and when we reached the zoo I did."[5] Little emotion accompanied this last step for him. His mind, intellect, and imagination had been settling into it for a very long time.

It is perhaps not so remarkable that two years passed between his belief in God and trust in Christ. It is certainly remarkable, however, that he believed in God a full year before he believed in immortality. He did not come to faith, as I had, out of fear of Hell or the promise of Heaven, but out of intellectual honesty in recognizing that God and Jesus were what the Bible claimed them to be. Lewis saw this element of his conversion process—believing in Jesus before believing in immortality—as a great advantage for him because he learned to obey God, not anticipating reward or punishment, but simply because it was right.

Something else happened on Lewis's journey from theism to Christianity that he saw as a false start but a great help in the long run. He tried with all his might to keep the moral law and inevitably failed. It was, he could see, by the mercy of Christ and his forgiveness alone that he or any of us would be saved, not by our own goodness. He had the cart before the horse: We don't get good before God accepts us; rather, God accepts us, places us under new management, and *then* we begin to have a moral life that comes from the inside out. We can see, with Lewis, not only how this sequence of faith before works is necessary, but how it misses the whole point if moral living is our goal. God's focus is relationship, not religious observance. But the relationship requires that we acknowledge the plain fact that God is at the center and not we ourselves In our fallen human nature, we act as though we belong to ourselves and not to God. "In other words," Lewis says, "fallen man is not simply an imperfect creature who needs improvement: he is a rebel who must lay down his arms." It is called repentance and involves "unlearning all the self-conceit and self-will that we have been training ourselves into."[6] And it can't be done on our own steam; nor can we will ourselves to be born of God. He must father us. As Lewis puts it, "what man, in his natural condition, has not got, is Spiritual life—the higher and different sort of life that exists in God."[7] How could we possibly think we could work our way into spiritual life?

This is exactly what Paul teaches in Romans: that the Law (morality) functions as a tutor to show us our failings and bring us to Christ for mercy. How can we be joined to a holy God when we are sinful? That is where the mercy of Christ comes in. God's way of giving us right standing and spiritual life is through his incarnate death on the cross. When we trust in that sacrifice as the payment for our sin, God credits us with Jesus' perfectly lived life, pays our death penalty by his own on the cross, and makes us thereby fully acceptable to God, who gives us new life. This is "mere Christianity" and what must be accepted by faith.

In the book *Mere Christianity*, Lewis gives a valuable explanation of two kinds of faith, clarifying just what constitutes "saving faith."[8] The first kind of faith is intellectual assent to the truth of something. The Devil believes in Jesus with this kind of faith; that is, he knows the truth of it, but is still not saved by it. Lewis writes to Dom Bede Griffiths, his former pupil, now a priest: "Simply to accept the Redemption & Heaven & Hell as fact, when the climate of opinion makes such acceptance inevitable, need not be faith: the devils so accept it. Was it not a kind of 'knowing Christ according to the flesh?'"[9]

All of us must, Lewis rightly says, have this first kind of faith (intellectual assent) as a prerequisite, but there is a second kind of faith crucial to salvation. It is trust of the sort that makes a full commitment. placing our hope for living this life properly and for our eternal destiny in his hands, knowing that he will do in us what we cannot do for ourselves. This trust is anchored in Jesus Christ as presented in God's revealed Word, the Bible. Good works or righteous living then flow out of Christ's enablement through a true change of heart. The change cannot be manufactured by human effort. It comes from being supernaturally born of God, becoming his sons and daughters. Our part is to have faith; God's part is to make us alive in him.

Evidence abounds for the truth of Jesus Christ as God incarnate, "creator of heaven and earth"—much to be found in Lewis's work. But as Lewis saw and as St. Augustine and the Bible writers saw before him, faith must precede understanding; believing is seeing.[10] In *The Voyage of the "Dawn Treader,"* the Narnian adventurers come to the Island of the Star, at the beginning of the end of the world, where they meet Ramandu (the spirit of a star) and his daughter. Almost immediately they discover a table laden with food and drink and three men at the table in a deep sleep. The travelers are hungry, but in light of the enchantments they have met, they fear to eat, though the food and drink are inviting. Ramandu's daughter assures them it is all right. "'How are we to know you are a friend?'" Edmund asks. "'You can't know,' said the girl. 'You can only believe—or not.'"[11]

We are reminded of Jill in *The Silver Chair*, meeting Aslan for the first time. She is dying of thirst and wants to drink from a stream, but the great lion Aslan is between it and her. Fearing to advance, she asks Aslan to move aside. He won't. She asks for a promise that he will not eat her. He won't give it. She considers not drinking, but Aslan says, "then you must die of thirst. . . . There is no other stream."[12] It is, of course, a question of trust. The water is Jesus himself, the "living water."[13] "Whoever drinks of the water that I will give him will never be thirsty forever. The water that I will give him will become in him a spring of water welling up to eternal life," Jesus tells the Samaritan woman.[14] Jill must risk her life to drink this water—not a bad example of saving faith. Lewis says in *The Problem of Pain*:

> God gives what He has, not what He has not: He gives the happiness that there is, not the happiness that is not. To be God—to be like God and to share His goodness in creaturely response—to be miserable—these are the only three alternatives. If we will not learn to eat the only food that the universe grows—the only food that any possible universe ever can grow—then we must starve eternally.[15]

And what God has to give is Jesus. If Jesus is the answer to our deepest longings—to all our longings—and he has promised to come back, why doesn't he just explode on the scene right now and be done with it? For starters, he might. Quoting John Donne, Lewis poses as a rhetorical question, "what if this present were the world's last night?"[16] It may well be. But if he delays, we may know the reasons, the two most important suggested by Lewis. The first directs us to think of ourselves:

> God will invade. But I wonder whether people who ask God to interfere openly and directly in our world quite realize what it will be like when He does. When that happens, it is the end of the world. When the author walks on to the stage the play is over. . . . It will be too late then to choose your side. There is no use saying you choose to lie down when it has become impossible to stand up. That will not be the time for choosing: it will be the time when we discover which side we really have chosen, whether we realized it before or not. Now, today, this moment, is our chance to choose the right side. God is holding back to give us that chance. It will not last for ever. We must take it or leave it.[17]

If we already believe, there is another closely related reason that should transform every earthly pilgrimage. The reason comes from one of the best things Lewis ever wrote, a sermon entitled "The Weight of Glory."

> It may be possible for each to think too much of his own potential glory hereafter; it is hardly possible for him to think too often or too deeply about that of his neighbour. The load, or weight, or burden of my neighbour's glory should be laid on my back, a load so heavy that only humility can carry it, and the backs of the proud will be broken. It is a serious thing to live in a society of possible gods and goddesses, to remember that the dullest and most uninteresting person you can talk to may one day be a creature which, if you saw it now, you would be strongly tempted to worship, or else a horror and a corruption such as you now meet, if at all, only in a nightmare. All day long we are, in some degree, helping each other to one or other of these destinations. It is in the light of these overwhelming possibilities, it is with the awe and the circumspection proper to them, that we should conduct all our dealings with one another, all friendships, all loves, all play, all politics. There are no *ordinary* people. You have never talked to a mere mortal.[18]

There it is then. This short time on earth has been given us to prepare ourselves and help others on the way. The life of faith is not an escape from reality; it is an escape into reality. Scripture teaches, and I believe, that one day this present heaven and earth will pass away—dissolve, as I imagine, from the center of every atom, as every nucleus lets go of every proton, and every electron spins out of orbit, and the universe vanishes like a dream. And Christ the Creator will create a new heaven and a new earth. Then we will see that this world is the Shadowlands and Heaven is the true reality, the undeniable fact, more substantial and more durable than the seat you now sit in. "For the things that are seen are transient, but the things that are unseen are eternal."[19] Is there any doubt of this? Lewis counsels "A Lady" by letter that "the Bible itself gives us one short prayer which is suitable for all who are struggling with beliefs and doctrines. It is: 'Lord, I believe; help thou mine unbelief.'"[20]

NOTES

EPIGRAPHS

1. John Donne, *The Complete Poetry and Selected Prose of John Donne*, ed., with Introduction, Charles M. Coffin (New York: The Modern Library, 1952), 501.
2. C. S. Lewis, *The Last Battle* (New York: HarperCollins, 1994), 16:228.
3. Ibid., 15:213.

INTRODUCTION

1. 1 Peter 2:11 and Philippians 3:20.
2. Wayne Grudem, "The Unseen World Is Not a Myth," *Christianity Today* 30, no. 10 (July 11, 1986), 24.
3. C. S. Lewis, *The Problem of Pain* (New York: Macmillan, 1962), 10:145.
4. Christopher Mitchell treats this idea superbly in his article "The 'More' of Heaven and the Literary Art of C. S. Lewis," *Christianity and the Arts* 5, no. 3 (Summer 1998): 40-44. See also C. S. Lewis, "Transposition," in *"The Weight of Glory" and Other Addresses*, ed., with Introduction, Walter Hooper (New York: Simon & Schuster, 1996), 84; Joni Eareckson Tada has an excellent section on this point in *Heaven: Your Real Home* (Grand Rapids, Mich.: Zondervan, 1995), 26-29.
5. David Mills, *The Pilgrim's Guide: C. S. Lewis and the Art of Witness* (Grand Rapids, Mich.: Eerdmans, 1998), xiii.

CHAPTER 1—THE MYTHS OF HEAVEN EXPOSED

1. Colossians 3:1-4 (New Living Translation).
2. 1 Corinthians 2:9.
3. C. S. Lewis, *The Collected Letters of C. S. Lewis*, vol. 2, ed. Walter Hooper (San Francisco: HarperCollins, 2004), to Warfield M. Firor (August 17, 1949), 971.
4. C. S. Lewis, "Transposition," in *"The Weight of Glory" and Other Addresses*, ed., with Introduction, Walter Hooper (New York: Simon & Schuster, 1996), 83.
5. Psalm 16:11.
6. Harry Blamires, "Heaven: The Eternal Weight of Glory," *Christianity Today* 35, no. 6 (May 27, 1991), 33-34. The original prints *lovingkindness* as one word.
7. John Newton, "Glorious Things of Thee Are Spoken," *Hymns for the Living Church* (Carol Stream, Ill.: Hope Publishing Co., 1974), 209.
8. C. S. Lewis, *The Screwtape Letters* (San Francisco: HarperSanFrancisco, 2001), 9:44. I have chosen the Simon & Schuster edition because, unlike many recent versions, it includes Lewis's valuable explanatory Preface to the 1961 edition, along with the 1959 addition, "Screwtape Proposes a Toast."
9. David W. Fagerberg, "Between Heaven & Earth: C. S. Lewis on Asceticism & Holiness," *Touchstone* 17, no. 3 (April 2004), 33.
10. C. S. Lewis, *The Lion, the Witch and the Wardrobe* (New York: HarperCollins, 1994), 4:39.
11. Ibid., 9:95.
12. Fagerberg, "Between Heaven & Earth," 31.
13. C. S. Lewis, *Out of the Silent Planet* (New York: Macmillan, 1965), 12:73.
14. Ibid., 12:74.
15. Christopher Mitchell, "The 'More' of Heaven and the Literary Art of C. S. Lewis," *Christianity and the Arts* 5, no. 3 (Summer 1998), 43.

16. John Piper, "'Brokenhearted Joy': Taking the Swagger Out of Christian Cultural Influence," *World* (December 13, 2003), 51.
17. C. S. Lewis, *The Problem of Pain* (New York: Macmillan, 1962), 7:115. Where I have bracketed *pose*, the original has *oppose*.
18. Hebrews 12:22-23.
19. Joseph Bayly, *Heaven* (Elgin, Ill.: David C. Cook Publishing, 1977), 12.
20. Luke 19:17.
21. John G. Stackhouse, Jr., "Harleys in Heaven: What Christians Have Thought of the Afterlife & What Difference It Makes Now," *Christianity Today* 47, no. 6 (June 2003), 38.
22. John 17:24.
23. C. S. Lewis, "The Sermon and the Lunch," in *God in the Dock*, ed. Walter Hooper (Grand Rapids, Mich.: Eerdmans, 1970), III.3:286.
24. C. S. Lewis, *Mere Christianity* (New York: Macmillan, 1960), IV.9:174-175.
25. C. S. Lewis, *Miracles* (New York: Macmillan, 1978), see the chapters "Miracles of the Old Creation" (15:132-142) and "Miracles of the New Creation" (16:143-163).
26. Psalm 16:11.
27. Lewis, *Screwtape Letters*, 9:44.
28. Matthew 22:30.
29. C. S. Lewis, *Perelandra* (New York: Macmillan, 1965), 3:32-33. Here Lewis's narrator says, "In Ransom's opinion the present functions and appetites of the body would disappear, not because they were atrophied but because they were, as he said, 'engulfed.'"
30. Lewis, *Miracles*, 16:160.
31. Hugh Ross, *Beyond the Cosmos: The Extra-Dimensionality of God* (Colorado Springs: NavPress, 1996), 31-32.
32. Lewis has many intriguing speculations on how we might experience time differently after this earthly life. His creative liberty with the time lapse between earth and Narnia is one. In *Miracles*, he suggests that "time may not always be for us, as it is now, unilinear and irreversible" (16:153); in *Reflections on the Psalms* he hopes we will "finally . . . emerge, if not altogether from time (that might not suit our humanity) at any rate from the tyranny, the unilinear poverty, of time" (15:137-138). Lewis also suggests that time might have something like a variable thickness, implying another dimension or two. The entire chapter "Miracles of the New Creation" in *Miracles* is relevant to not only this segment (Myth #2) but to the whole book.
33. Ross, *Beyond the Cosmos*, 203.
34. Lewis, "The Weight of Glory," in *"The Weight of Glory" and Other Addresses*, 26.
35. C. S. Lewis, *The Four Loves* (New York: Harcourt Brace Jovanovich, 1960), 5:158. Jeffrey Russell gives a similar view: "Heaven is the state of being in which all are united in love with one another and with God. It is an *agape*, a love feast. . . . Heaven is the community of those whom God loves and who love God. All retain their personal character, but woven together in perfect charity, so that in God's generous embrace each person among the millions whom God loves[,] loves each other person among the millions whom God loves. It is like a weaving in which each thread touches every other thread in a spark of loving light, so that the whole web shines like a field of stars." Jeffrey Burton Russell, *A History of Heaven* (Princeton, N.J.: Princeton University Press, 1997), 5-6.
36. Lewis, "Transposition," in *"The Weight of Glory" and Other Addresses*, 84.
37. Philippians 3:20-21.
38. Robert L. Sassone, *The Tiniest Humans* (Stafford, Va.: American Life League, 1995), viii; quoted in Joni Eareckson Tada, *Heaven: Your Real Home* (Grand Rapids, Mich.: Zondervan, 1995), 37.
39. Lewis, *Miracles*, 11:92.
40. Ibid., 16:147.
41. Ibid., 16:161.
42. Tada, *Heaven: Your Real Home*, 39.
43. Lewis, *Miracles*, 16:148.
44. Ross, *Beyond the Cosmos*, 46-47.
45. Lewis, *Perelandra*, 10:130.
46. Lewis, *Miracles*, 16:153.

47. C. S. Lewis, "Man or Rabbit?" in *God in the Dock*, I.12:112. Compare with Eustace's un-dragoning in *The Voyage of the "Dawn Treader,"* discussed in the Narnia section.
48. Lewis, *Miracles*, 16:149.
49. Ibid., 161.
50. Philippians 1:6.
51. Lewis, *Problem of Pain*, 152-153.
52. Ibid., 147-148.
53. Ibid., 150.
54. Lewis, *Perelandra*, 14:173.
55. Lewis, *Problem of Pain*, 123.
56. Lewis, *Collected Letters of C. S. Lewis*, to Dom Bede Griffiths OSB (July 28, 1936), vol. 2, 202.
57. Colin Duriez, *The C. S. Lewis Encyclopedia* (Wheaton, Ill.: Crossway Books, 2000), 88.
58. 1 Peter 1:3-5.
59. Lewis, *Mere Christianity*, III.10:121.
60. Lewis, "'Horrid Red Things,'" in *God in the Dock*, I.6:68.
61. Ibid., 69.
62. Lewis, *Screwtape Letters*, Preface to 1961 edition, 10.
63. Kenneth Kantzer, "Afraid of Heaven," *Christianity Today* 35, no. 6 (May 27, 1991): 38.
64. Ezekiel 1—3:15.
65. Lewis, *Miracles*, 9:67.
66. Ibid., 14:123.
67. Clarence F. Dye, "The Evolving Eschaton in C. S. Lewis," Ph.D. diss. (New York: Fordham University, 1973), 236.
68. Lewis, "The Weight of Glory," in *"The Weight of Glory" and Other Addresses*, 30-31.
69. Anne Graham Lotz, *Heaven: My Father's House* (Nashville: W Publishing Group, Thomas Nelson, 2001), 85.
70. 1 Corinthians 2:9.
71. 2 Corinthians 4:16-18.
72. Lewis, "Man or Rabbit?," in *God in the Dock*, I.6:108-109.
73. Ibid., 112.
74. Lewis, *Mere Christianity*, II.3:56.
75. Flannery O'Connor, "A Good Man Is Hard to Find," *Heath Introduction to Fiction* (New York: Houghton Mifflin, 2000), 651-663.
76. Romans 11:36.
77. John 14:6.
78. Romans 3:23; 6:23.
79. Lewis, *Problem of Pain*, 145.
80. C. S. Lewis, *Surprised by Joy* (New York: Harcourt Brace & Co., 1955), 232.
81. C. S. Lewis, *Reflections on the Psalms* (New York: Harcourt, Brace & World, 1958), 41.
82. Ibid., 42.
83. Lewis, "The Weight of Glory," in *"The Weight of Glory" and Other Addresses*, 27.
84. Lewis, *Miracles*, 16:155.
85. Matthew 6:33.
86. Michael Cromartie, "'Salvation Inflation': A Conversation with Alan Wolfe," *Books & Culture* 10, no. 2 (March/April 2004): 18-19.
87. See, for example, St. Augustine, *The City of God* (London: Penguin, 1984); Martin Luther, "The Freedom of a Christian," in Luther's *Works*, Vol. 31; *Career of the Reformer*, ed. Harold J. Grimm (Philadelphia, Pa.: Muhlenberg Press, 1957), 327-377; and H. Richard Niebuhr, *Christ and Culture* (New York: Harper and Row, 1951).
88. Lewis, *Mere Christianity*, III.10:118.
89. Lewis, "Some Thoughts," *God in the Dock*, 147.
90. Ibid., 150.
91. George Weigel, "Europe's Problem—and Ours," *First Things* 140 (February 2004): 5.
92. Mark 12:13-17.
93. Weigel, "Europe's Problem," 7-8.

94. Ibid., 8.
95. Ibid., 11.
96. Lewis, "Answers to Christianity," *God in the Dock*, I.4:49.

CHAPTER 2—MAKING THE MYTHS OF HEAVEN AND HELL

1. C. S. Lewis, "Sometimes Fairy Stories May Say Best What's to Be Said," *Of Other Worlds*, ed. with a Preface, Walter Hooper (New York: Harcourt Brace Jovanovich, 1966), 38.
2. Harry Blamires, "Heaven: The Eternal Weight of Glory," *Christianity Today* 35, no. 6 (May 27, 1991): 32.
3. Ibid., (Celestial or Heavenly Encyclopedia).
4. Ibid.
5. Colin Duriez, *The C. S. Lewis Encyclopedia* (Wheaton, Ill.: Crossway Books, 2000), 88.
6. David Downing, *The Most Reluctant Convert: C. S. Lewis's Journey to Faith* (Downers Grove, Ill.: InterVarsity Press, 2002), 147-148.
7. "Myth Became Fact," in *God in the Dock*, ed. Walter Hooper (Grand Rapids, Mich.: Eerdmans, 1970), I.5:66. See also "Is Theology Poetry?" a stunning piece in a collection of stunning pieces in *"The Weight of Glory" and Other Addresses*, ed., with Introduction, Walter Hooper (New York: Simon & Schuster, 1996). For a good scholarly study, see Maria Kuteeva's chapter, "Myth," in *Reading the Classics with C. S. Lewis*, ed. Thomas L. Martin (Grand Rapids, Mich.: Baker, 2000).
8. Matthew 13:34.
9. C. S. Lewis, *Experiment in Criticism* (Cambridge: Cambridge University Press, 1961), 43-44. This statement from one of Lewis's notebooks might be helpful: "A *Myth* is the description of a state, an event, or series of events, involving superhuman personages, possessing unity, not truly implying a particular time or place, and dependent for its contents not on motives developed in the course of action but on the immutable relations of the personages." Walter Hooper, "Past Watchful Dragons," quoted in Charles Huttar, ed., *Imagination and the Spirit* (Grand Rapids: Eerdmans, 1971), 286.
10. "Is Theology Poetry?" in *"The Weight of Glory" and Other Addresses*, 83, gives a short, effective response to the evolutionary view.
11. Quoted in Duriez, *C. S. Lewis Encyclopedia*, 155.
12. C. S. Lewis, *Perelandra* (New York: Macmillan, 1965), 11:144.
13. C. S. Lewis, "On Stories," in *"On Stories" and Other Essays on Literature*, ed. Walter Hooper (New York: Harcourt Brace Jovanovich, 1982), 19-20.

CHAPTER 3—RECLAIMING THE HEAVENS FOR HEAVEN:
OUT OF THE SILENT PLANET

1. Psalm 8:3.
2. The series is often called the "space trilogy," but the last of the books stays at home in England.
3. David Downing, *Planets in Peril* (Amherst, Mass.: University of Massachusetts Press, 1992), 35.
4. C. S. Lewis, "On Three Ways of Writing for Children," in *"On Stories" and Other Essays on Literature*, ed. Walter Hooper (New York: Harcourt Brace Jovanovich, 1982), 42.
5. Clyde Kilby, *The Christian World of C. S. Lewis* (Grand Rapids, Mich.: Eerdmans, 1964), 89-90.
6. C. S. Lewis, *Out of the Silent Planet* (New York: Macmillan, 1965), 18:124.
7. C. S. Lewis, "Myth Became Fact," in *God in the Dock*, ed. Walter Hooper (Grand Rapids, Mich.: Eerdmans, 1970), I.5:67.
8. C. S. Lewis, *Miracles* (New York: Macmillan, 1978), 16:158.
9. Ibid.
10. George Musacchio, *C. S. Lewis: Man & Writer* (Belton, Tex.: University of Mary Hardin-Baylor, 1994), 53. This book contains excellent discussions of the Ransom trilogy, especially Lewis's extensive use of the medieval worldview.
11. Lewis, *Out of the Silent Planet*, 5:32.
12. Ibid., 39.

13. Ibid., 40.
14. Ibid., 99.
15. Ibid., 42.
16. Evelyn Underhill Moore, in *The Collected Letters of C. S. Lewis*, vol. 2, ed. Walter Hooper (San Francisco: HarperCollins, 2004), to C. S. Lewis (October 26, 1938), 234, n. 34; and letter to Mrs. Stuart Moore (Evelyn Underhill), (October 29, 1938), 235.
17. Lewis, *Out of the Silent Planet*, 94.
18. Ibid., 121.
19. Ibid., 58.
20. Ibid., 154.
21. C. S. Lewis, *The Collected Letters of C. S. Lewis*, vol. 2, ed. Walter Hooper (San Francisco: HarperCollins, 2004), to Sister Penelope SCMV (July [August] 9, 1939), 262.
22. Lewis, *Out of the Silent Planet*, 20:139.
23. Ibid., 75.
24. Philippians 1:21.
25. Lewis, *Out of the Silent Planet*, 16:100.
26. Ibid., 18:123.
27. C. S. Lewis, *Mere Christianity* (New York: Macmillan, 1960), II.5:62. Lewis didn't believe in evolution; he merely grants it here to make a larger point. For his views on evolution see the satirical poem "Evolutionary Hymn" and the essays "Is Theology Poetry?" in *"The Weight of Glory" and Other Addresses*, ed., with Introduction, Walter Hooper (New York: Simon & Schuster, 1996) and "The Funeral of a Great Myth" in *Christian Reflections* (Grand Rapids, Mich.: Eerdmans, 1967).
28. Lewis, *Out of the Silent Planet*, 19:131.
29. Ibid., 19:132.
30. Ibid., 20:139-140.

CHAPTER 4—PARADISE REGAINED: *PERELANDRA*

1. Genesis 3:17 and Revelation 22:3.
2. C. S. Lewis, *Perelandra* (New York: Macmillan, 1965), 1:18.
3. C. S. Lewis, *Out of the Silent Planet* (New York: Macmillan, 1965), 18:119.
4. Lewis, *Perelandra*, 1:10.
5. Ibid., 1:13.
6. Ibid., 1:19.
7. Lewis, *Out of the Silent Planet*, 18:122.
8. Ibid., 72.
9. C. S. Lewis, "Christianity and Culture," in *Christian Reflections*, ed. Walter Hooper (Grand Rapids, Mich.: Eerdmans, 1967), 33.
10. Ibid., 110.
11. C. S. Lewis, *Surprised by Joy* (New York: Harcourt Brace & Co., 1955), 237.
12. Lewis, *Perelandra*, 11:149.
13. Lewis says in *A Grief Observed*. "Heaven will solve our problems, but not. I think, by showing us subtle reconciliations between all our apparently contradictory notions. The notions will all be knocked from under our feet. We shall see that there never was any problem." (New York: Bantam, 1976), 4:83.
14. Lewis, *Perelandra*, 17:214.
15. Though sexless, the Oyaresu of Mars and Venus are gendered, male and female, respectively.
16. Lewis, *Perelandra*, 16:197.
17. Ibid.

CHAPTER 5—THE FULFILLMENT OF HUMAN POTENTIAL: *THE GREAT DIVORCE*

1. C. S. Lewis, *The Letters of C. S. Lewis to Arthur Greeves (1914-1963)*, ed. Walter Hooper (New York: Macmillan, 1979), February 22, 1944, 501. Lewis uses "Xt" to abbreviate "Christ."

2. C. S. Lewis, "The Weight of Glory," in *The Weight of Glory" and Other Addresses*, ed., with Introduction, Walter Hooper (New York: Simon & Schuster, 1996), 8.
3. See Lewis's spiritual autobiography *Surprised by Joy* (New York: Harcourt Brace & Co., 1955).
4. Ecclesiastes 3:11.
5. William Blake, *The Marriage of Heaven and Hell*, ed. Geoffrey Keynes (New York: Oxford University Press, 1975), xviii.
6. C. S. Lewis, *The Great Divorce* (New York: Macmillan, 1946), Preface:6.
7. I have coined the term "hellian" as a convenient way of referring to someone from Hell, avoiding the common spelling "hellion" because it connotes an outward rowdiness, which applies to only a few.
8. Lewis, *Great Divorce*, 3:28.
9. Ibid., 9:72-73.
10. C. S. Lewis, *The Problem of Pain* (New York: Macmillan, 1962), 128.
11. Lewis, *Great Divorce*, 3:27.
12. Ibid., 13:122-123.
13. Ibid., 1:14.
14. C. S. Lewis, "Christianity and Culture," *Christian Reflections*, ed. Walter Hooper (Grand Rapids, Mich.: Eerdmans, 1967), 33.
15. Evan K. Gibson, *C. S. Lewis, Spinner of Tales: A Guide to His Fiction* (Grand Rapids, Mich.: Eerdmans, 1980), 116.
16. Ibid., 112.
17. John Milton, *Paradise Lost*, I, 254-255.
18. Ibid., IV, 75.
19. Lewis, *Great Divorce*, 9:75.
20. Lewis, *Problem of Pain*, 125.
21. 1 Corinthians 2:9.
22. Lewis, *Great Divorce*, 13:121.
23. For a fuller presentation of Frank and pity, see the section on *The Great Divorce* in the part of this book dealing with Hell.
24. Lewis, *Great Divorce*, 12:107.
25. Ibid., 14:128.

CHAPTER 6—LAND OF WONDER AND DELIGHT: THE CHRONICLES OF NARNIA

1. Psalm 37:4.
2. See Christin Ditchfield's valuable guide for biblical allusions throughout The Chronicles of Narnia: *A Family Guide to Narnia* (Wheaton, Ill.: Crossway Books, 2003); this allusion 96-97.
3. C. S. Lewis, *Prince Caspian* (New York: HarperCollins, 1994), 5:71.
4. Ibid., 5:72.
5. Ibid., 6:80.
6. C. S. Lewis, *Letters to Children*, ed. Lyle W. Dorsett and Marjorie Lamp Mead (New York: Macmillan, 1988), to Patricia (June 8, 1960), 92.
7. The name for Aslan's father varies slightly within and among the Chronicles, e.g., "Emperor-Beyond-the-Sea" and "Emperor-over-the-Sea."
8. C. S. Lewis, *The Magician's Nephew* (New York: HarperCollins, 1994), 6:88.
9. Ibid., 6:90.
10. A preliminary look at Michael Ward's work in progress was reported in the "Planet Narnia," *Times Literary Supplement* (April 25, 2003), 15.
11. Lewis, *Magician's Nephew*, 3:33. The Wood between the Worlds is not a place to stay, however, and with the children's drowsiness may owe something to the Lotus Eaters of Tennyson and Homer; for them staying is a temptation that works against their returning home.
12. Ibid., 13:149.
13. Ibid., 14:207.

14. Two passages serve to illustrate the biblical background for the Beatific Vision: "For God, who said, 'Let light shine out of darkness,' has shone in our hearts to give the light of the knowledge of the glory of God in the face of Jesus Christ" (2 Corinthians 4:6); "No longer will there be anything accursed, but the throne of God and of the Lamb will be in it, and his servants will worship him. They will see his face, and his name will be on their foreheads. And night will be no more. They will need no light of lamp or sun, for the Lord God will be their light, and they will reign forever and ever" (Revelation 22:3-5).
15. C. S. Lewis, *The Lion, the Witch and the Wardrobe* (New York: HarperCollins, 1994), 8:85.
16. Ibid.
17. Ibid., 8:86.
18. Augustine's *Confessions* IX.10.25; translation from Colm Luibheid's Preface to John Climacus, *The Ladder of Divine Ascent* (Paulist Press, 1982), xvii, in David W. Fagerberg, "Between Heaven & Earth: C. S. Lewis on Asceticism & Holiness," *Touchstone* 17, no. 3 (April 2004): 30-35.
19. C. S. Lewis, *Perelandra* (New York: Macmillan, 1965), 9:111.
20. Lewis, *Letters to Children*, to Mrs. K (May 6, 1955), 52.
21. Lewis, *Magician's Nephew*, 15:212-213.
22. Ibid., 15:213.
23. John 14:6.
24. Lewis, *The Lion, the Witch and the Wardrobe*, 7:74.
25. C. S. Lewis, *The Problem of Pain* (New York: Macmillan, 1962), 4:61.
26. Philippians 2:10-11.
27. Psalm 16:11.
28. Lewis, *The Lion, the Witch and the Wardrobe*, 12:140.
29. Romans 3:23; 6:23.
30. Lewis, *The Lion, the Witch and the Wardrobe*, 15:179.
31. Philippians 1:21.
32. Lewis, *The Lion, the Witch and the Wardrobe*, 15:177-178.
33. Ibid., 15:178.
34. Ibid., 15:179.
35. Ibid., 15:180.
36. Ibid., 17:201.
37. 1 Peter 5:5.
38. C. S. Lewis, *The Horse and His Boy* (New York: HarperCollins, 1994), 10:161.
39. Ibid., 161-162.
40. C. S. Lewis, *Mere Christianity* (New York: Macmillan, 1960), III.8:109.
41. C. S. Lewis, *Christian Reflections*, ed. Walter Hooper (Grand Rapids, Mich.: Eerdmans, 1967), 7.
42. C. S. Lewis, *Letters of C. S. Lewis*, ed. W. H. Lewis (New York: Harcourt Brace Jovanovich, 1975), To a Lady (June 20, 1952), 242.
43. Lewis, *The Horse and His Boy*, 11:172.
44. Ibid., 11:174.
45. Ibid., 10:157.
46. Hebrews 13:5, quoting several Old Testament passages.
47. Galatians 4:7.
48. Romans 8:16-17.
49. Lewis, *The Horse and His Boy*, 10:158.
50. Ibid., 11:177.
51. Ibid., 11:177-178.
52. Ibid., 12:184.
53. See God speaking to Moses: Exodus 3:13-14; road to the Transfiguration: Matthew 17:1-8; Emmaus: Luke 24:13-35; Peter rebuked: John 21:18-22; examples on baptism: Matthew 28:18, Acts 8:36-39; river in Heaven: Revelation 22:1-2.
54. Lewis, *The Horse and His Boy*. 14:214-215.
55. Ibid., 11:176.
56. Exodus 3:14. Aslan often identifies himself this way. In *The Silver Chair*, Jill asks Aslan,

"'Then are you Somebody, Sir?'" to which Aslan replies simply, "'I am.'" (New York: HarperCollins, 1994), 2:23.
57. Lewis, *The Horse and His Boy*, 11:176.
58. Lewis, *Problem of Pain*, 10:147-148.
59. "To the one who conquers I will give some of the hidden manna, and I will give him a white stone, with a new name written on the stone that no one knows except the one who receives it" (Revelation 2:17).
60. Lewis, *Prince Caspian*, 10:148.
61. Ibid., 15:228.
62. C. S. Lewis, *Preface to "Paradise Lost"* (New York: Oxford University Press, 1961), 102-103.
63. Lewis, *Prince Caspian*, 15:231.
64. C. S. Lewis, *Collected Letters of C. S. Lewis*, ed. Walter Hooper (San Francisco: HarperCollins, 2004), to Dom Bede Griffiths OSB (May 8, 1939), vol. 2, 258.
65. Anne Jenkins, March 5, 1961, in Roger Lancelyn Green and Walter Hooper, *C. S. Lewis: A Biography* (London: HarperCollins, 2002), 323-324.
66. C. S. Lewis, *Voyage of the "Dawn Treader"* (New York: HarperCollins, 1994), 2:21.
67. Ibid., 14:231.
68. Daniel 3:17-18.
69. Job 13:15.
70. Lewis, *Voyage of the "Dawn Treader,"* 2:22.
71. Acts 1:8 (KJV).
72. Matthew 28:19-20 (KJV).
73. Lewis, *Voyage of the "Dawn Treader,"* 1:15.
74. Paul A. Karkainen, *Narnia Explored* (Old Tappan, N.J.: Revell, 1979), 69.
75. See Myth #7, "Heavenly Minded, But No Earthly Good," in chapter 1 of this book.
76. Lewis, *Voyage of the "Dawn Treader,"* 1:1.
77. Ibid., 7:108.
78. Ibid., 7:109.
79. Ibid., 7:110.
80. Ibid.
81. "Now war arose in heaven, Michael and his angels fighting against the dragon. And the dragon and his angels fought back, but he was defeated and there was no longer any place for them in heaven. And the great dragon was thrown down, that ancient serpent, who is called the devil and Satan, the deceiver of the whole world—he was thrown down to the earth, and his angels were thrown down with him" (Revelation 12:7-9).
82. Lewis, *Voyage of the "Dawn Treader,"* 8:136.
83. Ibid., 6:93.
84. Ibid., 7:117.
85. Ibid.
86. Ibid., 7:117-118.
87. Ibid., 7:118.
88. Michael Ward, "The Path to Sympathy: Reflections on *Till We Have Faces*," presented July 14, 2000, at St. Anne's, Oxford; a copy in the Wade Center, Wheaton College, Wheaton, Ill., unpublished paper, 2. Several ideas from the next three paragraphs come from this paper.
89. Lewis, *Problem of Pain*, 3:41, 46.
90. Lewis, *Voyage of the "Dawn Treader,"* 10:167.
91. Ibid.
92. Ibid., 10:171.
93. Ibid., 11:174.
94. Ibid., 11:181-182.
95. Hebrews 11:16.
96. Isaiah 6:5.
97. Lewis, *The Lion, the Witch and the Wardrobe*, 8:86.
98. Lewis, *The Voyage of the "Dawn Treader,"* 16:269.
99. Lewis, *The Silver Chair*, 15:239.

Notes

100. Revelation 22:1; Romans 6:4.
101. Lewis, *The Silver Chair*, 16:251.
102. Lewis, *Mere Christianity*, III.9:118.
103. Lewis, *The Silver Chair*, 16:253.
104. Ibid., 8:124.
105. In a letter to Dom Bede Griffiths, January 8, 1936, Lewis says, "What indeed can we imagine Heaven to be but unimpeded obedience. I think this is one of the causes of our love of inanimate nature, that in it we see things which unswervingly carry out the will of their Creator, and are therefore wholly beautiful: and though their *kind* of obedience is infinitely lower than ours, yet the degree is so much more perfect that a Christian can see the reason that the Romantics had in feeling a certain holiness in the wood and water. The Pantheistic conclusions they sometimes drew are false: but their feeling was just and we can safely allow it in ourselves now that we know the real reason" (Hooper, *Collected Letters of C. S. Lewis*, vol. 2, 177-178).
106. Virgil, who has been the character Dante's guide up to now, says: "no longer await any word or sign from me: free, upright, and whole is your will, and it would be a fault not to act according to its intent. Therefore you over yourself I crown and mitre." Dante Alighieri, *Purgatorio*, in *The Divine Comedy*, ed. and trans. Robert M. Durling, 3 vols. (New York: Oxford University Press, 2003), canto 27, lines 139-42, 463.
107. C. S. Lewis, *The Last Battle* (New York: HarperCollins: 1994), 15:212.
108. Ibid., 10:139.
109. Paul F. Ford, *Companion to Narnia*, 3rd ed. (New York: Macmillan, 1986), 166, and Martha C. Sammons, *A Guide Through Narnia* (Wheaton, Ill.: Harold Shaw Publishers, 1979), 145. In "Narnia: The Domain of Lewis's Beliefs," an appendix in Kathryn Lindskoog's *Journey into Narnia* (Pasadena, Calif.: Hope Publishing House, 1998), M. A. Manzalaoui, of Arabic descent and a former pupil of Lewis, nominates himself as part of the inspiration for the character Emeth, 218-219.
110. Lewis, *The Last Battle*, 12:161.
111. Ibid., 10:140-141.
112. Ford, *Companion*, 407.
113. Lewis, *The Last Battle*, 15:204.
114. Exodus 20:3.
115. See the parable of the wheat and tares in Matthew 13:24-30.
116. C. S. Lewis, *Letters of C. S. Lewis*, ed., with a Memoir, by W. H. Lewis (New York: Harcourt Brace Jovanovich, 1966), to a Lady (January 8, 1952), 238.
117. Ibid., to a Lady (January 31, 1952), 238.
118. C. S. Lewis, *The Great Divorce* (New York: Macmillan, 1946), 13:124.
119. For example, in a letter to Joan Bennett, April 5, 1939, Lewis says, "Seriously, I don't pretend to have any information on the fate of the virtuous unbeliever. I don't suppose this question provided the solitary exception to the principle that actions on a false hypothesis lead to some less satisfactory result than actions on a true. That's as far as I would go" (Hooper, *Collected Letters of C. S. Lewis*, Vol. 2, 256).
120. See "Last Things: An Epilogue on Who Goes to Heaven," chapter 15 in this book.
121. Lewis, *The Last Battle*, 15:205-206.
122. Lewis says in one letter that he has not been able to harmonize other biblical teaching on righteousness through faith with Matthew 25:31-46. His approach in such cases was to believe both sides of a paradox until it got resolved. It seems easy enough to harmonize from the epistle of James, however: "For as the body apart from the spirit is dead, so also faith apart from works is dead." The passages on faith look at salvation before the fact: Believe to be saved. The passages on works look at salvation after the fact, showing what a saved person is like.
123. Paul F. Ford has a helpful list of such letters in his article on *The Last Battle* in *The C. S. Lewis Readers' Encyclopedia*, 232 (April 5, 1939; December 8 [not "9" as printed], 1941; January 31, 1952; November 8, 1952; August 3, 1953; and February 18, 1954). See also Lewis's comment in *Mere Christianity*, II.5.65; a short treatment in *The Four Loves* (New York: Harcourt Brace Jovanovich, 1960), 6:178; and Will Vaus's excellent discussion of the

221

issue in his *Mere Theology: A Guide to the Thought of C. S. Lewis* (Downers Grove, Ill.: InterVarsity Press, 2001), 104-108, the last of these pages dealing specially with Emeth.

124. Lewis, *Letters of C. S. Lewis*, to a Lady (November 8, 1952), 247.

125. Lewis, *Letters to Children*, to Patricia (June 8, 1960), 93. Lewis is aware that he has not harmonized this view with the whole counsel of Scripture. In a letter to Emily McLay (*Letters of C. S. Lewis*, August 3, 1953, 251), before referring to Jesus' words on the sheep and goats, he writes: "I take it as a first principle that we must not interpret any part of Scripture so that it contradicts other parts," though he immediately implies a contradiction in saying he wishes to give priority to Jesus' words over an apostle. A correct interpretation would have to accommodate the many references to salvation by faith (including Jesus' own words), as well as passages explicitly excluding works as a condition, like Ephesians 2:8-9, cited elsewhere in the book: "For by grace [unmerited favor] you have been saved through faith. And this is not your own doing; it is the gift of God, not a result of works, so that no one may boast."

126. Lewis, *The Last Battle*, 191.

127. Ibid., 8:111.

128. Ibid., 15:211.

129. Ibid., 15:212.

130. Colin Manlove, *The Chronicles of Narnia: The Patterning of a Fantastic World* (New York: Twayne, 1993), 109-110.

131. Ibid., 213.

132. 2 Peter 3:10.

133. Lewis, *The Last Battle*, 13:183.

134. Ibid., 13:172.

135. C. S. Lewis, *The Collected Letters of C. S. Lewis*, vol. 2, ed. Walter Hooper (San Francisco: HarperCollins, 2004), to Arthur Greeves (July 27, 1949), vol. 2, 960.

136. Lewis, *The Last Battle*, 16:227.

137. Ibid., 16:228.

138. Ibid.

139. Ibid., 15:211.

140. Ibid., 16:228.

CHAPTER 7—WHEN SEEING IS NOT BELIEVING:
TILL WE HAVE FACES

1. John 6:35-36.

2. C. S. Lewis, "The Weight of Glory," in *"The Weight of Glory" and Other Addresses*, ed., with Introduction, Walter Hooper (New York: Simon & Schuster, 1996), 15-16.

3. For a superb account of Joy or desire and its significance, see Lewis's sermon "The Weight of Glory" (perhaps the best thing he ever wrote) and his autobiographical treatment in *Surprised by Joy* (New York: Harcourt, Brace, & World, 1955). For a very readable scholarly treatment of Lewis's journey to belief, see David Downing's *The Most Reluctant Convert: C. S. Lewis's Journey to Faith* (Downers Grove, Ill.: InterVarsity Press, 2002).

4. C. S. Lewis, *The Collected Letters of C. S. Lewis*, vol. 2, ed. Walter Hooper (San Francisco: HarperCollins, 2004), Ruth Pitter to Herbert Palmer (November 15, 1945), vol. 2, 685n.

5. A familiar example of a story similarly working on multiple levels is *Gulliver's Travels*, which can be read by children as a fantasy story, by adults with no knowledge of the eighteenth century as a satire on human nature, and by the historically informed as a satire on Swift's political contemporaries. But so masterful is the integrity of the story that no reader feels left out by puzzling mysteries at any other level.

6. C. S. Lewis, *Till We Have Faces* (New York: Harcourt Brace & Company, 1984), I.2:23.

7. Ibid., I.7:72-73.

8. C. S. Lewis, "Five Sonnets," in *Poems*, ed. Walter Hooper (New York: Harcourt Brace Jovanovich, 1964), 126-127. This connection was suggested by Michael Ward, "The Path to Sympathy: Reflections on *Till We Have Faces*," presented July 19, 2000, at St. Anne's, Oxford; a copy is in the Wade Center, Wheaton College, Wheaton, Illinois, unpublished paper.

9. C. S. Lewis, *The Great Divorce* (New York: Macmillan, 1946), Preface: 6.
10. See ibid., chapters 10 and 11.
11. Ibid., 9:71.
12. Ibid., 9:81.
13. Ibid., 9:81-82.
14. John 12:24-25.
15. Lewis, *Till We Have Faces.*, II.4:294.
16. Ibid., II.4:305.
17. Ibid., II.4:307.

CHAPTER 8—THE MYTHS OF HELL EXPOSED

1. Matthew 23:37.
2. C. S. Lewis, *The Problem of Pain* (New York: Macmillan, 1962), 8:127.
3. Harris Poll on "The Religious and Other Beliefs of Americans 2003," *Skeptical Inquirer*, Vol. 27 (July/August 2003): 5; quoted in Henry M. Morris, "The Lake of Fire," *Back to Genesis*, no. 184 (April 2003), a.
4. Matthew 7:13-14.
5. C. S. Lewis, *The Problem of Pain* (New York: Macmillan, 1962), 8:119. Several ideas in the next few paragraphs are, like this one, paraphrased from the chapter on "Hell."
6. Don Richardson notes that the Old Testament mentions "Hell" thirty-one times, "once for every 774 verses," while among the New Testament's 7,992 verses, "Hell" and the nouns "perdition" and "fire" (when "fire" means "hell," not "zeal" or "revival") occur seventy-four times, which is once for every 120 verses. In *Secrets of the Koran* (Ventura, Calif.: Regal, 2003), 93.
7. Lewis, *Problem of Pain*, 8:119-120.
8. Ibid., 121-122.
9. Ibid., 123.
10. Ibid., 127.
11. C. S. Lewis, *The Four Loves* (New York: Harcourt Brace Jovanovich, 1960), 6:176.
12. C. S. Lewis, *Letters of C. S. Lewis*, ed., with a Memoir, by W. H. Lewis (New York: Harcourt Brace Jovanovich, 1966), to a Lady (undated, 1951?), 231.
13. C. S. Lewis, *Surprised by Joy* (New York: Harcourt, Brace, & World, 1955), 226.
14. Mark 5:1-20.
15. C. S. Lewis, "Divine Justice," in *Poems*, ed. Walter Hooper (New York: Harcourt Brace Jovanovich, 1964), 98.
16. Lewis, *Problem of Pain*, 124-125.
17. Here Lewis cites Matthew 25: 34, 41: "Then the King will say to those on his right, 'Come, you who are blessed by my Father, inherit the kingdom prepared for you from the foundation of the world'"; and "Then he will say to those on his left, 'Depart from me, you cursed, into the eternal fire prepared for the devil and his angels.'"
18. Lewis, *Problem of Pain*, 8:125.
19. Ibid., 126.
20. C. S. Lewis, *The Collected Letters of C. S. Lewis*, vol. 2, ed. Walter Hooper (San Francisco: HarperCollins, 2004), to Warren Lewis (January 28, 1940), vol. 2, 334-335.
21. C. S. Lewis, *The Pilgrim's Regress* (Grand Rapids, Mich.: Eerdmans, 1958), 181.
22. Ibid., 181.
23. Ibid.
24. The relevant lines from the poem "Divine Justice" read: "God in His mercy made / The fixed pains of Hell. / That misery might be stayed"; see C. S. Lewis, *Poems* (Grand Rapids, Mich.: Eerdmans, 1958), 98, or *Pilgrim's Regress*, 180.
25. Ibid. I'm grateful to Walter Hooper, whose *C. S. Lewis Companion & Guide* (San Francisco: HarperCollins, 1996) steered me to the right places. See 281.
26. John Milton, *Paradise Lost* I, 254-255.
27. C. S. Lewis, *The Great Divorce* (New York: Macmillan, 1946), 9:69.
28. Lewis, *Collected Letters of C. S. Lewis*, to Arthur Greeves (May 13, 1946), vol. 2, 710.

29. T. S. Eliot, *The Cocktail Party* (New York: Harcourt, Brace & World, 1950), 98 (act 1, scene 3).
30. Revelation 21:8.
31. Clarence F. Dye, "The Evolving Eschaton in C. S. Lewis," Ph.D. diss. (New York: Fordham University, 1973), 219.
32. Harry Blamires, *Knowing the Truth About Heaven and Hell: Our Choices and Where They Lead Us* (Ann Arbor, Mich.: Servant Books, 1988), 149-150.
33. Ibid., 150.
34. C. S. Lewis, *Preface to "Paradise Lost"* (New York: Oxford University Press, 1961), 13:102-103.
35. Kenneth Kantzer, "Afraid of Heaven," *Christianity Today* 35, no. 6 (May 27, 1991): 38.
36. Joshua 24:15.
37. Lewis, *Great Divorce*, 9:72-73.
38. Reformed or Calvinist views stress God's sovereignty in directing everything that happens in his creation, while an Arminian view stresses free will and human choice.
39. For more on this idea, see the chapter "Time and Beyond Time" in C. S. Lewis, *Mere Christianity* (New York: Macmillan, 1960), IV.3:145-149.
40. C. S. Lewis, *Perelandra* (New York: Macmillan, 1965), 11:147.
41. Ibid., 11:149.
42. Lewis, *Problem of Pain*, 125-126.
43. Ibid.
44. C. S. Lewis, *The Screwtape Letters* (San Francisco: HarperSanFrancisco, 2001), 28:101.
45. C. S. Lewis, *Out of the Silent Planet* (New York: Macmillan, 1965), 16:102.
46. Ibid., 20:139.
47. C. S. Lewis, *The Magician's Nephew* (New York: HarperCollins, 1994), 15:202-203.
48. For more on this point, see the discussion of Romans chapter one in the Hell section, Myth #1, and the Dwarfs in the segment on Narnia, *The Last Battle*, chapter 13.
49. Richard B. Cunningham, *C. S. Lewis: Defender of the Faith* (Philadelphia: Westminster, 1967), 125.
50. Ibid.
51. C. S. Lewis, "The Trouble with 'X' . . . ," in *God in the Dock*, ed. Walter Hooper (Grand Rapids, Mich.: Eerdmans, 1970), I.18:154-155.
52. Lewis, *Pilgrim's Regress*, 181-182 and *Poems*, 102-103.
53. Revelation 21:4.
54. Lewis, *Great Divorce*, 12:109.
55. Ibid., 13:120. The psalm is reminiscent of Psalm 91.
56. Ibid., 13:121. Much of the paragraph is a paraphrase of this page.
57. Ibid.
58. Lewis, "Dangers of National Repentance," *God in the Dock*, II.1:191n; Luke 14:26 KJV.
59. Matthew 22:23-33.
60. See also the discussion under the Heaven section, Myth #2 in chapter 1.
61. Lewis, *Problem of Pain*, 127-128.
62. Lewis, *Great Divorce*, 13:120.

CHAPTER 9—THE PHILOSOPHY OF HELL: *THE SCREWTAPE LETTERS*

1. 1 Peter 5:8.
2. C. S. Lewis, *Screwtape Letters* (San Francisco: HarperSanFrancisco, 2001), Preface to the 1961 edition, 7.
3. C. S. Lewis, *Perelandra* (New York: Macmillan, 1965), 10:128.
4. Lewis, *Screwtape*, Preface to the 1961 edition, 7.
5. Ibid., 84.
6. Ibid., 7.
7. Lewis, *Preface to "Paradise Lost"* (New York: Oxford University Press, 1961), 104-105.
8. Ibid., 107.
9. Lewis, *Screwtape Letters*, Preface to the 1961 edition, 7-8.

10. Ibid., 70-71.
11. C. S. Lewis, *Mere Christianity* (New York: Macmillan, 1960), III.8:109.
12. Matthew 22:36-40; see also Philippians 2:1-11.
13. Lewis says flat out that he believes in devils—that is, in angels who have made themselves enemies of God "by the abuse of their free will." That makes Satan "the opposite, not of God, but of Michael." See *The Screwtape Letters*, Preface to the 1961 edition, 6.
14. Ibid., 8:41.
15. Ibid., 18:71.
16. Ibid., 22:82-3.
17. Screwtape's transformation into a centipede has important literary precedents in both Dante's *Inferno*, where thieves metamorphose into serpents, and in Milton's *Paradise Lost* (on which Lewis wrote a book-length *Preface*), where the devils turn into serpents while listening to Satan's account of tempting Adam and Eve.
18. Lewis, *Screwtape*, 19:73.
19. Ibid., 22:83.
20. Ibid., 31:109.
21. Ibid., 31:110.
22. Walter Hooper, Lecture to Wheaton College group, St. Anne's, Oxford, July 2003.
23. Lewis, *Screwtape*, 31:110.
24. John 14:6.
25. Lewis, *Screwtape*, 31:111.
26. Ibid., 12:54.
27. C. S. Lewis, "A Slip of the Tongue," in *"The Weight of Glory" and Other Addresses*, ed., with Introduction, Walter Hooper (New York: Simon & Schuster, 1996), 142.
28. Exodus 20:3.
29. C. S. Lewis, *Letters to Malcolm: Chiefly on Prayer* (New York: Harcourt Brace Jovanovich, 1964), 4:22.
30. C. S. Lewis, *Four Loves* (New York: Harcourt Brace Jovanovich, 1960), 6:170-171.
31. George Sayer. *Jack: A Life of C. S. Lewis* (Wheaton, Ill.: Crossway, 1994), 276.
32. These are partial lists. For a comprehensive treatment of names and their meanings, see David G. Clark's article, "A Brief Discussion of the Designation for Persons in *The Screwtape Letters*," *The Lamp-Post of the Southern California CS [sic] Lewis Society* 26, No. 3-4 (Fall-Winter 2002): 19-32.
33. Ibid., 27.
34. Ibid., 25.

CHAPTER 10—EVIL IN PARADISE: *PERELANDRA*

1. 1 Corinthians 15:21 KJV.
2. Romans 6:23.
3. C. S. Lewis, *Perelandra* (New York: Macmillan, 1965), 9:110.
4. Ibid., 7:93.
5. Ibid., 7:96.
6. See the companion discussion in the Heaven section, chapter 4, for a fuller explanation of why the defeat of Weston and evil took a physical form.

CHAPTER 11—THE SOCIOLOGY OF HELL: *THAT HIDEOUS STRENGTH*

1. Romans 1:21-22.
2. Thomas Howard, "The Triumphant Vindication of the Body: The End of ism in *That Hideous Strength*," *The Pilgrims' Guide: C. S. Lewis and the Art of Witness*, ed. David Mills (Grand Rapids, Mich.: Eerdmans, 1998), 133.
3. There are characters, however, who have been to alternate worlds. Ransom has been to Malacandra and Perelandra; Merlin has been to King Arthur's Logres, a mythical place of goodness and justice. I include *The Pilgrim's Regress* in the fourteen, though it is allegorized autobiography.
4. Howard, "Triumphant Vindication of the Body," 141.

5. This quote from St. Augustine fairly summarizes the two opposing cities, St. Anne's and Belbury, in *That Hideous Strength*: "I classify the human race into two branches: the one consists of those who live by human standards, the other of those who live according to God's will. I also call these two classes the two cities, speaking allegorically. By two cities I mean two societies of human beings, one of which is predestined to reign with God for all eternity, the other doomed to undergo eternal punishment with the Devil." From *City of God* (New York: Penguin, 1984), Book XV.1.595. Thomas Howard identifies the struggle as "the ancient fight between Hell and Heaven" in "Triumphant Vindication of the Body," 142.

6. Lewis's great friend Charles Williams, in his *The Figure of Beatrice: A Study in Dante* (New York: Noonday Press, 1961 [c.1943]), brilliantly sets out the theme of love in Dante's *Divine Comedy*.

7. Augustine, *City of God*, XIV.28.593.

8. Matthew 5:14, 16.

9. C. S. Lewis, *That Hideous Strength* (New York: Macmillan, 1965), 9 (section 4):196.

10. Ibid., 9 (section 2):188.

11. Good summaries are available in Walter Hooper's *C. S. Lewis Companion & Guide* (San Francisco: HarperCollins, 1996) and *The C. S. Lewis Readers' Encyclopedia*, ed. Jeffrey D. Shultz and John G. West, Jr. (Grand Rapids, Mich: Zondervan, 1998).

12. Lewis, *That Hideous Strength*, 8 (section 3):177.

13. Ibid.

14. Ibid., 179.

15. Howard, "Triumphant Vindication of the Body," 138.

16. C. S. Lewis, *The Great Divorce* (New York: Macmillan, 1946), 13:125.

17. C. S. Lewis, "The Dark Tower," in *"The Dark Tower" and Other Stories* (New York: Harcourt Brace Jovanovich, 1977), 49.

18. Lewis, *That Hideous Strength*, 16 (section 4):353. The series of philosophical ideas Frost pursues are those current in Lewis's day, which this novel and many other works stand against. Here is Frost's complete philosophical trail: "He had passed from Hegel to Hume, thence through Pragmatism, and thence through Logical Positivism, and out at last into the complete void."

19. Ibid., 16 (section 6):358.

20. Ibid., 17 (section 3):367.

21. Ibid., 13 (section 5):289.

22. One of the most valuable parts of Lewis's *The Abolition of Man*, a prescient look into the consequences of abandoning God-given morality, is the appendix demonstrating that all civilizations at all points in history have recognized the existence of absolute moral truths and acted on them. A good analysis of the fragmentation resulting from abandonment of the moral law is Leslie P. Fairfield, "Fragmentation and Hope: The Healing of the Modern Schisms in *That Hideous Strength*" in David Mills, *The Pilgrim's Guide: C. S. Lewis and the Art of Witness* (Grand Rapids, Mich.: Eerdmans, 1998).

CHAPTER 12—HELL IS A CHOICE, TOO: THE GREAT DIVORCE

1. C. S. Lewis, *The Problem of Pain* (New York: Macmillan, 1962), 148.

2. C. S. Lewis, *The Great Divorce* (New York: Macmillan, 1946), 2:20.

3. Ibid., 9:75.

4. Owen Barfield, *Owen Barfield on C. S. Lewis*, ed. G. B. Tennyson (Middletown, Conn.: Wesleyan University Press, 1989), 88.

5. Ibid., 3:27.

6. Ibid.

7. Lewis, *Great Divorce*, 4:32.

8. Ibid., 4:34.

9. Ibid. There is some controversy over the etymology of *bloody* as a slang term.

10. Ibid., 4:36.

11. Lewis, *Great Divorce*, 9:69-70.

Notes

CHAPTER 13—DESCENT INTO HELL: THE CHRONICLES OF NARNIA

1. Matthew 7:13, 15.
2. I am putting the treatment of *The Lion, the Witch and the Wardrobe* first because Jadis is such a seminal representation of evil, and her strongest characterization comes from this book. Some of the Chronicles are not treated here as they don't all contribute strongly to this theme, but all are dealt with under the Heaven section. Cross-referencing the two sections on each book may prove of some value.
3. Jadis figures directly in *The Magician's Nephew* and *The Lion, the Witch and the Wardrobe* and indirectly in *The Silver Chair*.
4. C. S. Lewis, *The Lion, the Witch and the Wardrobe* (New York: HarperCollins, 1994), 13:149.
5. C. S. Lewis, *The Magician's Nephew* (New York: HarperCollins, 1994), 10:141.
6. Ibid., 13:192.
7. Ibid.
8. Ibid., 14:207-208.
9. Ibid., 15:212.
10. Ibid., 14:203.
11. The case of Uncle Andrew is discussed further in the section "A Good God Couldn't Send Anyone to Hell," chapter 8.
12. C. S. Lewis, *The Horse and His Boy* (New York: HarperCollins, 1994), 15:231.
13. Paul F. Ford, *Companion to Narnia*, 3ʳᵈ ed. (New York: Macmillan, 1985), 342.
14. C. S. Lewis, *The Voyage of the "Dawn Treader"* (New York: HarperCollins, 1994), 6:97.
15. Ibid., 6:98.
16. Ibid.
17. Ibid.
18. Ibid., 12:201.
19. C. S. Lewis, *The Great Divorce* (New York: Macmillan, 1946), 9:68-69.
20. C. S. Lewis, *The Silver Chair* (New York: HarperCollins, 1994), 10:160
21. Ibid., 10:149.
22. Ibid., 10:156.
23. Ibid. In Dante's *Inferno*, over the gate of Hell is written: "Through me the way into the grieving city, / Through me the way into eternal sorrow, / Through me the way among the lost people. / Justice moved my high maker; / Divine Power made me, / Highest wisdom, and primal love. / Before me were no things created / Except eternal ones, and I endure eternal. / Abandon every hope, you who enter." Dante, *Inferno*, ed. and trans. Robert M. Durling, Canto 3, lines 1-9, 55.
24. As some will see right away, the imagery owes a good deal to Plato.
25. Lewis, *Silver Chair*, 16:250.
26. John 8:44.
27. Lewis, *Great Divorce*, 9:69.
28. C. S. Lewis, *The Last Battle* (New York: HarperCollins: 1994), 10:131.
29. Matthew 7:1; 12:33.
30. C. S. Lewis, *The Problem of Pain* (New York: Macmillan, 1962), 123.
31. Lewis, *Last Battle*, 13:185-186.

CHAPTER 14—IS PURGATORY PLAN B?

1. Matthew 5:8.
2. C. S. Lewis, *The Great Divorce* (New York: Macmillan, 1946), 9:67.
3. Ibid.
4. C. S. Lewis, *Mere Christianity* (New York: Macmillan, 1960), III.9:118.
5. C. S. Lewis, *English Literature in the Sixteenth Century, Excluding Drama*, in The Oxford History of English Literature (Oxford: Oxford University Press, 1973), 172.
6. C. S. Lewis, *Letters to Malcolm: Chiefly on Prayer* (New York: Harcourt Brace Jovanovich, 1964), 20:107-108.
7. Lewis, *Letters to Malcolm*, 20:108-109.

8. C. S. Lewis, *Letters of C. S. Lewis*, ed., with a Memoir, W. H. Lewis (New York: Harcourt Brace Jovanovich, 1966), to Sister Penelope, C.S.V.M. (September 17, 1963), 307.
9. Lewis, *English Literature in the Sixteenth Century*, 163.
10. Lewis, *Great Divorce*, 11:91-92.
11. For an excellent article on Lewis's debt to Dante, see Dominic Manganiello, "*The Great Divorce*: C. S. Lewis's Reply to Blake's Dante," *Christian Scholar's Review*, 27, no. 4 (Summer 1998): 475-489.
12. Lewis, *English Literature in the Sixteenth Century*, 163.
13. As, for example, in Titus 3:4-5: "But when the goodness and loving kindness of God our Savior appeared, he saved us, not because of works done by us in righteousness, but according to his own mercy, by the washing of regeneration and renewal of the Holy Spirit, whom he poured out on us richly through Jesus Christ our Savior, so that being justified by his grace we might become heirs according to the hope of eternal life."
14. Isaiah 1:18.
15. 1 Corinthians 15:52.
16. Lewis, *Letters to Malcolm*, 20:109.
17. Ibid., 20:109.
18. Lewis, *Mere Christianity*, IV.5:156.
19. C. S. Lewis, *The Last Battle* (New York: HarperCollins: 1994), 5:67.
20. Lewis, *Great Divorce*, 5:42.
21. Sebastian D. Knowles, "A Purgatorial Flame: British Literature of the Second World War," Ph.D. diss. (Princeton, N.J.: Princeton University, 1987), 7.
22. Lewis, *Great Divorce*, 9:69.
23. C. S. Lewis, "Screwtape Proposes a Toast," in *The Screwtape Letters* (San Francisco: HarperSanFrancisco, 2001), 119-120.
24. C. S. Lewis, *The Problem of Pain* (New York: Macmillan, 1962), 124n.
25. For this chapter, see *The Pilgrim's Regress* (Grand Rapids, Mich.: Eerdmans, 1958), 178-180.
26. C. S. Lewis, *The Collected Letters of C. S. Lewis*, vol. 2, ed. Walter Hooper (San Francisco: HarperCollins, 2004), to Joan Bennett (April 5, 1939), 256.

CHAPTER 15—LAST THINGS: AN EPILOGUE ON WHO GOES TO HEAVEN

1. Hebrews 9:26-28.
2. For a full account of Lewis's journey to Christianity see David Downing, *The Most Reluctant Convert: C. S. Lewis's Journey to Faith* (Downers Grove, Ill.: InterVarsity Press, 2002).
3. Diana Glyer records that Lewis wrote sympathetically to one correspondent, "I don't wonder that you got fogged in *Pilgrim's Regress*. It was my first religious book and I didn't then know how to make things easy. I was not even trying to." See "A Reader's Guide to Books about C. S. Lewis" in David Mills, *The Pilgrim's Guide: C. S. Lewis and the Art of Witness* (Grand Rapids, Mich.: Eerdmans, 1998). Kathryn Lindskoog's *Finding the Landlord: A Guidebook to C. S. Lewis's "Pilgrim's Regress"* (Chicago: Cornerstone Press, 1995), offers a basic interpretation.
4. C. S. Lewis, *Surprised by Joy* (New York: Harcourt Brace, 1955), 228-229. Magdalen is the Oxford college where Lewis was a young don (tutor).
5. Ibid., 237.
6. C. S. Lewis, *Mere Christianity* (New York: Macmillan, 1960), II.4:59.
7. Ibid., IV.1:139.
8. See ibid., III, chapters 11 & 12, both entitled "Faith," 121-131.
9. C. S. Lewis, *The Collected Letters of C. S. Lewis*, ed. Walter Hooper (San Francisco: HarperCollins, 2004), to Dom Bede Griffiths (July 7, 1949), vol. 2, 953-954.
10. Lesslie Newbigin is especially good on this subject. See his *A Proper Confidence* (Grand Rapids, Mich.: Eerdmans, 1995); *Truth to Tell* (Grand Rapids, Mich.: Eerdmans, 1991); and/or *Foolishness to the Greeks* (Grand Rapids, Mich.: Eerdmans, 1986).
11. C. S. Lewis, *The Voyage of the "Dawn Treader"* (New York: HarperCollins, 1994), 13:217.
12. C. S. Lewis, *The Silver Chair* (New York: HarperCollins, 1994), 2:21.
13. John 4:10.

Notes

14. John 4:14.
15. C. S. Lewis, *The Problem of Pain* (New York: Macmillan, 1962), 53-54.
16. C. S. Lewis, "The World's Last Night," *"The World's Last Night" and Other Essays* (New York: Harcourt Brace Jovanovich, 1987), 109.
17. Lewis, *Mere Christianity*, II.5:56.
18. C. S. Lewis, "The Weight of Glory," in *"The Weight of Glory" and Other Addresses*, ed., with Introduction, Walter Hooper (New York: Simon & Schuster, 1996), 18-19.
19. 2 Corinthians 4:18. When *heaven* has a lower case *h*, it refers to the sky or space. With a capital *H*, *Heaven* means the permanent dwelling of God and the redeemed.
20. *Letters of C. S. Lewis*, To a Lady (March 18, 1952), 239. Quoted passage: Mark 9:24 KJV.

WORKS CITED

Alighieri, Dante. *The Divine Comedy*. Ed. and trans. Robert M. Durling, 3 vols. New York: Oxford University Press, 2003.

Augustine, Saint. *Confessions* IX.10.25; translation from Colm Luibheid's preface to John Climacus, *The Ladder of Divine Ascent* (Paulist Press, 1982), p. xvii. Quoted in David W. Fagerberg, "Between Heaven & Earth: C. S. Lewis on Asceticism & Holiness." *Touchstone* 17, no. 3 (April 2004): 30-35.

Barfield, Owen. *Owen Barfield on C. S. Lewis*. Ed. G. B. Tennyson. Middletown, Conn.: Wesleyan University Press, 1989.

Blake, William. *The Marriage of Heaven and Hell*. Ed. Geoffrey Keynes. New York: Oxford University Press, 1975.

Blamires, Harry. "Heaven: The Eternal Weight of Glory." *Christianity Today* 35, no. 6 (May 27, 1991): 30-34.

_____. *Knowing the Truth About Heaven and Hell: Our Choices and Where They Lead Us*. Ann Arbor, Mich.: Servant Books, 1988.

Donne, John. *The Complete Poetry and Selected Prose of John Donne*. Ed., with introduction, Charles M. Coffin. New York: The Modern Library, 1952.

Clark, David G. "A Brief Discussion of the Designation for Persons in *The Screwtape Letters*." *The Lamp-Post of the Southern California CS* [sic] *Lewis Society* 26, no. 3-4 (Fall-Winter 2002): 19-32.

Cromartie, Michael. "'Salvation Inflation': A Conversation with Alan Wolfe." *Books & Culture* (March/April 2004): 18-19.

Cunningham, Richard B. *C. S. Lewis: Defender of the Faith*. Philadelphia: Westminster, 1967.

Ditchfield, Christin. *A Family Guide to Narnia: Biblical Truths in C. S. Lewis's The Chronicles of Narnia*. Wheaton, Ill.: Crossway, 2003.

Downing, David. *The Most Reluctant Convert: C. S. Lewis's Journey to Faith*. Downers Grove, Ill.: InterVarsity Press, 2002.

_____. *Planets in Peril: A Critical Study of C. S. Lewis's Ransom Trilogy*. Amherst, Mass.: University of Massachusetts Press, 1992.

Dye, Clarence F. "The Evolving Eschaton in C. S. Lewis." Ph.D. diss. New York: Fordham University, 1973.

Duriez, Colin. *The C. S. Lewis Encyclopedia*. Wheaton, Ill.: Crossway Books, 2000.

Eliot, T. S. *The Cocktail Party*. New York: Harcourt, Brace & World, 1950.

Ford, Paul F. *Companion to Narnia*, 3rd ed. New York: Macmillan, 1986.

Fagerberg, David W. "Between Heaven & Earth: C. S. Lewis on Asceticism & Holiness." *Touchstone* 17, no. 3 (April 2004): 30-35.

Gibson, Evan K. *C. S. Lewis, Spinner of Tales: A Guide to His Fiction*. Grand Rapids, Mich.: Eerdmans, 1980.

Goffar, Janine. *C. S. Lewis Index: Rumours from the Sculptor's Shop*. Riverside, Calif.: La Sierra University Press, 1995.

Grudem, Wayne. "The Unseen World Is Not a Myth." *Christianity Today* 30, no. 10 (July 11, 1986): 24.

Harris Poll on "The Religious and Other Beliefs of Americans 2003." *Skeptical Inquirer* 27

Works Cited

(July/August 2003): 5. Quoted in Henry M. Morris. "The Lake of Fire." *Back to Genesis*, no. 184 (April 2003): a-d.

Hooper, Walter. *C. S. Lewis Companion & Guide*. San Francisco: HarperCollins, 1996.

Howard, Thomas. "The Triumphant Vindication of the Body: The End of Gnosticism in *That Hideous Strength*." In David Mills, *The Pilgrim's Guide* (see below), 133-144.

Huttar, Charles, ed. *Imagination and the Spirit*. Grand Rapids, Mich.: Eerdmans, 1971.

Kantzer, Kenneth. "Afraid of Heaven." *Christianity Today* 35, no. 6 (May 27 1991): 38-39.

Karkainen, Paul A. *Narnia Explored*. Old Tappan, N.J.: Revell, 1979.

Kilby, Clyde. *The Christian World of C. S. Lewis*. Grand Rapids, Mich.: Eerdmans, 1964.

Knowles, Sebastian D. "A Purgatorial Flame: British Literature of the Second World War." Ph.D. diss. Princeton, N.J.: Princeton University, 1987.

Lewis, C. S. "Answers to Christianity." In *God in the Dock* (see below), 48-62.

_____. "Christian Reunion: An Anglican Speaks to Roman Catholics." In *C. S. Lewis: Essay Collection and Other Short Pieces*. Ed. Lesley Walmsley, 395-397. London: HarperCollins, 2000.

_____. "Christianity and Culture." In *Christian Reflections*. Ed. Walter Hooper, 12-36. Grand Rapids, Mich.: Eerdmans, 1967.

_____. "Dangers of National Repentance." In *God in the Dock* (see below), 189-192.

_____. "The Dark Tower." In *The Dark Tower & Other Stories*. Ed. Walter Hooper, 15-91. New York: Harcourt Brace Jovanovich, 1977.

_____. *English Literature in the Sixteenth Century, Excluding Drama*. In The Oxford History of English Literature. Oxford: Oxford University Press, 1973.

_____. *Experiment in Criticism*. Cambridge: Cambridge University Press, 1961.

_____. *The Four Loves*. New York: Harcourt Brace Jovanovich, 1960.

_____. *God in the Dock*. Ed. Walter Hooper. Grand Rapids, Mich.: Eerdmans, 1970.

_____. *The Great Divorce*. New York: Macmillan, 1946.

_____. *A Grief Observed*. New York: Bantam, 1976.

_____. *The Horse and His Boy*. New York: HarperCollins, 1994.

_____. *The Last Battle*. New York: HarperCollins, 1994.

_____. *Letters: C. S. Lewis, Don Giovanni Calabria: A Study in Friendship*. Trans. and ed. Martin Moynihan. Ann Arbor. Mich.: Servant Books, 1988.

_____. *Letters of C. S. Lewis*. Ed., with a Memoir, W. H. Lewis. New York: Harcourt Brace Jovanovich, 1966.

_____. *The Letters of C. S. Lewis to Arthur Greeves (1914-1963)*. Ed. Walter Hooper. New York: Macmillan, 1979.

_____. *Letters to Children*. Ed. Lyle W. Dorsett and Marjorie Lamp Mead. New York: Macmillan, 1988.

_____. *Letters to Dom Bede Griffiths*. Wade Center, Wheaton College, Wheaton, Ill.

_____. *Letters to Malcolm: Chiefly on Prayer*. New York: Harcourt Brace Jovanovich, 1964.

_____. *The Lion, the Witch and the Wardrobe*. New York: HarperCollins, 1994.

_____. *The Magician's Nephew*. New York: HarperCollins, 1994.

_____. "Man or Rabbit?" In *God in the Dock* (see above), 108-113.

_____. *Mere Christianity*. New York: Macmillan, 1960.

_____. *Miracles*. New York: Macmillan, 1978.

_____. "Myth Became Fact." In *God in the Dock* (see above), 63-67.

_____. *Of Other Worlds: Essays & Stories*. Ed., with Preface, Walter Hooper. New York: Harcourt Brace Jovanovich, 1966.

_____. "On Stories." In *"On Stories" and Other Essays on Literature*. Ed. Walter Hooper, 3-20. New York: Harcourt Brace Jovanovich, 1982.

_____. "On Three Ways of Writing for Children." In *"On Stories" and Other Essays on Literature* (see above), 31-44 and *Of Other Worlds* (see above), 35-38.

_____. *Out of the Silent Planet*. New York: Macmillan, 1965.

_____. *Perelandra*. New York: Macmillan, 1965.

_____. *Poems*. Ed. Walter Hooper. New York: Harcourt Brace Jovanovich, 1964.

_____. *Preface to "Paradise Lost."* New York: Oxford University Press, 1961.

_____. *Prince Caspian*. New York: HarperCollins, 1994.

_____. *The Problem of Pain*. New York: Macmillan, 1962.

_____. *The Screwtape Letters*. New York: Simon & Schuster, 1996.

_____. "The Sermon and the Lunch." In *God in the Dock* (see above), 282-286.

_____. *The Silver Chair*. New York: HarperCollins, 1994.

_____. "A Slip of the Tongue." In *"The Weight of Glory" and Other Addresses* (see below), 137-143.

_____. "Some Thoughts." In *God in the Dock* (see above), 147-150.

_____. *Surprised by Joy*. New York: Harcourt, Brace, & World, 1955.

_____. *Till We Have Faces*. New York: Harcourt Brace, 1984.

_____. "Transposition." In *"The Weight of Glory" and Other Addresses* (see below), 72-89.

_____. "The Trouble with 'X.'" In *God in the Dock* (see above), 151-155.

_____. *The Voyage of the "Dawn Treader."* New York: HarperCollins, 1994.

_____. "The Weight of Glory." In *"The Weight of Glory" and Other Addresses* (see below), 25-42.

_____. *"The Weight of Glory" and Other Addresses*. Ed., with Introduction, Walter Hooper. New York: Simon & Schuster, 1996.

_____. "The World's Last Night." In *"The World's Last Night" and Other Essays* (see below), 93-113.

_____. *"The World's Last Night" and Other Essays*. New York: Harcourt Brace Jovanovich, 1987.

Lindskoog, Kathryn. *Finding the Landlord: A Guidebook to C. S. Lewis's "Pilgrim's Regress."* Chicago: Cornerstone Press Chicago, 1995.

_____. *Journey into Narnia*. Pasadena, Calif.: Hope Publishing House, 1998.

Lotz, Anne Graham. *Heaven: My Father's House*. Nashville: W Publishing Group, Thomas Nelson, 2001.

Manganiello, Dominic. "*The Great Divorce*: C. S. Lewis's Reply to Blake's Dante." *Christian Scholar's Review* 27, no. 4 (Summer 1998): 475-489.

Manlove, Colin. *The Chronicles of Narnia: The Patterning of a Fantastic World*. New York: Twayne, 1993.

Manzalaoui, M. A. "Narnia: The Domain of Lewis's Beliefs." In Lindskoog, *Journey* (see above), 205-22.

Martin, Thomas L., ed. *Reading the Classics with C. S. Lewis*. Grand Rapids, Mich.: Baker Book House, 2000.

Mills, David. *The Pilgrim's Guide: C. S. Lewis and the Art of Witness*. Grand Rapids, Mich.: Eerdmans, 1998.

Milton, John. *The Complete Poems and Major Prose*. Ed. Merritt Hughes. New York: Odyssey Press, 1957.

Mitchell, Christopher W. "The 'More' of Heaven and the Literary Art of C. S. Lewis." *Christianity and the Arts* 5, no. 3 (Summer 1998): 40-44.

Morris, Leon. "Hell: The Dreadful Harvest." *Christianity Today* 35, no. 6 (May 27, 1991): 34-38.

Musacchio, George. *C. S. Lewis: Man & Writer*. Belton, Tex.: University of Mary Hardin-Baylor, 1994.

Piper, John. "'Brokenhearted Joy': Taking the Swagger Out of Christian Cultural Influence." *World* (December 13, 2003): 51.

Richardson, Don. *Secrets of the Koran*. Ventura, Calif.: Regal, 2003.

Works Cited

Ross, Hugh. *Beyond the Cosmos: The Extra-Dimensionality of God.* Colorado Springs: NavPress, 1996.

Russell, Jeffrey Burton. *A History of Heaven.* Princeton, N.J.: Princeton University Press, 1997.

Sammons, Martha C. *A Guide Through Narnia.* Wheaton, Ill.: Harold Shaw Publishers, 1979.

Sassone, Robert L. *The Tiniest Humans.* Stafford, Va.: American Life League, 1995. Quoted in Joni Eareckson Tada. *Heaven: Your Real Home* (see below), 37.

Sayer, George. *Jack: A Life of C. S. Lewis.* Wheaton, Ill.: Crossway, 1994.

Schakel, Peter J. *Reading with the Heart: The Way into Narnia.* Grand Rapids, Mich.: Eerdmans, 1979.

Schultz, Jeffrey D. and John G. West, Jr., eds. *The C. S. Lewis Readers' Encyclopedia.* Grand Rapids, Mich.: Zondervan, 1998.

Stackhouse, John G., Jr. "Harleys in Heaven: What Christians Have Thought of the Afterlife, & What Difference It Makes Now." *Christianity Today* 47, no. 6 (June 2003): 38-41.

Tada, Joni Eareckson. *Heaven: Your Real Home.* Grand Rapids, Mich.: Zondervan, 1995.

Vaus, Will. *Mere Theology: A Guide to the Thought of C. S. Lewis.* Downers Grove, Ill.: InterVarsity Press, 2001.

Ward, Michael. "The Path to Sympathy: Reflections on *Till We Have Faces.*" Presented July 19, 2000, at St. Anne's, Oxford. A copy in the Wade Center, Wheaton College, Wheaton, Ill.

————. "Where Dreams Don't Come True: Reflections on *The Voyage of the Dawn Treader.*" Presented July 14, 2000, at St. Anne's, Oxford. A copy in the Wade Center, Wheaton College, Wheaton, Ill.

Weigel, George. "Europe's Problem—and Ours." *First Things* 140 (February 2004): 18-25.

INDEX

234

Index

Index